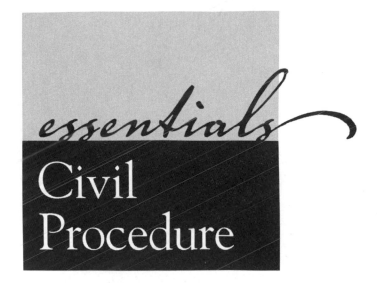
essentials

Civil
Procedure

Editorial Advisors

Vicki Been
Elihu Root Professor of Law
New York University School of Law

Erwin Chemerinsky
Alston & Bird Professor of Law
Duke University School of Law

Richard A. Epstein
James Parker Hall Distinguished Service Professor of Law
University of Chicago Law School
Peter and Kirsten Bedford Senior Fellow
The Hoover Institution
Stanford University

Ronald J. Gilson
Charles J. Meyers Professor of Law and Business
Stanford University
Marc and Eva Stern Professor of Law and Business
Columbia Law School

James E. Krier
Earl Warren DeLano Professor of Law
The University of Michigan Law School

Richard K. Neumann, Jr.
Professor of Law
Hofstra University School of Law

David Alan Sklansky
Professor of Law
University of California at Berkeley School of Law

Kent D. Syverud
Dean and Ethan A. H. Shepley University Professor
Washington University School of Law

Elizabeth Warren
Leo Gottlieb Professor of Law
Harvard Law School

ASPEN PUBLISHERS

essentials

Civil
Procedure

Suzanna Sherry
Herman O. Loewenstein Professor of Law
Vanderbilt University Law School

Jay Tidmarsh
Professor of Law
Notre Dame Law School

Wolters Kluwer
Law & Business

AUSTIN   BOSTON   CHICAGO   NEW YORK   THE NETHERLANDS

Aspen Publishers
Attn: Permissions Department
76 Ninth Avenue, 7th Floor
New York, NY 10011-5201

To contact Customer Care, e-mail customer.care@aspenpublishers.com, call 1-800-234-1660, fax 1-800-901-9075, or mail correspondence to:

Aspen Publishers
Attn: Order Department
PO Box 990
Frederick, MD 21705

Printed in the United States of America.

1 2 3 4 5 6 7 8 9 0

ISBN 978-0-7355-6426-8

Library of Congress Cataloging-in-Publication Data

Sherry, Suzanna.
    Civil procedure : essentials / Suzanna Sherry, Jay Tidmarsh.
        p. cm.
    Includes bibliographical references and index.
    ISBN 978-0-7355-6426-8 (pbk. : alk. paper)   1. Civil procedure–United States.
    I. Tidmarsh, Jay, 1957-   II. Title.

KF8840.S483 2007
347.73'5–dc22

                                                                        2007011446

About Wolters Kluwer Law & Business

Wolters Kluwer Law & Business is a leading provider of research information and workflow solutions in key specialty areas. The strengths of the individual brands of Aspen Publishers, CCH, Kluwer Law International and Loislaw are aligned within Wolters Kluwer Law & Business to provide comprehensive, in-depth solutions and expert-authored content for the legal, professional and education markets.

CCH was founded in 1913 and has served more than four generations of business professionals and their clients. The CCH products in the Wolters Kluwer Law & Business group are highly regarded electronic and print resources for legal, securities, antitrust and trade regulation, government contracting, banking, pension, payroll, employment and labor, and healthcare reimbursement and compliance professionals.

Aspen Publishers is a leading information provider for attorneys, business professionals and law students. Written by preeminent authorities, Aspen products offer analytical and practical information in a range of specialty practice areas from securities law and intellectual property to mergers and acquisitions and pension/benefits. Aspen's trusted legal education resources provide professors and students with high-quality, up-to-date and effective resources for successful instruction and study in all areas of the law.

Kluwer Law International supplies the global business community with comprehensive English-language international legal information. Legal practitioners, corporate counsel and business executives around the world rely on the Kluwer Law International journals, loose-leafs, books and electronic products for authoritative information in many areas of international legal practice.

Loislaw is a premier provider of digitized legal content to small law firm practitioners of various specializations. Loislaw provides attorneys with the ability to quickly and efficiently find the necessary legal information they need, when and where they need it, by facilitating access to primary law as well as state-specific law, records, forms and treatises.

Wolters Kluwer Law & Business, a unit of Wolters Kluwer, is headquartered in New York and Riverwoods, Illinois. Wolters Kluwer is a leading multinational publisher and information services company.

To our students — past, present, and future

S.S. and J.T.

Table of Contents

CHAPTER 3
Jury Trial   63

CHAPTER 4
Accuracy   99

CHAPTER 5

Procedural Fairness   135

CHAPTER 9

Epilogue: Beyond Civil Procedure   255

Preface

When the publishers at Aspen asked us to consider writing this book — the first in a new series called *Essentials* — they described their vision for the series in a number of ways: "a look at the forest rather than the trees"; "a view of Civil Procedure from 30,000 feet"; "the eight or ten words that capture the field"; and "what you hope your students *really* take away from Civil Procedure." We liked the challenge: writing a book that is short and readable but still sophisticated enough to add value for the student. Many works already exist to help students understand the course, but their primary purpose is not to place the procedural system in a larger frame of reference or show how different doctrines relate to each other and to the underlying goals of the American procedural system.

We believe that students cannot really understand Civil Procedure until they have this larger frame of reference — in other words, until they understand the ideas and arguments that underpin the doctrines. More than in most classes, these deeper ideas and arguments are not accessible from reading the cases. Moreover, professors have a limited number of credit hours to teach the basics of this foreign language of procedure and cannot spend as much classroom time on these ideas and arguments as they would like.

Hence this book. It is meant to help students answer some basic questions that underlie the typical Civil Procedure course: Why have we Americans designed our civil justice system as we have? What choices have we made, what are the benefits and drawbacks of these choices, and what other choices might we make to improve the procedural system in the future? We try to give students a sense of the purposes behind the rules, to show how seemingly different rules have common motivations, and to describe how the tensions among our procedural goals lead to changes in the rules. If we have succeeded, this book is a true supplement to the casebook and the classroom, shedding a new light on the course material and providing a new depth of understanding.

We created this book so that it can be used in conjunction with any casebook. You can use it in either (or both) of two ways. First, individual chapters can be assigned as you complete various topics, bringing together the ideas connecting those topics. We include two charts, on pages 5 and 6, that link the chapters of this book with the topics of a typical Civil Procedure course. The book can also be used as a way to wrap up and review the entire course, simultaneously deepening the students' understanding. If students read it during the last week or two of the course, they will necessarily be reviewing the doctrinal basics, but classroom discussion during that time can also focus on the deeper questions we address.

Many people have helped us in the preparation of this book. We thank Steve Errick, Carol McGeehan, and Taylor Kearns for their development of the *Essentials* project, for their unwavering support, and for their insights on our manuscript. We are humbled by the efforts of seven anonymous reviewers — our procedural colleagues — who took the time to read a draft of the manuscript and provide incisive comments. Teresa Horton was a wonderful copy editor, and Carmen Corral-Reid, our senior manuscript editor, helped make the publication process smooth and easy. Our administrative assistants, Janelle Steele and Debbie Blasko, were ever helpful. We are grateful for the research funding and support that we received from Vanderbilt Law School and Notre Dame Law School. Finally, we took our inspiration from the many students in our Civil Procedure classes over the years. While we wrote, we always imagined that we were talking directly to them.

If you have questions or comments about how this book might be used in your Civil Procedure class, please get in touch with either or both of us. And after you have used the book we welcome your reactions.

Nashville, Tennessee
Notre Dame, Indiana
April 2007

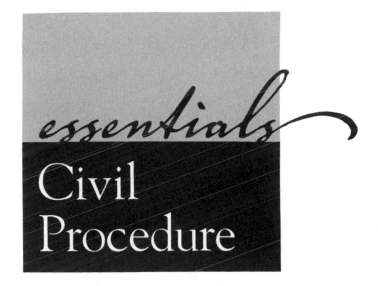

essentials
Civil
Procedure

⁀ Introduction ⁀

How This Book Will Help You Learn Civil Procedure

One of the questions first-year students commonly ask is "What am I supposed to get out of this course?" On one level, you face the minutiae of rules, exceptions, and multifactor tests. On another level, class discussions often focus on broad themes and principles, not nitty-gritty details. Of all first-year classes, nowhere is the sense of disconnection between the doctrine and what the course seems to be "really" about stronger than in Civil Procedure. It is so easy to focus on the trees, branches, and twigs that you can no longer see the forest.

This book tries to paint the picture of the Civil Procedure forest. It is intended to give you a broad overview rather than a detailed accounting. It does not dwell on procedural detail, nor provide a doctrine-by-doctrine rehashing of your Civil Procedure course. You can — with careful reading — glean most of the basic doctrines from this book, but that is not our purpose. Our purpose is to give you a way of connecting parts of the course that do not seem to be connected, and thus both to understand the individual bits of doctrine *and* to have a framework that allows you to understand their relation to each other. Imagine that your Civil Procedure course is a maze (that shouldn't be too much of a stretch!): You are walking through the maze, but you could negotiate the maze more easily if you could climb a nearby hill and look down at it. This book offers a guided tour from the hill.

The book is designed to help you understand what might be called the superstructure of Civil Procedure: the underlying principles, themes, and connected ideas that wind through the doctrines of your Civil Procedure course. These principles do not necessarily track the chapters in your casebook or the units on your syllabus, but are instead woven into the very fabric of our procedural system. Each concept may intersect with several different doctrinal areas discussed in class, and many of the doctrines covered in class implicate more than one of the concepts in this book.

You might wonder, especially if you are just starting your legal education, how understanding Civil Procedure's super-structure can help you. Our experience in teaching beginning law students leads us to suggest three ways in which a view of the forest (or the view of the maze from the hill, if you prefer) helps students understand the material more thoroughly and perform better on exams.

First, reading about the forest inevitably helps you learn and remember each tree. As you read through this book and encounter familiar (but perhaps only partially understood or vaguely remembered) doctrines, placing them in the context of their underlying principles will help cement them in your mind. For example, if you have only a fuzzy grasp of how Rules 14 and 19 — both about party joinder — differ, reading about their common underlying principle and their separate and distinctive departures from that principle will increase your understanding. Diversity jurisdiction comes alive when you understand the principles that animated its eighteenth-century creators and modern interpreters.

Second, themes and principles make sense of what otherwise might seem like unconnected and often arbitrary rules. Why do some claims have to be related in order to be joined, and others not? What makes pretrial discovery so controversial, why does it work so poorly in some cases, and how can I get a handle on the rules' mind-numbing detail? Without underlying principles, it is difficult to answer such questions. Pure memorization of the individual rules and doctrines is tedious and time-consuming and is not always the best way to learn. You have certainly encountered this before law school. Apparently random dates or events in a history course fall into place if you can construct a timeline that puts the historical events in context. Physics formulas make more sense when you put them together with broad principles about natural forces. Rules of music composition become understandable in light of music theory. Law is no different, but the underlying principles are often taught in class much more indirectly. This book will help you identify these principles and make sense of Civil Procedure.

Finally, drawing connections among different doctrines by exposing their underlying principles will enable you to make arguments that go beyond or behind the doctrine. And it is that ability that primarily distinguishes a solid exam answer from a spectacular one, and a good lawyer from a great one. When the black-letter law runs out (and it always does eventually, especially on first-year exams), there is no single right answer to a legal question. The best answer, though, will be the one that is most persuasively connected to the underlying principles that animate the existing doctrines.

So how should you use this book for maximum advantage? You will benefit most from this book by reading each chapter as a whole — or, better still, by considering the entire book as a single explanation — to see how the various parts of Civil Procedure are interrelated. For that reason, this book will be most helpful toward the end of your Civil Procedure course, after you have studied the basic doctrines. Reading this book as you prepare your course outline and study for the final exam will help you review, as it also helps you organize and synthesize the course.

Of course, as you will probably learn in your Torts class, not everybody uses a product as directed. So if you want to dip into this book a doctrine or two at a time, the following chart will help you (we also include an index at the back of the book). We have organized the chart according to the stages of a lawsuit, from the very first decisions that a lawyer makes even before the case is filed all the way to the end of the case and beyond. In the second column, you will see the doctrines that are involved at each of these stages — these are probably the subjects that appear on the syllabus for your course. The third column tells you the principles that these doctrines invoke, and thus the chapters in this book where you will find discussion of each doctrine. The final column tells you more precisely the pages in the chapter where the doctrine is discussed.

Steps in the litigation process	Topics included in a typical course	Procedural principles involved	Page numbers in text
Choosing a court	Subject matter jurisdiction Personal jurisdiction Venue	Transactionalism, federalism Procedural fairness, federalism Efficiency	206-214, 225-236 136-139, 237-243 169-171
Choosing the parties	Joinder Class actions	Adversarial system, transactionalism Procedural fairness, transactionalism	41-44, 184-206 158-162, 201-206
Choosing the law to apply	Choice of law (*Erie*)	Procedural fairness, federalism	140-141, 243-254
Pleading	Complaint Answer Amendment Abuse	Accuracy, procedural fairness Accuracy, procedural fairness Accuracy, procedural fairness, transactionalism Adversarial system	107-111, 151-155 112-114, 151-155 114-118, 151-155, 214-216 51-55
Disclosure and discovery	Disclosure and discovery	Adversarial system, accuracy	55-57, 118-127
Other pretrial issues	Judicial case management Summary judgment Settlement and ADR	Adversarial system, procedural fairness Jury trial, accuracy Procedural fairness, efficiency	57-60, 155-156 89-94, 128-130 156-158, 176-180
Trial	Right to jury trial Judgment as a matter of law	Jury trial Jury trial	66-74 83-89
Post-trial issues	Renewing a motion for judgment as a matter of law New trial Appeal Preclusion	Jury trial Jury trial Efficiency Adversarial system, procedural fairness, efficiency, transactionalism	83-89 80-83 172-176 41-44, 144-147, 175-176, 187-194

Again, if you are trying to understand a doctrine in context, we do not recommend that you necessarily go right to the relevant pages and read just about that one doctrine. We are trying to show you how larger themes connect doctrines to each other and thus make each doctrine more comprehensible. So it is usually best to wait until you have completed a group of related doctrines, and then read the whole chapter. You will get maximum benefit from the book if you read certain chapters after you complete the study of specific subject areas. The following chart gives our recommendation for when to read each chapter.

Chapter 1 (Designing a Procedural System)	≡	At any time during or after the first two weeks of class
Chapter 2 (The Adversarial System)	≡	After you have covered pleading, discovery, and case management
Chapter 3 (Jury Trial) and Chapter 4 (Accuracy)	≡	After you have covered the topics above plus summary judgment, trial, and post-trial motions
Chapter 5 (Procedural Fairness)	≡	After you have covered the topics above plus personal jurisdiction
Chapter 6 (Efficiency)	≡	At any time, although the short sections on venue, appeal, and preclusion will make the most sense after you have covered those subjects

Chapter 7 (Transaction- alism)	≡	After you have covered joinder and preclusion, although the second half of the chapter is best read after you have also covered subject matter jurisdiction
Chapter 8 (Federalism)	≡	After you have covered personal jurisdiction, subject matter jurisdiction, and choice of law (*Erie*)
Chapter 9 (Epilogue)	≡	After you have read the rest of the book

The particular rules and doctrines that govern civil procedure continue to evolve. (One of the most important lessons you will learn in Civil Procedure — and in all your first-year courses — is how to teach yourself, so that your knowledge does not become obsolete as the law changes.) The fundamental principles we discuss in this book are more enduring. Although there might be changes in how they are translated into rules and doctrines, the principles themselves guide those changes. If you understand these principles, and how they work in today's procedural context, you will be better able to understand — and to use to your clients' advantage — the procedural regimes of the future.

↜ 1 ↝

Designing a
Procedural System

Before we can explore the fundamental principles underlying the American procedural regime, it is helpful to
have an overview of the basic structure of American
civil procedure and how it came to be. We need to know, in
other words, what issues and options arise in the design of any
system of dispute resolution, and then how the United States
came to choose its particular procedural structures. This chapter
thus first asks two basic questions: What is adjudication for, and
what are the possible structural approaches to accomplish its
goals? Once we have laid out the choices in the abstract, we
turn to history to provide the necessary context for understanding
our own procedural regime.

DESIGN QUESTIONS

The Point of Adjudication

At its most basic level, Civil Procedure is about the process that
courts do and should follow when they adjudicate cases.
*Adjudication** is simply a way to make a decision between

---

* We italicize terms of art or common procedural phrases when we first use
them in a chapter. We include most of these italicized phrases in the Glossary.

competing alternatives. Adjudication places the decision about which alternative is best into the hands of a third person who has a less immediate stake in the choice than the people most affected by the decision. Typically adjudication is associated with the court system (although sometimes it can be done through *arbitration* or *administrative proceedings*). The competing alternatives involve a claim of legal right or remedy by one party and a denial of that right or remedy by another. A third person — the judge — determines the "correct" alternative, and enters a *judgment* that binds the parties to the result. The power of the government stands behind the judgment, ready to enforce it against a recalcitrant losing party.

In reality, this model is too simple. It assumes that there is only one judge, when in fact the judicial function is often divided between trial and appellate courts, and the trial function can be divided between judge and *jury*. It assumes that there are only two parties, with two diametrically opposed legal positions, when in fact a legal dispute can involve multiple parties and nuanced differences among legal positions. We will explore some of these complications as we go through this book. For now, let us assume a simple two-person dispute over a legal entitlement, and a single judge as the adjudicator.

Let us also assume that the judge wants to resolve this dispute as accurately as possible. Although this assumption seems self-evident, stop a moment to think about it. Why do we want judgments to be accurate? Suppose we handed judges two-sided coins, and told them to make decisions by flipping them. Think of how many lawsuits a judge could resolve in a day! Think of how cheap litigation would become! The problem with a coin flip, of course, is that the judge is likely to make the wrong decision a lot of the time. Being frequently wrong imposes costs. To take a recent example, consider the many lawsuits against the Merck pharmaceutical company for harms allegedly caused by the drug Vioxx. If our society resolved suits like these with a coin flip, that would make litigation less expensive — and more enticing. Because every person who sued Merck would have a 50–50 chance of winning, there would be many false or trumped-up claims. Merck would have to pay millions of dollars even if Vioxx is completely safe. In such a world, what incentive does Merck have to develop new drugs? What incentive does anyone have to be productive and accumulate wealth if it might be lost with the flip of a coin? The coin-based procedural system would also be unfair to people who were actually harmed by Vioxx, because half of them would likely remain uncompensated. So although we want adjudication to be swift and inexpensive, it also needs to be accurate — but not necessarily perfectly accurate. If we assumed that we could resolve each case with perfect accuracy at a cost of $10 million, the expense would not be worth it for disputes worth less than $10 million. But we do want results that are reasonably accurate.

To resolve disputes with reasonable accuracy, adjudication must accomplish several things. The law specifies certain standards of behavior for people living within a society, and then enforces those standards against transgressors. Therefore, adjudication first must determine the relevant legal standards. To continue with our earlier example, we have to decide how safe Merck must make its products, what risks it must disclose, and how the behavior of patients or doctors might change Merck's liability. As your courses in substantive law teach you, this task is not always easy. No big book precisely identifies how we should act in every particular situation on every occasion. American law contains conflicting, overlapping, and often incomplete expectations of behavior that the adjudicatory process must distill into the appropriate "rules" to follow in instances like the Vioxx litigation.

Next, adjudication must determine the facts of the dispute. The appropriate legal rule can often be written in this form: When a person does X and Y, then legal consequence Z

attaches. Adjudication must determine, as a matter of fact, whether X and Y occurred. Again, this process is not always simple. Eyewitnesses might have different memories, documents might be incomplete about important details, or the most valuable evidence on X and Y might be unavailable. Sometimes, determining even the most basic facts—for instance, whether a person actually started to take Vioxx before suffering from a fatal heart attack—can be a tricky business.

Adjudication must then apply the law to the facts. This process might sound mechanical; once the court has determined that X and Y happened, and has further determined that Z is the legal consequence for such behavior, then the outcome is clear. But in many cases applying the law to the facts is the most difficult part of the job. Often legal rules operate at a level of generality removed from the particulars of a dispute. For instance, one legal rule is this: When a defendant manufactures a defective product that causes physical injury, the defendant is liable. Suppose Merck had spent many millions of dollars investigating the safety of Vioxx, which alleviated the severe symptoms of thousands of arthritic patients but doubled the risk of a patient suffering a heart attack. On these facts, is Vioxx defective or not defective? (Obviously, if the legal rule was "When a manufacturer's product causes five or more heart attacks, then the product is defective," the process of applying the law to the facts would be mechanical. But legal rules are rarely so precise.)

Finally, adjudication must determine the appropriate remedy. Sometimes money will be compensation enough. Sometimes it will not be, but it will be all that the legal system can provide: Merck cannot relieve the pain or disabilities of a patient who suffered a heart attack, or bring back a loved one who died. In these cases, the court orders the defendant to pay money, or *damages*. In other cases, however, an *injunction* of some sort might be appropriate: Merck might be ordered to take Vioxx off the market, or to perform certain tests on its other products. An adjudicatory system must deal with the potential mismatch between what people want from adjudication and what it can give them.*

So now we have at least four functions that adjudication must perform if it is to render reasonably accurate judgments: Find the facts, declare the law, apply the one to the other, and determine an appropriate remedy. Behind these four central functions lie subsidiary tasks that are equally vital to accurate adjudication. First, for the facts to be "found," some person (or people) must investigate what happened, accumulate any additional relevant information, and then organize and present the most salient aspects of the dispute in a way that helps the adjudicator. Second, to determine the relevant legal principles, some person (or people) must research the law, and describe for the adjudicator the merits of the possible legal principles or approaches that might apply to the dispute.

At this point, the rules of procedure come into play. Procedural rules provide structure for the process of adjudication. They decide who must, and who may, participate in the adjudication, and in which court or courts the adjudication must, or may, take place. They determine which participants must fulfill which responsibilities for determining the facts and the law, for applying the facts to the law, and for investigating, researching, and presenting the evidence and arguments. Procedural rules also specify the methods or mechanisms that the participants must, or may, use to discharge their

---

* Your class in Civil Procedure will not focus much on the issue of remedies. Your school might offer an upper level class on Remedies, and classes like Torts and Contracts will probably devote some time to the damages or injunctive relief that an injured person can receive. In the real world, the question of remedies is critical to the functioning of an adjudicatory system. Most clients care only about the bottom line. Thus, plaintiffs will typically litigate only when the net remedy (calculated by multiplying the amount of the remedy by the probability of obtaining it, and then subtracting the expenses of litigation), is (1) greater than zero, and (2) greater than they could achieve through *alternative methods of dispute resolution* such as arbitration or settlement.

responsibilities. Some procedural rules are positive commands—they describe how a particular adjudicatory task
must be performed. Just as often, they are negative commands
or guidelines—they outlaw certain practices but leave to the
relevant participants some choice about whether and how to
perform their tasks. Obviously, there are many possible
procedural permutations. In allocating the tasks of adjudication,
however, two principal procedural models—one highly centralized and one highly decentralized—have emerged over time.

Two Models for Adjudication: Inquisitorial and Adversarial

With respect to the central functions of determining the facts
and the law, applying the law to the facts, and declaring the
remedy, the adjudicator is in control; otherwise, it would not be
adjudication. But who should be in charge of the subsidiary
tasks of investigation, research, and presentation of the
evidence and arguments? Keeping in mind that we want the
ultimate decision to be reasonably accurate, the candidates with
the most incentive to ensure that the investigation, research,
and presentation are effective are the judge and the parties.

Both choices have some merit. If we centralize the tasks of
investigation, research, and presentation in the judge, we can
expect that the work will usually be performed with a degree of
impartiality. Moreover, because he or she will be the ultimate
decision maker, the judge is likely to keep the preliminary tasks
of research and investigation tightly bound to the ultimate task
of making a decision. The conscientious judge has an incentive
to do everything necessary to decide the case, and no more.

If we place the parties in charge of investigation, research,
and presentation, we must split the task between them,
because we cannot trust either of the parties to be disinterested
enough to do a good job for both sides. Having two parties
rather than one judge perform these tasks might seem wasteful,

but that is not necessarily true. The parties probably know more about the circumstances of the case than the judge, so they can streamline the investigation and research. Moreover, because they pay for their share of investigation and research, the parties are often in a better position to decide whether particular lines of research and investigation are worthwhile. Keeping the judge neutral while the case is investigated, researched, and presented also might make the judge's decision more accurate; early judicial involvement carries with it the risk that the judge will begin to prejudge the case before all the facts are in.

The centralized approach — having the judge research, investigate, and present the case — is usually called the *inquisitorial* approach to adjudication. The decentralized approach — placing the parties in charge of the preliminary adjudicatory tasks — is usually called the *adversarial* approach to adjudication.* Different legal systems around the world use one approach or the other. The inquisitorial approach is dominant in continental Europe and in other countries with legal systems that are influenced by the continental systems. The adversarial approach derives from English common law

---

* Sometimes the inquisitorial approach is also called the *civil law* (or *civilian*) system, and the adversarial approach is called the *common law* system. Civil law systems usually use a foundational legal document, such as a code, to specify legal rules and entitlements; prior similar cases can be helpful guides, but only the code itself is binding authority on the judge. Common law systems treat prior cases as a binding statement of the law (*precedent*), which judges in subsequent cases must follow except in unusual circumstances. Whether a code or a case is the source of binding law presents a question distinct from the question of whether the judge or the parties should handle the preliminary tasks in adjudication. Nonetheless, as a matter of history, those legal systems that adopted the inquisitorial process have tended to be civil law systems, and those legal systems that adopted the adversarial process have tended to be common law systems.

You should not confuse the civil law system with the civil justice system in America. "Civil" is one of those words with multiple meanings. As is true of many countries, the American legal system contains a basic division between criminal and civil (i.e., noncriminal) law. Thus, "civil procedure" refers to the procedures used to resolve noncriminal cases, not the procedures used in civil law countries.

practice, and is used mostly in those legal systems around the world influenced by the English system. In the real world, no legal system is purely inquisitorial or purely adversarial; even the most inquisitorial system allows the parties to suggest lines of investigation and research to the judge, and even the most adversarial system expects the judge to assist in the development of factual and legal issues. Overall, inquisitorial civil justice systems are more prevalent. As descendants of the English system, however, American courts inherited the adversarial approach to adjudication. Indeed, on the spectrum from more inquisitorial to more adversarial, the United States today is arguably the most adversarial system in the world. It makes the plaintiff the *master of the complaint* by putting him or her in charge of such fundamental tasks as deciding whether, when, where, against whom, and on which legal claims to file suit, and it expects both parties to be the principal forces investigating, researching, and driving the case forward to trial.

Whether the inquisitorial or the adversarial approach is "better" is a topic much debated among lawyers, judges, and academics. Chapter 2 examines the consequences and merits of our choice of an adversarial approach. But if both inquisitorial and adversarial systems are defensible — and if the inquisitorial system is more common (and, according to some, better) — why is American procedure so adversarial? Thereby hangs the tale of the next section, which describes the history of American procedure that underlies the rest of the book.

A BRIEF HISTORY OF CIVIL PROCEDURE

Our English Heritage

Litigation as we know it began with the Norman invasion of England in 1066. The Romans — with their great system of centralized *civil law* governed by detailed written codes — had, much earlier, ruled England for over three centuries. But when the Romans left in 407, the various disunited tribes remaining on (and invading) what ultimately became the British Isles developed their own law, which was based on local custom rather than on written codes. Roman law would later reappear in different guise, but for the next 600 years, England had a localized, informal, and somewhat irrational dispute resolution system that often depended on supernatural signs to reveal the truth of the dispute. Some of the irrationality survived even into the American colonies: Throwing suspected witches into the water to see whether they would float (a witch) or drown (not a witch) was a remnant of this early system. The rejection of the Roman system of civil law also persists today in both English and American law, which are still based more on *common law* — made case-by-case by judicial decisions (including decisions interpreting written statutes), which then become *precedent* for the next case — than on detailed written codes that are designed to answer every legal question in advance.

The Normans gradually regularized and centralized the English legal regime. The king, and later the royal courts, heard disputes and corrected errors committed by the local courts (which the Normans retained for some time as useful for the day-to-day administration of the law). Because the Normans were French, the language of the royal courts was an Anglicized version of French called *Law French*. It is from Law French that we inherited words such as *plaintiff* and *defendant* — and even "court," which comes from the *courtiers* who were the advisors to the king and the earliest decision makers of what became the royal courts. The development of the various royal courts and their interactions, against the background of the centuries-long power struggle between the king and Parliament, is a fascinating story but only marginally relevant to modern civil procedure.

Much more important is the Norman introduction of what has become a key feature in Anglo-American law: *trial by jury*.

Instead of looking for divine guidance, the law began turning to members of the community to resolve disputes. That innovation in turn drove many other features of the system, and, as we will see in Chapter 3, still does. Citizen-jurors are not trained in the law or in resolving disputes; an individual might sit on only a single jury in his or her whole life. Medieval English jurists (both judges and lawyers) therefore did not fully trust the jury to get it right, nor did the king and his advisors. English law after the Norman conquest gradually responded to this problem by narrowing the scope of the jury's authority in two ways: It limited the kinds of claims that could be brought and it relied on procedures that would pare each claim down to a single, and preferably simple, issue for the jury to decide.

writ
system

The claim-limiting function was performed by the *writ* system. A writ was a piece of parchment, issued by the *chancellor,* the king's most trusted advisor. It entitled its bearer to be heard on his claim in a royal court; without it, the court had no *jurisdiction* over the dispute. Each writ was limited to one type of claim: There was one writ if you claimed that your neighbor trespassed on your property, another if he stole your cow, and a third if you claimed to own the land his house stood on. (Most cases involved property disputes of one sort or another.) The writ enabled the royal court — and the jury — to know exactly what sort of claim was at stake in any particular case.

This administrative gatekeeper worked well as long as the chancellor had the flexibility to issue writs for whatever disputes happened to arise. Through about the middle of the thirteenth century, the chancellor retained this flexibility, and the number of writs gradually multiplied as new types of claims arose and old writs morphed into new ones. Some of the basic substantive principles established under this system have survived, and you might even read some old English writ cases in your Property or Torts classes.

During the latter half of the thirteenth and into the fourteenth century, however, the writ system ossified. Mistrust of juries and a corresponding desire to limit the types of claims they could hear was only part of the cause. A second factor was that, as wealth began to accumulate in forms other than land, new types of disputes were continually arising and it became harder to adapt an old writ to a new purpose. The third, and probably most important, factor was the king's ongoing battles with Parliament and with his own courts, which were becoming more independent. The Statute of Westminster, enacted by Parliament in 1285, forbade the chancellor from issuing new writs unless they were similar to existing writs. The royal courts began *quashing* — denying the validity of — writs issued by the chancellor if they were not close enough to existing writs. Without a valid writ, the case could not be heard.

Complementing the increasingly rigid writ system was the equally rigid procedural system, which revolved around the *pleadings* and was designed to leave the judge or the jury with but a single easy issue to decide. The plaintiff's opening plea was dependent on which writ he was using. From there, the defendant had to choose a single response: He could raise some procedural challenges with a *dilatory plea* and others with a *special demurrer*. Denying that he did what the plaintiff accused him of doing was pleading the *general issue*. A *general demurrer* meant that he was claiming that his action was not a legal wrong, and a *special plea* argued that he was justified in his action. (We should warn you that the italicized terms in the preceding three sentences are unimportant in federal civil procedure today,* but are included to give you a flavor of the complexity of the pleading system. They are not included in our glossary, but you can look them up in *Black's Law Dictionary* if you'd like — although we advise against it!) Further pleading followed, with each plea dependent both on what it

---

* Some state systems still retain these or similar terms, although the devices they describe do not usually operate in the way that demurrers and pleas had operated at common law. In any event, the study of state procedural systems is beyond the scope of most Civil Procedure courses.

was responding to and the particular argument it was intended to raise.

At each stage, the party had to choose a single plea and could not change it later. Once a defendant started down the road of alleging a procedural defect with a special demurrer, for example, he or she could never use a general demurrer to claim that he or she did not act as alleged, and he or she could not make both pleas together. Not only that, but each writ had its own procedures, so that a pleading that worked with one writ did not necessarily work the same way with another. One historian gives a flavor of the variations:

> Each form of action [or writ] . . . had its own form of general denial, so called because it imported an absolute and complete denial by a defendant of each and every allegation in a plaintiff's declaration. For example, in trespass either vi et armis or on the case the appropriate form of general denial was not guilty; in debt, owes nothing; in debt on a bond, it is not the defendant's deed; in assumpsit, never promised. If the defendant pleaded the wrong general issue, as not guilty to a plea of assumpsit or owes nothing to a plea of trespass, . . . then judgment would be given on demurrer for the plaintiff.[1]

The goal of this mandatory precision was to narrow the case to a single issue for the judge or jury to decide, but it did so at great cost. As one description summarizes it, "Pleading was a game — a very serious game — in which mistakes were common. Specialists in the art of pleading thrived on an opponent's miscues."[2] Because there was no going back, mistakes were not only common but fatal, and many meritorious claims or defenses were *dismissed* solely because a lawyer used the wrong writ or the wrong plea, or simply made a bad choice among available claims or defenses. From these inauspicious beginnings came our adversarial system.

The English common law system of writs and pleading had two other weaknesses, neither as spectacular as the rigidity that prevented claimants from obtaining justice when justice was due. First, there was almost no way for the parties to ferret out facts unless they paid for an investigation—and, of course, the opposing party would do its best to hide any useful evidence. Second, because the writ system had hardened in the late thirteenth century, the types of relief that could be awarded were limited. In an economically developing society, limiting relief to such things as the payment of money or the transfer of land was insufficient.

Nevertheless, this system did not begin to change until the nineteenth century. How could such an inefficient and unjust system have survived for so long? A number of factors contributed to its longevity,* but the most important for our purposes is that the common law regime was not the only game in town.

Go back to the Norman beginnings, and the chancellor. Claimants could always *petition* the chancellor to hear their cases directly instead of issuing a writ that sent them to the royal courts, although at first such petitions were rarely granted. But as the writ system became more ossified, the chancellor began to hear more claimants whose claims did not fit an existing writ or who could not get relief in the common law courts. The chancellor was originally an ecclesiastical official, trained in canon law, which itself derived from Roman law. (We told you Roman law would be back.) He was therefore not bound by the writ system or common-law pleading. He had no jury, and instead decided cases himself. He borrowed from canon law the inquisitorial processes of *subpoena* and *deposition,* commanding the production of evidence and the testimony of witnesses. He could also award relief—such as ordering a party to perform an act—

---

* Hindsight is 20–20, but it was harder for people immersed in the system to see its flaws. Moreover, for a good period of this time the system did a respectable job of resolving the most common types of disputes. Finally, the jury trial—inextricably linked to the whole procedural morass—became the pride of the English legal system, and its benefits were thought to outweigh any costs.

that the law courts could not. It might be useful to recall that Roman law was crafted by the Caesars, who were not known for accepting limits on their authority!

This alternative system of adjudication by the chancellor was known as *chancery* or *equity*.* It was formalized in the *Court of Chancery*, although the chancellor or his chief assistant — the master of the rolls — always maintained control over the final decision. By the middle of the fifteenth century, the Court of Chancery rivaled the common law courts. Because Chancery was within the control of the king, and the common law courts (originally the royal courts) had become much more independent, the rivalry between the two sets of courts was intertwined with the battles between the king and Parliament. Each court remained powerful, however, and both law and equity were very much part of the English legal system from the time America was colonized through (and after) it became independent.

Like the courts of law, equity had its drawbacks. Justice in the Court of Chancery was measured, in a commonly used phrase, by "the chancellor's foot" — in other words, by the chancellor's own sense of justice, which could differ considerably from chancellor to chancellor. It was also exceedingly slow and expensive. The chancellor decided every case individually, and could always ask for more information, which often produced the kind of interminable case that Charles Dickens described in *Bleak House*. As the case dragged on, moreover, every chancery official who collected information or performed some required administrative task had to be paid by the parties, and the costs of litigation mounted. Finally, although never as rigid as the common law, equitable pleading also became less

---

* Aside from the common law courts and equity, the English system had other courts of limited jurisdiction — an *admiralty* court, ecclesiastical courts, local courts, and other courts with a narrow subject-matter focus. Common law and equity were, however, the two court systems that exercised the greatest influence over modern American procedure.

flexible as time went on, which deprived equity of one of its major advantages over the common law courts.

From this brief description, you should be able to identify four primary, and interrelated, differences between equity and (common) law. First, and probably most important, while the common law system revolved around procedural form rather than substantive justice, equity was "impatient of pedantry and inclined to place substance before form."[3] Second, law was adversarial, while chancery — at least in its early years — was inquisitorial: In the courts of law, the parties were in control and the judges (and juries) were neutral arbiters, while in the Court of Chancery the judge collected the evidence, questioned the parties, and retained complete control over both the proceedings and the decision. Third, because the chancellor sat without a jury, litigation in equity was a meandering sequence rather than a single trial. The chancellor asked for evidence, made decisions about some issues, then perhaps looked at more evidence to make further decisions, and could even reopen a case at will if he thought justice had not been done. You will see in the Federal Rules and in modern civil procedure generally an attempt to combine the best features of both systems.

Finally, law and equity differed in the type of relief that was afforded. As noted earlier, the chancellor, unlike the common law courts, could directly order the parties to take action or refrain from taking action. But relief in chancery was also limited: Because the chancellor supposedly worked only on the "conscience" of the parties, he could *only* tell the parties what to do and could not order the transfer of property or money. This remedial distinction lives on in the substantive law of remedies: Damages are legal remedies, and injunctions (as well as specific performance of contracts, restitution, accounting, and various other things) are equitable relief. This distinction rarely makes more than a semantic difference, with one large and one small exception. Under the Seventh Amendment to the United States Constitution, parties are entitled to a jury trial if and only if their dispute would have been tried at law rather than in equity in 1791, when the Amendment was ratified. And because equity originally arose to fill the holes in the common law regime, a party cannot get any form of relief that is considered to be equitable unless he or she can show that he or she has no adequate remedy at law.

This, then, is how the law of England — and of the American colonies — stood at the time of the American Revolution. We turn in the next section to what the new United States did with its legal heritage.

Transplantation and Growing Dissatisfaction

Almost all the newly independent states initially adopted the English system, complete with the writ and pleading regime and the distinction between law and equity. The addition of a system of federal courts, as part of the national government apart from the individual states, complicated matters somewhat, as we explore in detail in Chapter 8. The federal system retained the distinction between law and equity, and by and large conformed to the procedures adopted in state courts.* And of course the federal Constitution, as well as the constitutions of the states, entrenched the pride of the English system, the jury.

America's unique geographic and sociological conditions, however, quickly began to influence its legal development. With vast uncultivated land, expanding commercial opportunities, and a mobile population, the United States desperately needed a coherent body of substantive law to govern the increasingly complex relationships among citizens. The writ system, tied as it was to procedure rather than substantive

---

* This is a very simplified description; we give a fuller description of the convoluted and evolving relationship between state and federal courts in Chapter 8.

law, could not fill this need. As one commentator put it: "By the early nineteenth century . . . the emerging concern in pleading was with substance, not with form. This concern was of great significance, for it compelled the bench and bar to think about law in substantive categories, such as 'tort' and 'contract,' rather than in the old procedural categories of trespass, assumpsit, and the like."[4] A second aspect of the new concern with substance was a demand for *trans-substantive* procedure — that is, a common procedural system for all the different categories of substantive law. These concerns moved the legal system away from both the writ system and common-law pleading, and also allowed for some *amendment* of the pleadings to give litigants somewhat greater procedural flexibility.

This new American focus on substantive law had two enduring consequences for our procedural regime. First, it affected the relationship between judge and jury. Recall that one goal of the English common law system was to narrow and simplify the claims that juries could hear. Once American courts began moving away from that system, they had to confront a choice between allowing the jury more authority or devising other methods of jury control. They chose the latter course. This choice was assisted by the American preference for divided authority: Balancing power between judge and jury came naturally to a society whose Constitution divided power between the federal and state governments and among the branches of the federal government. Many of the nineteenth-century jury-control innovations have survived in the form of the distinction between fact and law, evidentiary rules that limit what the jury can see and hear, and rules of procedure that allow the judge to take some factual decisions away from the jury.

The second consequence of a changing legal focus was felt in Britain as well as the United States: increasing dissatisfaction with common-law pleading and writs, and with the separation of law and equity. New York was the first to act, abolishing its chancery court in 1846 and adopting the *Field Code* (the brainchild of David Dudley Field, a lawyer and reformer) in 1848. Taken together, these two developments merged law and equity, created a single form of action to replace the multiplicity of writs, and replaced common-law pleading rules with what came to be known as *code pleading*: "If the common law may be termed *issue pleading*, since its main purpose was the framing of an issue, code pleading may be referred to as *fact pleading*, in view of the great emphasis placed under the codes upon getting the facts stated."[5] By the end of the nineteenth century, 27 states had adopted some version of code pleading, more had retained common-law pleading but relaxed its procedural rigidity, and even Great Britain, in the Judicature Acts of 1873 and 1875, had brought law and equity closer together and greatly relaxed and simplified pleading in both.

Code pleading, however, was far from a panacea. In some ways, it combined the worst aspects of law and equity. It made no provision for either a narrowing of the issues (as the common law had) or the discovery of evidence (as equity had) at the *pretrial* stage. Thus the parties might arrive at trial with multiple issues and little or no idea of what evidence would be presented. And although code pleading was simpler and more flexible than common-law pleading, it was still relatively complex, and it grew both more complex and more rigid with time. As with the common law system, the complexity and rigidity meant that small mistakes were both easy to make and likely to be fatal to one's case. The merger of law and equity in some states, moreover, deprived litigants of any alternative system of adjudication. The upshot was that by the beginning of the twentieth century, justice was almost as hard to obtain under code pleading as it had been under the old system of common law and equity.

Enter a new cadre of reformers, led by Roscoe Pound. Pound later became dean of the Harvard Law School (in

1916), but he began his crusade in 1906 when he delivered a speech to a meeting of the American Bar Association (ABA) entitled "The Causes of Popular Dissatisfaction with the Administration of Justice." In that speech—which the ABA almost refused to publish—Pound laid out the principles that eventually came to undergird the Federal Rules of Civil Procedure. It is to the long gestation and birth of those Rules that we turn in the next section.

The Federal Rules of Civil Procedure

Pound's reform efforts focused on three related defects of the administration of justice under both code pleading and common-law pleading. First, he decried what he called the "sporting theory of justice":

> The inquiry is not, What do substantive law and justice require? Instead, the inquiry is, Have the rules of the game been carried out strictly? If any material infraction is discovered . . . our sporting theory of justice awards new trials, or reverses judgments, or sustains demurrers in the interest of regular play.[6]

Second, he made a plea for the kind of judicial *discretion* that had been available in courts of equity. He criticized what he called the "mechanical operation of legal rules,"[7] and suggested that adjudication "involves, not logic merely, but discretion."[8] Finally, he believed that procedural rules should, in the words of one of his contemporaries, be "the 'handmaid rather than the mistress' of justice."[9] According to Pound, "rules of procedure should exist only to secure to all parties a fair opportunity to meet the case against them and a full opportunity to present their own case; and nothing should depend on or be obtainable through them except the securing of such opportunity."[10]

The heart of Pound's vision, then, was very close to the original system of equity: a judge with great discretion and

27

control, whose goal was to do justice between the parties rather than enforce procedural rules. Ultimately, most of his vision was implemented, although it took more than 30 years.

The first change came in a backwater of American jurisprudence: the still functioning but mostly inconsequential federal equity system. (Although there was only one set of federal courts, there was still a division between cases at law and cases in equity, with different rules governing each.) Using authority that had been granted to it in the early nineteenth century, the Supreme Court promulgated a comprehensive set of Equity Rules in 1912. Because cases at law far outnumbered those in equity, the new rules had little practical effect, but they are significant as precursors of the Federal Rules of Civil Procedure.

The 1912 Equity Rules adopted virtually all of Pound's principles. Pleading was simplified to require only a bill of complaint and an answer in most cases, and those needed only to describe the parties' dispute in "short and plain" or "short and simple" terms. No longer tied to a single writ or claim, parties could join multiple claims or raise multiple defenses. And the Equity Rules were shot through with opportunities for the judge to exercise discretion and excuse procedural mistakes in the interest of justice. The 1912 Rules also added an important innovation that Pound had not thought of: They permitted parties to discover information from each other before trial by requesting the production of documents, answers to written questions called *interrogatories*, and even live testimony through depositions.

Pound, joined by others including Charles Clark (dean of the Yale Law School, later appointed to the United States Court of Appeals for the Second Circuit) and Edson Sunderland (a professor at the University of Michigan Law School), continued to advocate procedural reform. In 1934, their efforts bore fruit: Congress passed the Rules Enabling Act,[11] which authorized the Supreme Court to promulgate one set of rules for both law and equity and directed that any such rules "shall neither abridge, enlarge, nor modify the substantive rights of any litigant." Congress retained the power to veto any rule. The Supreme Court immediately appointed a committee, led by Clark and Sunderland, to draft new federal rules of procedure. The committee drafted a comprehensive set of rules, which were issued by the Supreme Court without change and took effect in 1938. Thus were born the Federal Rules of Civil Procedure.

The Rules merge law and equity into a single form of action, the "civil action."[12] Otherwise, however, they look very similar to the 1912 Equity Rules, especially with regard to the simplicity of pleading, the availability of pretrial *discovery*, and the discretion of the judge. As one modern commentator has put it:

> The underlying philosophy of, and procedural choices embodied in, the Federal Rules were almost universally drawn from equity rather than common law. The expansive and flexible aspects of equity are all implicit in the Federal Rules. Before the rules, equity procedure and jurisprudence had applied to only a small percentage of the totality of litigation. Thus the drafters made an enormous change: in effect the tail of historic adjudication was now wagging the dog. . . .
>
> When one looks at the disgruntlement over unwieldy cases, uncontrolled discovery, unrestrained attorney latitude, and judicial discretion, . . . the pattern is clear. These are not the complaints about the rigor and inflexibility associated with the common law, but the opposite. The symptoms sound like what one would expect from an all-equity procedural system.[13]

To say that the Federal Rules are "all equity" is an exaggeration, as the 1938 Rules retained two important aspects of common law adjudication: the idea of a party-driven adversarial system with the judge as neutral arbiter, and the jury trial as the centerpiece of litigation. As we will see in the next two chapters, however, both of these common law holdovers sometimes sit uncomfortably within the largely equitable system created by the Federal Rules, even as they are central to it. And both have been somewhat diluted by subsequent amendments and interpretations of the Rules.

As you go through your Civil Procedure course — and as you read the rest of this book — you should keep this history closely in mind. This book follows the lead of most Civil Procedure courses by focusing on the history and development of the Federal Rules of Civil Procedure, as well as related federal procedural doctrines. Although the Federal Rules apply only in federal courts, and each state adopts its own rules for its state courts, they have heavily influenced the rules of procedure in every state; indeed, about half of the state courts have state rules of procedure that are nearly identical to the Federal Rules. Thus, the Federal Rules provide a common language for discussing how procedural principles have intersected with procedural doctrine. The history is relevant to both; because the Federal Rules of Civil Procedure are an amalgam of common law and equity rules (although heavy on the equity), many of the problems that arose under each of those systems might be replicated under the Rules. And the very act of trying to combine two very different systems creates problems of its own. One reason the Rules have been amended many times is to repair some of the problems. Your Civil Procedure class is likely to explore how well today's Rules navigate the pitfalls of law and equity, and whether (and how) they should be changed. It is impossible to answer those questions without an understanding of where the Rules came from.

THE PRINCIPLES OF PROCEDURE

From this history of American procedure, we can identify seven fundamental principles that together shape the structure of modern American civil procedure. From our common law heritage, we draw the *adversarial system* and the centrality of a *trial by jury*. The crucial insight from equity is that cases should not turn on procedural technicalities, but instead should be decided with an emphasis on *accuracy*. The drafters of the Federal Rules also had to make new choices in combining law and equity, and we are still making choices. First, equity's strength was dispensing justice, but it was terribly slow, expensive, and inefficient. The law courts were ruthlessly efficient, but often at the cost of justice. Balancing the two requires us to explore both *procedural fairness* and *efficiency*. Procedural fairness also implicates the *Due Process Clause* of the United States Constitution, which requires certain minimum procedural guarantees. Second, if cases can combine multiple claims and multiple parties (as equity permitted) but still must be tried before a single jury (as law required), what principles should govern the size of the lawsuit? The primary limiting principle in our system is *transactionalism*. Finally, the constitutional division of authority between the state and federal governments means that we have multiple courts, multiple procedural regimes, and multiple substantive legal doctrines. The interactions among them are mediated by principles of *federalism*. How each of these principles undergirds, intersects with, and influences the different parts of our procedural system is the subject of the next seven chapters.

～ 2 ～

The Adversarial
System

This book examines how we have—and how we should—design the American civil justice system. Over the next two chapters, we examine two design choices—*adversarial process* and *jury trial*—that influence every aspect of civil procedure and set the table for many of the doctrines that we study in succeeding chapters. These choices are critical because they allocate adjudicatory power in a way that establishes the boundaries within which litigation occurs. Jury trial divides the decision-making power between judge and jury, and the adversarial process hands the preliminary tasks of investigation, research, and presentation principally to the litigants and their lawyers. Both remove power from the judge. Both are enormously controversial. And both are quintessentially American: The United States is the only country to use civil juries with regularity, and it operates the most adversarial civil justice system in the world.

In this chapter, we examine the ways in which the adversarial system dictates the structure of American procedure, the benefits and drawbacks of the American adversarial system, and the way in which the ongoing controversy over the adversarial system drives some of the most significant recent reforms in American procedure.

THE PROCEDURAL CONSEQUENCES
OF AN ADVERSARIAL SYSTEM

Adversarialism is the foundational, and arguably the most critical, principle for the entire system of American civil justice. From the level of constitutional structure to the level of procedural and substantive detail, the adversarial system places its invisible hand over all of American law. Although we could debate the benefits and drawbacks of the adversarial system as an abstract matter, we think it better to defer that discussion until we explore the ways in which adversarial process matters in modern American litigation.

The Roles of the Judge, the Parties, and the Lawyers

In the classic adversarial model, the parties investigate, research, and present their cases. The judge remains detached, neutral, and passive until the time for a decision. At the presentation the judge listens, asking no questions and maintaining an open mind until the last scrap of evidence is in and the last argument made. The judge decides only the matters that the parties raise; even if the judge sees a better argument or claim than the one the parties make, the judge must not raise it. The parties' cases rise or fall on their own wits. The judge merely umpires the dispute.

This umpireal approach has significant political and legal consequences. Politically, the adversarial system establishes an expectation of judicial modesty and passivity. A great deal of power that a government might assert through its judicial branch — investigating alleged breaches of the government's laws and developing the evidence and arguments about those possible breaches — is instead entrusted to the parties. Judges are not supposed to be social reformers; they are resolvers of private disagreements. The attitude of the adversarial system toward those seeking legal redress is decidedly laissez-faire: If the parties want a particular result, they should expect no help from the government (the judge) in achieving it. Indeed, the debate in modern America over judicial activism has its roots in assumptions about the restrained nature of the judiciary that derive from our historical acculturation to the adversarial system.

Legally, the adversarial system means that the responsibility for sharpening the issues for decision lies with the parties. For this system to work, the parties must not have the same set of interests. One of the clearest rules in American law, derived from the adversarial ideal, is that a court cannot hear a "friendly" lawsuit. The parties must also have a real, live dispute between them; it cannot be moot or hypothetical or contrived. The parties also need to have a significant legal interest in the outcome of the case; your affection for your dear Aunt Mabel gives you no right to sue her neighbor when the neighbor's dog gives Aunt Mabel a fitful night's sleep. In Constitutional Law, you will learn that, in the federal courts, a case cannot be *moot, unripe*, or *advisory*, and that the parties must have *standing* (a sufficient legal interest) to bring the case. All of these constitutional doctrines derive from America's historical commitment to adversarial process.

The influence of adversarial process extends beyond a few doctrines in constitutional law to the whole of the American procedural system. When parties have differing interests, each has a big incentive to win. That incentive creates some assurance that the parties will adequately investigate and research the case, and will present their best claims and arguments. It also creates the dark underbelly of the adversarial system: the possibility that, in their desire to win, the parties might cheat, distort, or destroy information, and otherwise fail to cooperate with their opponent. After all, when the plaintiff's lawsuit seeks to put the defendant in a worse position, what incentive does the defendant have to help the plaintiff in any way?

Conversely, why should the plaintiff cooperate with a defendant who wants to deprive him or her of a remedy? We want judgments to be reasonably accurate, but how is accuracy possible when so much depends on the cooperation of parties with little incentive to cooperate?

To address these concerns, an adversarial system requires strict rules of behavior during the course of the lawsuit; it requires, in other words, rules of procedure and ethics. But these rules become yet another thing for the parties to fight over and to seek adversarial advantage in. Regardless of the content of the rules, grappling for procedural advantage is endemic to an adversarial system; and resolving disputes over procedural compliance becomes a common judicial activity. Adversarial process has something of the quality of a sporting contest, and we expect the judicial umpire to enforce the rules of the sport strictly, equally, and without regard to who "ought to win" on the merits. As a result, and as the history of common law procedure shows, procedure can come to dominate substance as the focal point of legal disputes. Creating procedural rules that induce appropriate behavior among adversaries without losing sight of the substance of the dispute is a constant challenge in an adversarial system.

In part because it is likely to be procedurally complex, an adversarial system also invites a new set of participants into the lawsuit. So far we have spoken about the judge and the parties as the only participants. When the law is complex, however, the parties are likely to turn to specialists. Lawyers take over the responsibilities for developing the case and determining the best claims and arguments to make. The lawyer becomes the client's spokesperson, and conducts the legal fight on the client's behalf. Ethical rules describe the litigator's role as one of "zealous" advocacy "within the bounds of the law." Sometimes the lawyer is described as a "hired gun," a nod in the direction of the mythology of the Old West, which, together with a love of sports and competition, have so inclined the American mind to adversarial legal combat.

Hiring a legal gunslinger does not decrease the existing incentives to lie, cheat, and distort; if anything, it splits the moral costs of such behavior between the client and the lawyer and makes such behavior more likely. Even worse, lawyers have their own interests (for example, to be well paid and to be acknowledged for their superior legal skills) that make them imperfect agents of either the client's will or society's desire to see that justice is done. Because of lawyers' specialized knowledge, monitoring their fidelity to the interests of their clients and the courts is also difficult. Therefore, an adversarial system must necessarily impose on lawyers a strong set of ethical duties that are intended to vault the interests of clients and courts over the interests of the lawyers themselves. These duties typically demand, without explicit recognition of the contradiction, that a lawyer be both a *zealous advocate* for the client and an *officer of the court* who acts with the interests of justice always in mind. The course in Professional Responsibility that you take in law school will help to sort out these obligations, which owe their existence largely to our use of the adversarial system. So do other constraints on lawyerly conduct that you encounter in your Civil Procedure course, such as Rule 11 of the Federal Rules of Civil Procedure.

The effects of the adversarial system extend beyond these areas. For an adversarial system to work well, the client and the lawyer must work as a team, and must therefore be assured of the privacy of their conversations — hence the *attorney–client privilege*. Just as a coach's game plan is kept secret from the other side, a lawyer must be able to prepare a case without fear that the opposing lawyer is borrowing his or her wits — hence the *work-product doctrine*.

The adversarial system, then, establishes a web of constitutional doctrines, procedural rules, ethical duties, and evidentiary privileges that derive from the roles that the system expects of the participants. Because the principal focus of this book is on the procedural system, the remainder of this section discusses a number of more specific procedural consequences that follow from an adversarial system.

The Structure of Legal Processes

Using an adversarial system does not help much in terms of filling in the nitty-gritty details of a procedural code (for example, whether a defendant should have 20 or 30 days to answer a complaint). In a number of ways, however, it establishes the framework for the procedural system as a whole.

The Dialectical Form of Litigation To resolve disputes, the adversarial system invites the use of dialectical reasoning — reasoning by question and answer, by point and counterpoint — to achieve a correct synthesis. One side presents its best case, and the other side attacks that case. Then the roles reverse, and the other side presents its best case while the first side challenges those assertions. Like a sport, one side gets the ball trying to score and the other defends; then the other side gets the ball. Adversarial process is more literary than logical. Like a storytelling contest, each side uses certain facts and builds a story from them, trying to persuade the listener that its version of the facts is more compelling than the other side's yarn. Each side's natural tendency to tell a tall tale is held in check only by the other side's ability to interrupt and say, "That's not how it was." Back and forth, examination and cross-examination, closing argument pitted against closing argument: This form of trial, which Americans take for granted, results from our commitment to adversarial process.

The rest of the litigation process reflects the same point and counterpoint found in the trial. To commence the case, the plaintiff files a *complaint*, the defendant an *answer*. When a party seeks something from the court that the other side will not or cannot provide voluntarily, he or she files a *motion*, and the other party files a *response* (sometimes followed by the first party then filing a *reply*). When one side wants information from the other side, it files a *discovery request*, and the other side *objects* or *responds*. Testimony can be taken from witnesses before the trial through *depositions*, at which one side asks questions on *direct examination*, followed by the other side asking questions on *cross-examination*. Again, this adversarial structure does not determine procedural specifics like what the complaint must say or how many depositions a party may take, but it establishes the broad expectation about how the litigation process moves to and through trial.

Notice and the Opportunity to Be Heard   The adversarial system presupposes a fairly passive judge, stirred to action only when the parties need the judge to resolve a dispute. The judge comes to a decision only after hearing the evidence and arguments of both sides. If only one side presents the dispute to the judge, the risk exists that the evidence and arguments will be unduly biased, and the judge, who is to perform no investigation of his or her own, will not know better. Having both sides present the evidence and the arguments both guards against overreaching by either party and provides the judge with a richer, more diverse set of possibilities than either side alone would likely present.

For this reason, giving each side the *opportunity to be heard* is absolutely essential to the working of the adversarial system. But the opportunity to be heard is meaningless unless the party that brings a dispute to the court's attention gives the opponent *notice* sufficiently far in advance that the opponent can prepare to meet the first side's arguments. This idea of notice and an opportunity to be heard is one of the bedrock concepts in adversarial justice.

Indeed, the concept of notice and an opportunity to be heard is so fundamental that it enjoys constitutional stature.

The United States Constitution contains two *Due Process Clauses*: One is contained in the Fifth Amendment, which applies to the federal government, and one is contained in the Fourteenth Amendment, which applies to state governments and their subdivisions (counties and cities). As you will learn in Civil Procedure, Constitutional Law, and other classes, the Due Process Clauses constrain many different kinds of government behavior. One government institution that they constrain is the judiciary. And one of the numerous constraints that the Due Process Clauses place on the judiciary is the requirement that a court provide notice and an opportunity to be heard before taking an action that might affect litigants' interests in life, liberty, and property. If a court fails to afford a constitutionally adequate notice and opportunity to be heard before issuing an order or judgment, then the order or judgment is a constitutional nullity, not deserving of obedience.*

Requiring notice and an opportunity to be heard does not specify exactly what the notice should say or how it should be communicated to the other side. Nor does the requirement of an opportunity to be heard precisely specify what that opportunity must consist of. Notice and opportunity to be heard do not typically define a certain way in which courts must always act, but they limit in important ways the actions that courts can take.

---

    * The last two sentences are slightly inaccurate. First, in emergency situations, a court can sometimes act without providing a defendant notice and an opportunity to be heard; thus, a court can order a short-term *temporary restraining order* or *attachment* (seizure) of a defendant's property. But the court must immediately follow such action with an opportunity to be heard, at which time the aggrieved litigant can challenge the court's pre-notice deprivation. Second, a party who believes that he or she was not afforded constitutionally adequate notice or opportunity to be heard cannot parade around and act like the order did not exist. Once an aggrieved party has notice of the allegedly deficient order or judgment, the party must challenge the order through the trial and appellate processes, and obey it in the meantime.

Joinder and the Binding Effect of Judgments Another
piece of the structural bedrock, which is related to notice
and an opportunity to be heard, is the effect of the adversarial
system on the size and scope of litigation. To see what we
mean, ask yourself these questions: Why don't we use lawsuits
to decide the level at which the Federal Reserve should set its
lending rate, or to decide how large an annual increase Social
Security recipients should get? A lot of good reasons exist,
among them respect for the workings of American democracy.
One of the other reasons is a sense that courts are not thought
to be institutionally competent to make these types of decisions. Why are they thought to be incompetent? Partly because
no legal (as opposed to economic or political) standard determines the answer, and partly because, in one way or another,
every person in the country feels the influence of a rise or fall in
the Federal Reserve's lending rate, or the increase in Social
Security payments. If we litigate such questions in an adversarial way, isn't each American citizen entitled to notice of the
government's proposed actions and an opportunity to be heard
before the agency acts?

Obviously, we cannot imagine conducting such amorphous, massive lawsuits — and that fact highlights how the
adversarial system constrains our imagination about what a
civil justice system does and should do. Under the adversarial
system, courts work best when the dispute involves a clearly
defined set of potentially applicable legal (as opposed to economic, political, social, or cultural) rules, a limited set of facts
that possibly bear on those rules, and a limited number of
people immediately affected by the court's decision. The dispute is confined in time, space, effect, and numbers of participants. To take a far more mundane example showing the
limits of the adversarial mind, perhaps you are being sued
for a car accident you got into. As fellow drivers and payers
of auto insurance premiums, we have an indirect interest in the
outcome of your case; if you lose, our premiums will go up a

tiny bit. But we have no right to participate in your lawsuit. Our interests are too indirect, so our contribution to a correct resolution of your lawsuit is likely to be small.

Put differently, affording some people the bedrock right of an adversarial system — the right to notice and an opportunity to be heard — means excluding other people from that privilege. The adversarial system requires us to decide who "counts" for purposes of litigation, who can present evidence and arguments and who cannot.

Reasonably enough, participation in civil lawsuits is initially limited to those whose interest in the dispute is more significant in kind or degree from the rest of us. These are the *parties* — the people who complain that a legal wrong was done to them (the *plaintiffs*) and those who supposedly committed the wrong (the *defendants*). Some legal linkage among these parties is also required; for instance, if one plaintiff got into an accident one day against one defendant, and another plaintiff got into another accident another day at another intersection against another defendant, this situation would usually be treated as two lawsuits rather than one.* Without something linking them together, the parties to the first accident have little incentive to provide evidence or arguments that will help the court decide the merits of the second accident accurately. Therefore, whatever else the lawsuit might contain, some legal *claim* must link all of the parties and give them an incentive to be heard either in favor of or against a particular outcome on that claim.

In short, an adversarial approach to adjudication suggests that a procedural system should have a fairly conservative

---

* You might have noticed that we used the words "initially" and "usually" in the first and third sentences of this paragraph. These are, quite intentionally, designed to be weasel words. In Chapter 7, we explore how other fundamental principles lead us to compromise on the adversarial preference in some situations.

attitude toward the questions of *claim joinder* and *party joinder*. If too many claims or parties become involved in a case, ensuring every claim and every party a full hearing while still excluding extraneous information becomes a more difficult task.

If parties joined in the case are the only ones entitled to notice and an opportunity to be heard, it seems fair that the parties should be the only ones bound to respect the judgment entered in that case. After all, the adversarial system is based on self-interest. We expect self-interested parties to advance their own positions, not the positions of others. The judge does not look out for anyone's interests — and certainly does not look out for the interests of people who are not even parties to the case. A nonparty has no notice, no opportunity to be heard, and no way to present or protect his or her particular interests. As we have seen, the Constitution's commitment to notice and an opportunity to be heard renders void an order or judgment entered against a party who fails to receive notice or an opportunity to be heard. *A fortiori*, as the Supreme Court has held on a number of occasions, the Due Process Clauses do not allow a court to bind a nonparty who receives neither notice nor an opportunity to be heard to an adverse judgment or order.*

Therefore, status as a party takes on a particular significance in the American adversarial system. Parties are bound to a court's decisions; nonparties are not bound. Assume that you and a friend are injured in a car accident. Your friend sues the driver of the other car, claiming negligence. Your friend loses. Now you sue the other driver in the same court. Because you were not a party to your friend's case, the court cannot force you to accept the result of that case. In other words, the

---

* A couple of exceptions to this rule exist. The only significant one for our purposes involves the *class action*, which we discuss later in the book.

judgment entered in your friend's case has no *preclusive* effect on your case. You are free to argue again that the other driver was negligent. And you might even win. The American adversarial system places such a priority on the individual's right to be heard that it is even willing to tolerate judgments that are inconsistent with each other.

The American version of party joinder and preclusion rules derives largely from the existence of our adversarial system.

The Constitutional Status of the Adversarial System

The Constitution is our most foundational document. No government official can lawfully act contrary to its commands, and no statute or rule of law inconsistent with the Constitution can stand. If a court acts contrary to constitutional strictures, its actions are null and void. As we have said, a number of doctrines that flow from the adversarial system (including mootness, ripeness, standing, notice and an opportunity to be heard, and binding effect only against parties) have constitutional stature. Therefore, courts must respect them.

Given that the adversarial ideal has spawned a number of constitutional doctrines, an interesting question is whether the adversarial system itself enjoys constitutional status. Put differently, would it be unconstitutional for American courts to adopt an *inquisitorial*, rather than an adversarial, approach to litigation, or to change any of the significant guarantees of the adversarial system? The answer matters a great deal, because reform of our present adversarial approach might be impossible if the approach has constitutional stature.

Thus far, however, the Supreme Court has never held that an adversarial approach to civil litigation is constitutionally compelled. Famous snippets in some Supreme Court opinions (many of them penned by either Justice Frankfurter or Justice Jackson) point in that direction, but most of these quotations arise in the criminal context, in which the stakes, and therefore the constitutional considerations, are different. In the most widely used modern approach to the question, the Supreme Court has suggested that the procedural guarantees of the Due Process Clauses are determined through a balancing test: Courts can alter adversarial procedures when the cost savings from a less adversarial procedure exceed the expected cost (if any) resulting from additional erroneous rulings that a less adversarial procedure will cause.[1]

Therefore, the adversarial system sits in an anomalous constitutional position: Some of its features, such as notice and opportunity to be heard, are constitutionally enshrined, but other features, such as the right to control the presentation of evidence and arguments, might not be required if a cheaper or better non-adversarial substitute can be found. That fact puts back into focus a question that we deferred when we began this section: Is the adversarial system a better method of adjudication than its alternatives?

THE ADVANTAGES AND DISADVANTAGES OF THE ADVERSARIAL SYSTEM

The debate over the benefits and drawbacks of the adversarial system has gone on for centuries, with no end in sight. The system has its strong adherents and its equally ardent detractors. Its supporters argue that the system better respects individual autonomy and choice, limits the power of government, increases acceptance of judicial decisions, and places the decision about how much to invest in the litigation in the hands of those with the most direct stake in the outcome. Some adherents also claim that the system does a better job of truth seeking because the other side is always ready to hold a deceptive party accountable and because judicial detachment guarantees greater neutrality in the ultimate decision. The most thoughtful philosophical support for the system came from Professor Lon Fuller. He argued that adjudication by its very nature was a decision-making process that required the affected parties to participate in the outcome by presenting evidence and arguments. Because the adversarial system better enabled the parties to do so, it was the most legitimate form of adjudication.

Adherents of the adversarial system point out that the system's main competitor, the inquisitorial system, suffers from exactly the flaws that the adversarial system remedies to advantage: too much judicial power, too little litigant control, too great a risk of judicial prejudgment, and so on. But detractors of the adversarial system claim that adherents fail to recognize the adversarial system's weaknesses, and unfairly minimize the advantages of inquisitorial process. The adversarial approach of motion and response, examination and cross-examination, is slow and expensive. An inquisitorial judge can cut to the heart of a case quickly, and can level the playing field when great disparity in wealth and resources handicaps the poorer side. Typically, detractors of adversarial process contend that an inquisitorial approach leads to more accurate outcomes. An inquisitorial judge can decide the case on its substantive legal merits, and need not be distracted by procedural smokescreens or silk-tongued obfuscation spun out by advocates with excessive loyalty to their clients' positions. The quaint claim that truth better emerges from an adversarial contest between two parties, each of whom has an incentive to lie (or at least tell only half the truth), is dubious at best, and flat wrong at worst. As detractors point out, no other major decision-making process — whether to invest in a particular company, to conduct open-heart surgery, or to build a sky-scraper in a neoclassical style — uses the adversarial method. It is a relic of days gone by, when litigation was a close substitute for combat. It turns the trial into a circus, relies too much on the wits of counsel, and creates a "win at all costs" gamesmanship that denigrates respect for justice. To use the phrase popularized by Roscoe Pound, it is a "sporting theory of justice."

The issue at the heart of this disagreement, whether the adversarial system advances or hinders the search for the truth, has never been resolved definitively. In most of the debates, "truth" refers to the correct state of the facts on which a legal decision can be based. But there also exists such a thing we might call "legal truth": Has the case been correctly decided after considering the best possible claims, defenses, and arguments? Some data, which are inconclusive (surprise!), bear on the question of whether the adversarial system or the inquisitorial system leads closer to factual truth, but little empirical work has ever been done on the question of each system's merits in determining legal truth. Both sides love to dredge up a parade of horrible injustices perpetrated by the other system, but be careful never to confuse anecdotes with data. Both systems have their flaws. For the time being, therefore, an objective observer is safest maintaining a healthy agnosticism about the truth-seeking benefits of either system.

Even if we could know with certainty that the adversarial system was less effective in finding the truth than the inquisitorial system, that fact would not end the debate. As we said in Chapter 1, we want our adjudicatory system to be reasonably, but not necessarily perfectly, accurate. We also want the system to advance other goals as well—for instance, to be as inexpensive and speedy as possible, and to conform to the political expectations that we have for the judiciary in our culture. Suppose that adversarial process led to accurate outcomes in 99.98 percent of all cases, and a non-adversarial process led to accurate outcomes in 99.99 percent of all cases. But suppose that the non-adversarial process eliminated your right to choose your own lawyer, and put the judge in charge of examining all witnesses, so that your lawyer had no rights of examination or cross-examination. Maybe you would be unwilling to sacrifice these cherished adversarial rights for a .01 percent gain in accuracy. Maybe you would make the trade. The point is that claims about the adversarial system and its alternatives cannot reduce only to a question about which system is better at determining truth. Other principles, a number of which we discuss elsewhere in this book, also bear on the adversarial system's merits.

In the end no single "best" procedural system exists. Every procedural system is embedded in a web of legal, cultural, political, economic, and social expectations, some of which the procedural system helped to create. Upsetting those expectations too much will be costly — perhaps even too costly — whatever the objective merits of a particular procedural reform. At any given moment, the best system for France is probably different from the best system for Japan or Kenya. One of the strongest arguments for the American adversarial system has nothing to do with its excellence in discerning the merits of factual or legal disputes. We are a market-driven, autonomy-protecting, contest-loving people distrustful of large concentrations of power in government or other institutions. The simple fact is that a strongly adversarial approach to litigation fits this national character better than other approaches. Any discussion about serious reforms to the American adversarial process must also be a discussion about changes in our national identity.

ONGOING REFORMS IN AMERICAN ADVERSARIAL PROCESS

Although outright abandonment of the adversarial system is unimaginable, calls to reform aspects of the American adversarial culture have had, and continue to have, a significant influence on the American procedural system. The most famous call to reform issued forth a century ago, when Roscoe Pound stridently attacked the adversarial system in the speech that catapulted him to national prominence and ultimately to the deanship of Harvard Law School. Pound's basic argument was that the "sporting theory of justice" had vaulted issues of procedure over the merits of disputes. To rebalance American law, lawyers and judges needed to recover the original spirit of *equity*, in which flexible and discretionary procedural rules advanced resolutions on the merits rather than became obstacles in the path of justice. Pound did not call for abolition of the adversarial system; he thought that an infusion of equitable principles could sufficiently cabin its obfuscatory tendencies. Nonetheless, the mix was bound to be unstable; recall that equity had been an inquisitorial process in its inception.

The ultimate result of Pound's speech was the adoption in 1938 of the Federal Rules of Civil Procedure. The Federal Rules still contemplated an adversarial approach to litigation; parties were firmly in control of choosing claims and defenses, making and responding to motions, and digging up and presenting evidence and legal arguments. But the Rules softened the adversarial system in important ways. The Rules tended to be more forgiving of procedural miscues. The Rules were loosely textured to give a judge considerable *discretion* to achieve the "just, speedy, and inexpensive determination of every action."[2] The judge was somewhat less an umpire and somewhat more a fellow explorer in the quest to achieve justice. The rigor of the *pleadings* — and the resulting opportunity for adversarial gamesmanship — was lessened. Rules of claim and party joinder followed the equity model, and were considerably more generous than the *common law* allowed. The great innovation of the Federal Rules involved the widespread use of discovery, through which each side, before the trial, could request almost any kind of evidence from opponents or third parties. Before the Federal Rules, discovery was often unavailable at common law, and the Federal Rules expanded on the devices that equity usually allowed. In its early years, one of the criticisms of this discovery system was its incompatibility with the adversarial spirit, because now lawyers and parties would have to help their opponents build their cases by providing them with potentially damaging information.

This blend of an essentially adversarial system with some non-adversarial impulses lasted for about 40 years. Pleading and discovery worked reasonably well for the run-of-the-mill cases of the 1930s, and the fear that discovery was the beginning of the end of the adversarial system proved unfounded. For various reasons, however, cases after World War II often became larger, messier, and more complex. Among the cases were antitrust and securities claims against businesses and civil rights claims against government institutions. In these cases, pleading often provided few clues about the dispute, and the discovery needed to uncover the true nature of the parties' contentions was extensive and expensive. A common claim was that businesses and government institutions were forced to settle cases not because they had done wrong but because they could not afford the expense of litigation (especially the expense of discovery). A system of pleading and discovery that had been designed to expose a case's merits had, critics claimed, metamorphosed into a system in which litigants blackmailed opponents into settlements without merit. At the same time, the common lore went, lawyers were shirking their obligations under the discovery rules by making groundless objections or refusing to hand over requested information. Giving and getting information had become a game in itself, as complex, contentious, expensive, and adversarial as anything that had happened in the bad old days of the common law. In short, according to this view, the lawyers were doing what lawyers in an adversarial system will always do: They were learning how to use procedural rules to achieve leverage over their opponents.

The truth of this portrayal is debatable and perhaps lies in the eye of the beholder. Its accuracy is beside the point. This image of adversaries using the Federal Rules to pervert the course of justice took hold in the judicial and legal imagination. By the 1970s, dissatisfaction with the original design of the Federal Rules was widespread, and most of the unhappiness centered on the pleading and discovery systems. In the early 1980s, a series of reforms to the pleading and discovery rules again rounded the sharp edges of adversarial culture. These new Rules became the first salvo in what has become a principal focus of American procedural reform for the past quarter of a century: creating disincentives for sharp adversarial practices by giving the judge more power during the *pretrial process*. This new direction merged with a second reforming impulse: making litigation more efficient by reducing cost and delay.

These reforms manifested themselves in amendments to the Federal Rules and comparable state procedural codes, as well as in legislation and judicial decisions. Here we focus on changes in four areas that you are likely to encounter in Civil Procedure: Rule 11, discovery, *mandatory disclosure*, and *case management*.

Changes in Rule 11

Rule 11 was a backwater until it was overhauled in 1983 and again in 1993. The purpose of the amended Rule 11 is to prevent the filing of pleadings, motions, or other papers that lack merit. Rule 11 accomplishes this goal by means of a requirement that each pleading, motion, or paper be signed by an attorney (or, in some cases, by the party). Rule 11(b) says that this signature constitutes a certification that the pleading, motion, or paper is not being filed for an improper purpose (for example, to harass or extort a groundless settlement) and that it has both legal and factual support. Although there is some disagreement among the courts, the usual view is that Rule 11 imposes an objective standard of liability (would a reasonable person have known that the offending document was harassing or meritless) rather than a subjective standard (did the signer in fact know that the document was harassing or meritless).

In one sense, Rule 11 does not seem all that remarkable. Even before Rule 11, ethical rules prevented lawyers from engaging in such behavior. Often, however, enforcement of ethical rules was lax. Ethical violations needed to be reported to an offending lawyer's disciplinary body, many of which displayed sympathy for fellow lawyers and all of which moved slowly. In short, there was little incentive to report a lawyer even for egregiously obstreperous behavior. Rule 11 created a far more immediate process. Bad behavior was reported directly to the presiding judge (and parties love to tattle on an opponent as a means of driving a wedge between the judge and the opponent). *Sanctions* were imposed in the case itself.

You still might wonder why so much attention is paid to Rule 11 in a Civil Procedure class. One reason to study Rule 11 is that it serves as a good vehicle to talk about the ethics of the adversarial system: about how far lawyers should go to represent their clients' interests, about what duties lawyers should owe to courts, and about the limits of creativity in advocacy. Moreover, Rule 11 is also a good vehicle to talk about the relationship between procedure and substance. After the 1983 amendment, one of the great criticisms of Rule 11 was its lack of neutrality: Although it appeared to be neutral on its face, in reality Rule 11 chilled the filing of certain types of lawsuits — especially civil rights and securities fraud cases — in which the plaintiffs often had little prefiling information about whether a legal wrong had been done. Next, Rule 11 can touch off an interesting debate about how open we want our courts to be (and therefore how litigious we want our society to be) — in other words, how much chaff we are willing to make our legal system sift through to find some wheat.

Lastly, Rule 11 provides a wonderful case study in how difficult procedural reform can be in an adversarial system. To explain, we need to give a bit of background. In the original 1983 amendment, a violation led to automatic sanctions against the offending party or lawyer. In addition to other penalties, a typical sanction included payment of the attorneys' fees that the other side had expended in dealing with the sanctionable pleading, motion, or paper. The award of attorneys' fees constituted an extraordinary shift in American litigation. Under the *American Rule*, each side in an American court pays its own attorneys' fees; the winning party cannot obtain fees from the losing party. (By statute, some legal claims permit the winner to obtain attorneys' fees, but these statutes are the exception.) The traditional argument for the American Rule is that it removes a bar to litigation and opens courts to average citizens. But the American Rule is unique; nearly every major legal system requires the loser to pay the winner's fees.

As a significant exception to the American Rule, Rule 11 suddenly became very popular. Winners saw a way to recover their litigation expenses from losers: All they needed to do was to convince the court that the loser's case was so weak that it was frivolous. Some parties also used real or threatened Rule 11 motions to browbeat a poorly financed opponent into withdrawing a case, claim, or argument; even if the opponent's side had some merit, the opponent was unable to bear the risk of a Rule 11 sanction. Soon, opponents fought back by filing Rule 11 motions against parties' allegedly frivolous filing of Rule 11 motions. Within a few years, Rule 11 had become a poster child for the adversarial behavior that it was supposed to prevent.

In 1993, this reality compelled the drafters of the Federal Rules of Civil Procedure to amend Rule 11 to its present form. The most important changes soften the sanctions in two ways. First, a sanction is no longer compulsory; and when a judge does order a sanction, Rule 11(c) limits the sanction to one that suffices to "deter repetition" of the offending conduct. Because an award of attorneys' fees is no longer nearly automatic, the incentive to use Rule 11 against an opponent drops markedly. Second, the 1993 amendment creates a *safe harbor* provision. A party who believes that an opponent has committed a Rule 11 violation must first call that fact to the opponent's attention. Rule 11(c) then affords the opponent a 21-day safe harbor within which to withdraw or amend the allegedly offending pleading, motion, or paper. Only if the opponent refuses to do so can the party move the court for a Rule 11 sanction.*

The 1983 and 1993 amendments tell a story as old as the adversarial system itself. After the 1983 amendment, lawyers were doing with Rule 11 what they will do with any procedural rule in an adversarial system: They were using a rule designed for an important public purpose (to deter frivolous litigation) to accomplish private objectives (to obtain fees or threaten opponents into submission). The effort to reduce certain sharp adversarial practices led to a rise in other sharp adversarial practices. The 1993 amendment beat a retreat, trying to preserve the core of the rule while reducing the side litigation and gamesmanship that the 1983 amendment had spawned. Of course, it also reduced the effectiveness of Rule 11 as a device to police the ethical practices of lawyers. The moral that you derive from the story of Rule 11 depends on your perspective. One moral is that efforts to rein in sharp adversarial practices are ultimately doomed to failure, so that the

---

* This safe harbor provision does not apply to potential Rule 11 sanctions that the judge notices on his or her own. A judge can enter an immediate order, called an *order to show cause*, asking a party to show why a sanction should not be entered because of an allegedly offensive pleading, motion, or other paper.

only solution is abandonment of the adversarial system. The converse moral is that efforts to chill adversarial zeal cloak a substantive political agenda in the clothing of procedural neutrality, so that the only sure guarantee of individual rights is an unfettered adversarial system.

Changes in Discovery

A second set of changes designed to temper the perceived adversarial excesses of the 1970s involved discovery. One change is the addition of Rule 26(g), which is the equivalent of Rule 11 for discovery requests and responses. Rule 26(g) requires every discovery request or response to be signed; this signature constitutes a certification that the request or response is not intended for an improper purpose, is not unduly burdensome, and is not frivolous. Second, some changes in discovery are designed to restrict at the margins the amount of information that a lawyer can obtain through discovery from an opponent or third parties. For instance, one restriction, put into place in 1983 and reinforced in 1993, 2000, and 2006, limits discovery only to information that is not unduly burdensome or expensive in light of the needs of the case.[3] Another amendment, put into place in 2000, precludes discovery dealing with the "subject matter" of the case unless the requesting party shows "good cause" for the discovery.[4] A third restriction limits the number and length of certain discovery devices.[5] Finally, a lawyer who objects to the production of discoverable documents can no longer simply file an objection — a simple matter — but is now put to the task of listing certain information about each such document, a more onerous task intended to discourage excessive objections.[6]

Most of these changes in discovery can be defended as *efficiency* measures, designed to streamline litigation and keep the lawyers focused on the heart of the case. Although they constrain the amount of information that lawyers can

2 2 ~ *The Adversarial System*

seek, none of them changes the basic adversarial structure of litigation, in which lawyers gather and craft the information and judges passively receive it. At the same time, these changes in discovery were put into place principally because of the perception that, left to its own devices, the adversarial system was making a hash out of the discovery system — that the public goal of discovery (to assist in the accurate resolution of a case) was being turned to the private goals of adversaries (to win by browbeating opponents with expensive discovery requests and refusing to provide reciprocal information).

The Addition of Mandatory Disclosure

A more direct challenge to adversarial roles occurred in 1993, with the adoption of the mandatory disclosure provisions of Rule 26(a). Rule 26(a) requires the disclosure — even without a request from an opponent — of three types of information: an initial disclosure of the identity of persons and documents that support the disclosing party's claims or defenses; a subsequent disclosure of the identity of expert witnesses and the substance of their opinions; and a disclosure shortly before trial of the identity of witnesses that a party expects to or may call at trial, the transcript of depositions that a party expects to use in lieu of testimony, and the identity of documents that a party expects to or may introduce at trial.[7] The rule regarding *initial mandatory disclosure* created such a controversy that Rule 26 originally allowed districts to opt out of the rule if they wished. About half did. In 2000, after some softening of its terms, the requirement of initial disclosure was made mandatory across all federal courts.

The disclosure provisions are intended as an antidote to excessively adversarial behavior. The discovery rules already entitled parties to obtain this information, and good lawyers always sought it out. In some cases, however, opponents or their lawyers stonewalled or dissembled. So, the argument went, why not make the requirement of disclosure come from the court? Lawyers would be far more loath to disobey a rule of the court than a request from an opponent. It sped up the process and removed a sharp adversarial practice.

So understood, it is hard to oppose mandatory disclosure. But opponents of the idea feared that initial disclosure might hand a party with a frivolous case a gold mine of information it could use for other purposes, and it would create a huge front-end expense that poorer litigants would be unable to pay. In addition, some argued that this provision was the camel's head under the edge of the tent (the camel's nose already having snuck under the tent through other amendments in the 1980s). The march from adversarial to inquisitorial justice was accelerating its pace. Like an inquisitor, the court was ordering the production of evidence rather than leaving the task to the adversaries.

The early experience with mandatory disclosure has shown that, except for the purist, the fears that these disclosures signaled the demise of the adversarial system are overdrawn. Perhaps, if the American system becomes inquisitorial in another century, the adoption of the mandatory disclosure provisions will be seen as an important event in the transition. For now, the lesson seems to be that the adversarial system is not perfectly compatible with the discovery system, and as long as we are committed to using discovery before trial, we constantly need to sand down the sharp edges of adversarial behavior.

Case Management

The final, and undoubtedly most significant, intrusion on the classic adversarial model has been the rise of case management. The concept of case management is to inject the judge into the process of managing the case at an early stage. In adversarial theory, the judge has little to do with the case until it is ready for trial; the judge rules on disputes, but otherwise remains passive for fear that exposure to scraps of information about the case might cause bias or prejudice.

Beginning with a spate of antitrust claims in the 1940s and civil rights litigation in the 1950s, courts grappling with larger, more complex social issues often had a difficult time resolving them. During the 1950s, a judicial consensus emerged: To resolve such complex cases, the judge could not sit back and let the parties slog through years of discovery, countless disputatious motions, and fruitless efforts to narrow claims. The judge had to help shape the litigation by clarifying disputed issues and controlling the amount and pace of discovery. The judge became the manager of the case.

Although the managerial role forced the judge to step outside the role assigned by the adversarial system, the results of managerial judging in complex cases were generally thought to be positive. As a result, when judicial dissatisfaction with perceived adversarial excesses and the resulting costliness of litigation set in during the 1970s, some judges and scholars found in case management an attractive, already tested solution. One of the criticisms of case management, however, was that it was largely "off-book" — the judge's more active role was nowhere authorized under the Federal Rules of Civil Procedure. Therefore, the 1983 amendments to the Federal Rules took Rule 16, another sleepy little Rule, and converted it into one of the longest and most significant of all the Federal Rules. A further amendment in 1993 confirmed and strengthened the managerial role.

The centerpiece of Rule 16 is the conference system. Although they are not required to do so, judges are encouraged to (and usually do) hold a *scheduling conference* shortly after the complaint and answer have been filed. Lawyers for both sides attend the conference, at which the judge begins to develop some familiarity with the factual and legal disputes of the case. Rule 16(b) requires the judge to establish deadlines for amending pleadings, completing discovery, and filing motions; these deadlines can be changed only for "good cause." The case management literature generally recommends keeping the deadlines short and firm, and judges tend to do so.

Rule 16(c) also provides that a judge can hold additional *pretrial* (or *case management*) *conferences*, and lists a total of 16 subjects concerning the "just, speedy, and inexpensive disposition of the action" that the judge and lawyers can discuss at any pretrial conference. Rule 16(e) requires the judge to memorialize decisions reached in these conferences in *case management orders* (CMOs). Rule 16(d) also encourages a *final pretrial conference* to be conducted shortly before trial; under Rule 16(e), the order that emerges from this conference, usually called the *final pretrial order,* can be modified only to prevent "manifest injustice."

A reading of Rule 16, which mostly contains lists of case management techniques that will or might be discussed at pretrial conferences, does not give a sufficient sense of the Rule's importance in modern litigation practice. CMOs often shape the course of litigation. Some experimental data show that different case management techniques can alter the outcome of a case. Thus, in choosing one management technique in one case, a judge can enhance the chance of a favorable outcome for the plaintiff; in choosing a different technique for another identical case, a different judge can enhance the chance of a favorable outcome for the defendant. Rule 16 does nothing to guide a judge's decision whether or not to use any case management techniques, or which case management techniques to use. Hence, case management is subject to the criticism that a judge's predisposition about a case might guide the judge to choose a technique that bears out the predisposition. Rather than shielding the judge from early exposure to evidence and arguments, as the adversarial system does, the case management approach expects the judge to start making decisions affecting the outcome of the case at the outset, based on limited information and with no protection against possible prejudgment. By design, case management gives trial judges a great deal of discretion to tailor management techniques to the needs of each case, and courts of appeal can overturn a trial judge's management decision only if the judge has abused his or her discretion. *Abuse of discretion* is a very difficult thing to show. Thus, the trial judge's power during the pretrial phase of the case is significant — a far cry from the restraints on pretrial judicial power that the classical adversarial model contemplates.

For these reasons, case management remains a controversial subject. The available data suggest that case management techniques do not result in quicker dispositions or less expense, but they have not lengthened lawsuits or added expense either. The savings that case management achieves in some cases offset the time and expense of unnecessary case management in others. Despite the ambivalent data, case management seems to be here to stay.

THE ADVERSARIAL SYSTEM IN CONTEXT

It was not a coincidence that case management began in earnest in 1983, in the same set of amendments that gave teeth to the sleepy Rule 11 and added new restraints on discovery under Rule 26. Taken together, these changes constitute a step in the direction of inquisitorial process. They also demonstrate the need to balance the principle of adversarial process against other important procedural principles such as resolving cases accurately and efficiently — a balance that is constantly being recalibrated. These are the reasons why your Civil Procedure class might dwell on recent changes in Rules 11, 16, and 26 more than on other Rules. They represent important adjustments to the classic adversarial model.

For now, however, the momentum in American law to move significantly further in the direction of inquisitorial process seems to have abated. Despite its recent rebalancing, the American legal system is still counted firmly among the systems most devoted to the adversarial method. Curiously, during the same time period as a more inquisitorial approach was being adopted in the United States, some inquisitorial systems (Germany, for example) began to take a few cautious steps in the direction of adversarial procedure. Whether these two great models, pressured by the needs of transnational litigation in a globalizing world, will ever meet in the middle will be one of the great procedural storylines of the twenty-first century.

✕ 3 ✕

Jury Trial

In the last chapter, we suggested that the shape of the procedural systems in American courts was determined largely by two variables: the *adversarial system* and *jury trial*. In this chapter, we explore the issues surrounding juries — in particular, what a jury does, when a jury is used, and why the jury system is so critical to the structure of the American legal system. We also provide some perspective on why the jury system is, and is likely to remain, one of the most controversial aspects of American civil justice.

THE JURY'S FUNCTION

An adversarial or *inquisitorial* system is only a means to an end. The end is to adjudicate disputes accurately and fairly. Adjudication has four principal tasks: determining the facts, determining the law, applying the facts to the law, and declaring the remedy. The Anglo-American legal system divides these tasks between the judge and the jury.

Before we look at that division, however, we must look a little more closely at the jury. What, exactly, is this "jury"? A jury is a group of ordinary citizens drawn from the court's geographical territory. Each court has rules about the exact size of the jury, but under our Constitution it cannot be fewer than

6 people, and is never more than 12. In a process known as *voir dire*, the judge or lawyers question prospective jury members before the trial begins in order to ensure that they have no biases or detailed knowledge of the controversy. The jury is supposed to be a *tabula rasa* — a blank slate on which the parties write the story of the dispute. After the trial, the jury deliberates in secret and then renders its decision, or *verdict*. In many American courts, the verdict must be unanimous; in other courts, one or two dissenters are allowed. The verdict does not end the case; the judge must still enter a *judgment* based on that verdict.

The division of adjudicatory responsibility breaks down this way. The judge, not the jury, determines the law.* The jury, not the judge, determines the facts. As for the application of the law to the facts — the *mixed question of law and fact*, as it is sometimes called — the allocation of responsibility is less definite. In most cases the jury applies the law to the facts. Similarly, the jury usually declares the appropriate remedy, although in some cases the judge does so.

The judge *instructs* the jury about the relevant legal principles, and sends the jury off to its secret deliberations. The expectation is that the jury will use the evidence, the arguments, and the instructions to determine the facts and decide who should win, and that it will not simply flip a coin. But we have no way of knowing that for sure. When the jury reaches its decision, it usually renders a *general verdict*. A general verdict

---

* In some states after the American Revolution, juries decided both the law and the facts, but that experiment was short-lived. In Criminal Law you might have studied *jury nullification*. Jury nullification occurs when the jury finds a defendant not guilty because it disagrees with the law being used to prosecute the defendant; effectively, the jury ignores the law. Because the prosecution cannot usually appeal from a verdict of not guilty, a jury has some de facto power to determine the law used in a particular case. Jury nullification, however, has no counterpart on the civil side. A civil jury is required to follow the law, and a judge can overturn its verdict when the jury has not done so. Jury nullification can occur only in civil cases in which the judge cannot detect that nullification occurred.

simply declares who wins (e.g., Defendant is liable and should pay Plaintiff $10,000). The verdict does not specify how the jury resolved each of the factual disputes in the case, or which legal theories the jury relied on. The jury's exact *factual findings,** and how the jury applied the law to them, must be inferred from the verdict. For instance, if the jury returns a verdict for the defendant in a case in which both sides claimed to have the green light, we can infer that the jury found that the defendant had the green light. But this is only an inference. For all we know, the jury flipped a coin, or sided with the defendant because it liked him or her.

Two devices allow a judge to exercise more control over the jury's functions. First, a judge can use a *general verdict accompanied by interrogatories.*[1] The jury renders a general verdict, but also tells the judge, by answering written interrogatories the judge gives it, exactly what its factual findings in the case were. This device provides a better sense of the jury's findings, and enables the judge to check that the jury properly applied the law to these findings. Second, the judge can remove from the jury the task of applying the law to the facts, and do the job himself or herself. By means of a device known as a *special verdict,*[2] a jury makes a separate finding for each of the factual disputes in the case. The judge then takes these findings and applies the legal standard to them. Neither of these two devices is commonly used in jury trials.

The jury's role, although critical, is limited. Because a jury exists only to resolve factual disputes and to apply the law to the facts, a jury is unnecessary when the dispute between the parties is purely a question of law. The judge can hear the parties' arguments and render a decision in such a case without a jury's input. Moreover, the jury is called into existence only

---

* It is typical to call the factual determinations rendered in a case the *findings* of the case, and the person or persons who determine the factual disputes the *fact finder*. Legal determinations are often called the *conclusions of law*.

when the trial begins. Until then, the jury has no role in the litigation process. It does not vote on who should win pretrial motions or set the deadlines in *scheduling orders*.

Indeed, even the jury's role in fact finding is subject to two important caveats. First, a judge can decide that no genuine factual dispute exists and override the jury's function. Suppose, for example, that the plaintiff claims the defendant was negligent in running a red light and hitting her. Twenty bishops who were standing on the street corner when the accident occurred are all willing to testify that the plaintiff, not the defendant, ran the red light; the video of a tourist who caught the entire accident on camera confirms this testimony. No witness other than the plaintiff, who happens to be a thrice-convicted perjurer, says that she had the green light. Do we need to go to the trouble of asking a jury what happened? As we discuss later in the chapter, judges can employ certain devices, such as *summary judgment* and *judgment as a matter of law*, to decide truly lopsided factual disputes without a jury's assistance, or to overrule a jury's contrary verdict.

Second, in certain civil disputes, juries are not used at all. The judge resolves all the legal *and* factual issues, and applies the law to the facts.* In the following section, we discuss when a jury is used at trial, and when it is not.

THE RIGHT TO A JURY TRIAL

The United States Constitution contains two provisions guaranteeing a right to trial by jury. The first, in the Sixth Amendment, applies in "all criminal prosecutions"; it need not concern us further. The other, in the Seventh Amendment, applies in civil cases. The Seventh Amendment does not guarantee a jury in all civil cases. Instead, it provides: "In Suits at common law,

---

* These cases are sometimes called *bench trials*, or *trials to the bench*.

where the value in controversy shall exceed twenty dollars, the right of trial by jury shall be preserved. . . ."* This is curious language. What is a "Suit at common law" — and what is not? Why use the word "preserved"? What, exactly, is to be preserved?

The answers to these questions matter. The United States Constitution is the foundational document of American government. Its dictates are supreme, and it takes precedence over any statute, rule, or order to the contrary. Like other constitutional guarantees such as notice and an opportunity to be heard, we have to respect the right to jury trial, and make sure the parties get it.

Despite the Seventh Amendment's opacity, a few points are clear. First, it was ratified in 1791, as one of the ten Bill of Rights. The original Constitution contained no guarantee of jury trial, and those who regarded juries as one of the bulwarks of freedom against tyrannical government leveled telling criticisms during the ratification debates in 1788. The Sixth and Seventh Amendments responded to some of these criticisms.

Second, in 1791, most American states followed the English system of justice. As we described in Chapter 1, the English system distributed civil disputes among various judicial organs. The principal ones were the common law courts and the Chancery. Most disputes went to one of the common law courts. The relief available at *common law* was almost always monetary. Common law actions were tried to a jury.

The Chancery handled many of the remaining disputes. The Lord Chancellor presided over this system of *equity*. Equity handled some unique branches of the law, such as the law of trusts, but for the most part its subject matter overlapped with that of the common law courts. A principal difference from common law was that, rather than money,

---

* The Seventh Amendment also contains a second clause, known as the Reexamination Clause, which provides: "[N]o fact tried by a jury, shall be otherwise reexamined in any Court of the United States, than according to the rules of the common law." We discuss this clause later in the chapter.

equity awarded *injunctions*. (For instance, if a seller breached a promise to sell you his or her house, you went to the law courts to obtain *damages* for the breach; if you wanted the house itself, you went to equity to get an injunction forcing the seller to go through with the deal.) Another difference was that equity did not use juries; the chancellor (aided by other functionaries) found the facts and applied the relevant equitable principles to them.

Over the course of centuries, common law and equity often collided, and the line between the authority of the two systems was always shifting. Perhaps what the Seventh Amendment was "preserving," however inartfully,* was the 1791 division in English law between common law and equity: If a case arose on the common law side, the parties had a right to trial by jury; if it arose on the equity side, no right to trial by jury existed.

That interpretation of the Seventh Amendment has some problems. First, in 1791, the line between law and equity was in flux, so the reason for freezing the constitutional right to jury trial at that exact moment is not evident. A second problem was the continued growth of the law after 1791. For instance, in 1938, Congress gave employees the right to sue employers who did not pay the minimum wage. Did employees have a right to a jury trial for such claims? Minimum wage claims did not exist in 1791, so answering the jury trial question by returning to eighteenth-century divisions among English courts is an anachronism. A third problem developed in the nineteenth century, as many states abolished separate systems for common law and equity. The federal system abolished the separate systems in 1938, when it adopted the Federal Rules of Civil Procedure.[3] Why should a constitutional right such as jury trial

---

* One problem is the language used in the Seventh Amendment. There was no such thing as a "Suit at common law." Common law cases were called "actions at law." Equity cases were called "suits in equity."

hinge on a historical distinction that has had no legal salience for the past 70 years?

Courts have struggled with these questions in the effort to give meaning to the Seventh Amendment. The interpretation of the Seventh Amendment has not yet come to its final resting place, and the Supreme Court issues a new decision refining or tweaking its analysis every few years. We can, however, provide a somewhat simplistic sketch of the present scope of the Seventh Amendment.

First, the Supreme Court has never applied the Seventh Amendment to state courts.* Second, a party who wants a jury must file a *jury demand*; otherwise, the right to jury trial is waived.[4] Third, the Seventh Amendment does not come into play when a federal statute grants a right to trial by jury. The Seventh Amendment establishes a floor, not a ceiling, so Congress can grant a right to jury trial even if the Constitution does not.[5] But statutes that require the use of juries are uncommon. When a statute is silent about the right to jury trial, or when it specifically entrusts fact finding to a judge, then the question reverts to the Seventh Amendment.

Fourth, the modern interpretation of the Seventh Amendment begins with *Ross v. Bernhard*,[6] in which the Supreme Court stated that three factors determine whether a claim contains a right to jury trial:

- The historical custom in the days before the merger of law and equity in 1938;
- The "remedy sought"; and
- The "practical abilities and limitations of juries."

---

* For the most part, the Seventh Amendment's inapplicability in state court is a moot point. Almost every state includes a right to civil jury trial in its own constitution. The right under state law is usually as broad as that under the Seventh Amendment, and some states use juries even more broadly than the Seventh Amendment requires.

The first factor makes the anachronistic inquiry described earlier. In cases subsequent to *Ross*, this factor has forced the Court to turn itself into a legal historian. The Court seeks the best historical analogue to a post-1791 claim by taking a snapshot of the types of cases that were tried at law and in equity in 1791, and then discerning whether a modern claim bears more resemblance to an old-fashioned law action or an equitable suit. The Court's historical analysis is usually abstruse. Often it is inconclusive. In a number of the Court's decisions, a dissent examining the same historical evidence comes to the opposite conclusion about whether the best analogue is legal or equitable. Unless you get excited about legal history or about the historical approach to interpreting the Constitution, reading the Court's efforts to shoehorn modern claims into ancient categories is tough going.

The second factor, the nature of the remedy sought, is more comprehensible. Using history as its inspiration, this factor is simple: If a claim seeks a monetary remedy, then the right to jury trial exists; if the remedy sought is injunctive, then the judge acts as fact finder.* Although this factor is not strictly faithful to history — law courts sometimes gave injunctive-like relief, and equity sometimes awarded money — it has the advantage of being easy to apply.

The third factor, the practical abilities and limitations of the jury, has proven the most controversial. Unlike the first two factors, which had been involved in the Court's Seventh Amendment jurisprudence for many years, dicta in *Ross* invented the third factor from whole cloth. Courts and scholars began to wonder if this factor signaled a cutback on jury trial rights: Even when the first two factors pointed toward a jury, could a jury be denied if the case was too complicated, too technical, or too lengthy for 12 ordinary citizens? Almost

---

* The Court has carved out a couple of exceptions in which a request for monetary relief does not result in a jury trial, but they do not often come into play.

20 years later, in *Granfinanciera, S.A. v. Nordberg*,[7] the Supreme Court in essence said "No." *Granfinanciera* limited the third factor to a narrow range of "public rights" cases, usually involving the government as a party, in which Congress could have delegated the fact-finding function to an administrative agency but instead entrusted the job to a judge. For the most part, when deciding whether a claim (as opposed to a particular issue that is part of a claim) must be tried to a jury, the third factor has now dropped out of the picture, leaving the jury trial question to be answered by application of the first two factors.

When both of these factors point either toward jury trial or away from it, the answer to the jury trial question is evident. But what happens when one factor points in one direction and the other in the opposite direction? *Granfinanciera* made clear the relationship between the first two factors: Of the two, the second is the more important. Given that the third factor rarely applies and the second factor outweighs the first, a fair question is whether we should replace the three-factor analysis of *Ross* with the simple, more or less historically faithful "remedy sought" test: Damages mean a jury, and injunction means a judge. Justice Brennan argued for that result, but the Court as a whole never went along with him. If anything, the Court's last significant Seventh Amendment case, *City of Monterrey v. Del Monte Dunes at Monterey, Ltd.*,[8] seems to emphasize the first factor a bit more. The Seventh Amendment analysis has become caught up in the factious question of whether the Constitution should be interpreted according to the original intent of those who ratified it or in light of modern circumstances. Until the Court comes to an equilibrium on that question, the Seventh Amendment analysis is also likely to drift.

The three-factor analysis is only the beginning of the Seventh Amendment's complexities. The three factors are designed to decide whether a jury should hear a particular claim. But a claim is usually made up of individual issues. For instance, with a car accident involving a driver who ran a red light, the claim sounds in tort. To prevail on this claim, the plaintiff will need to prove a number of facts: that the defendant ran the red light, that the defendant should have been paying attention, that the accident caused the plaintiff's injuries, and that there were lost wages, medical bills, and so on. Even though a jury must hear and decide the claim as a whole, a technically separate question is whether the jury must decide each and every factual dispute within that claim. Might the judge, for instance, be allowed to decide the proper amount of the medical bills, and the jury to decide the remaining factual disputes?

You might think that the answer to this question should be "no": If the Seventh Amendment says a jury is supposed to hear a claim, then the jury should decide every fact relevant to that claim. That entirely logical position is not, unfortunately, the law. In *Tull v. United States*,[9] the Court held that Congress can authorize judges to determine certain facts in a jury-tried claim, as long as "the substance of a common-law right to a trial by jury" or "the essence of the system of trial by jury" is not infringed. This unhelpful language received somewhat more definite shape in *Markman v. Westview Instruments, Inc.*,[10] in which the Court held that a judge, rather than a jury, should determine the meaning of a word that was used in a patent document. In allowing the judge to decide this factual issue, the Court examined three questions:

- Whether a jury would have decided this fact in 1791;
- Whether jury fact finding on this one issue was necessary "to preserve the substance of the common-law right as it existed in 1791"; and
- When neither history nor precedent provided an answer, whether there existed "functional considerations" that made a judge or a jury a better fact finder.

Because judges routinely construed legal documents, *Markman* held that functional considerations tipped the scale toward judicial fact finding on the meaning of the patent.

This result is confusing. *Granfinanciera* went out of its way to confine *Ross v. Bernhard*'s "practical abilities and limitations of the jury" factor. Then in *Markman*, the Court allowed "functional considerations" (i.e., the jury's competence to determine the facts) to creep back in. Isn't the Court guilty of taking away with one hand and giving back with the other? The issues in the two cases — whether a jury should hear a *claim* and whether a jury should determine each and every *factual dispute* contained within that claim — are technically distinct. Nevertheless, either a jury is competent to hear factual issues or it is not. *Granfinanciera* appears to take a different view of the jury's fact-finding capacity than *Markman*.

A final complexity in the jury trial analysis also developed from the collapse of the separate systems of law and equity. Today a person can assert both jury-tried and equitable claims in the same case.[11] Suppose that the plaintiff's neighbor has been playing loud music for a month, and seems to want to keep on doing so. The plaintiff might want to bring a nuisance suit against the neighbor, seeking both damages for the past harm and an injunction to prevent the playing of loud music in the future. One of the factual questions relevant to both forms of relief is whether the music is so loud that it is a nuisance. If the plaintiff had sought only damages, a jury would decide this question. If the plaintiff had sought only an injunction, the judge would have decided it. Who decides when the plaintiff seeks both remedies?

One solution — to let the jury and the judge each decide independently — is unappealing. It does not look good for the system of justice when the judge and the jury, after hearing exactly the same evidence, come to different results. Therefore, we need to have one of the fact finders (judge or jury) make the factual finding, and then bind the other fact finder to accept it. In *Beacon Theatres, Inc. v. Westover*,[12] the Supreme Court held that, except in extraordinary cases, the jury should decide factual issues that overlapped between the jury-tried and equitable portions of the case. The judge was then bound to accept those factual findings in deciding the equitable portion of the case.

Now that we have a basic understanding of when a jury is used and what it does, we can turn to the question of why the jury matters so much in the design of American litigation.

THE JURY'S INFLUENCE ON AMERICAN PROCEDURE

In one sense, the jury has shaped all of American civil law, both substantive and procedural. The story of many bodies of law that first developed in medieval England, such as torts, contracts, or property, is the story of the jury. As juries came to be used, medieval lawyers and judges concentrated considerable energy on designing procedures to check the jury's fallibility. The pleading system they developed to control juries eventually defined the elements of claims and defenses — the substantive law and doctrines you learn in other classes. Likewise, the great field of equity, which also shapes the doctrines you study in many classes, developed in large part because litigants petitioned the chancellor when they feared that a jury was incapable of delivering justice. Indeed, our present procedural system is in large measure a reaction to the deficiencies in the procedural systems that preceded it, and those systems received their shape from the jury's existence. It is no exaggeration to say that the shadow of the jury hangs over all of the modern American legal system.

But the importance of the jury is not limited to receding historical influences. Today the civil jury continues to exercise an enormous influence on the American procedural system. Starting at the structural level and proceeding to the more concrete level of doctrine, we discuss three ways in which the civil jury shapes American procedure and makes our system distinct from those in the rest of the world.

Juries and the Distribution of Adjudicatory Power

In functional terms, the jury removes certain adjudicatory powers (fact finding and, often, applying the facts to the law, and declaring the remedy) from the judge. The result is that the government, represented by the judge, becomes less powerful; and the people, represented by the jury, retain more power. This decentralization of power has important consequences. Most evidently, it aids in the workings of American-style democracy. Aside from voting and paying taxes, jury service is the most common way in which American citizens participate in the project of self-governance. Juries make the outcomes of court decisions more acceptable to the citizenry as a whole because people just like us shape those decisions, and they make the outcomes more acceptable to the parties because people just like them shape those outcomes.

This dispersal of power to the jury also reinforces other structural features of the American system. Just as the adversarial system acts as a check on judicial power, so do juries. One of Madison's insights in the way he crafted aspects of the Constitution was to distribute power among the branches of government, and between the state and federal government, in order to prevent any actor from becoming too powerful. In an adversarial system with a right to jury trial, lawyers and juries assume some of the functions that judges in a more inquisitorial system perform on their own.

We do not suggest that an adversarial system requires jury trial in civil cases. For example, Britain, which was the fountainhead of both the adversarial system and jury trial, has maintained the former while for the most part dispensing with the latter. But we do suggest that the adversarial system and the jury system complement each other. Moreover, the jury system is deeply ingrained in the American psyche. When you close your eyes to think about courtrooms and trials, don't you always see a jury? It takes some imagination for Americans to envision a procedural system without the jury.

Juries also significantly influence the scope of adjudicatory power in an indirect way. Many litigants regard juries as unpredictable. As a result, they often seek to avoid going to trial. Preferring to arbitrate rather than litigate, some parties enter into *arbitration agreements* before disputes even arise. Other parties settle or agree to enter *arbitration* or some other *alternative dispute resolution* (ADR) process after litigation commences but before the case comes to trial. Reliance on settlements and other forms of ADR, which has increased in recent years, shrinks the number of occasions on which judges and juries can exercise adjudicatory power. Many judges, lawyers, and scholars regard this as a positive development. Others worry that the movement away from adjudication weakens the rule of law. Whichever view is right, American perceptions about juries are an important cause of this trend.

The Structure of Pretrial and Trial

The jury system also has important and immediate consequences for the structure of American litigation. Because juries are drawn from the community, they are not legal professionals in the way that judges and lawyers are. We ask them to leave their ordinary occupations and families to render a verdict, and then we expect them to return to their lives. As a practical matter, this means that the trial has to be a single event, in which all the issues of law and fact are tried together and determined. Because the trial is the "whole enchilada," it also becomes a dramatic event, a piece of theater, the final act in a play. A culminating trial also means that there has to be a separate and distinct pretrial process, in which the legal and factual issues are investigated and researched and the legal issues are winnowed down to the crucial disputes.

The uniqueness of this form of adjudication is even more apparent when we examine European inquisitorial systems, which do not employ jury trial. Rather than having separate pretrial and trial phases, the European approach is to have a continuous trial, which is nothing more than a series of hearings before a judge. For example, the judge might hold a hearing one day to determine a particular fact. If the judge determines the fact one way, then the case proceeds down one path, and if the judge determines the fact the other way, the case proceeds down another path. After the hearing, the parties and the judge continue to make further inquiries and research, and then come together for another hearing, at which other points of fact or law are determined. This process of periodic hearings continues until enough points of fact and law have been determined that the claim of the plaintiff can be finally decided. Often the case ends with a whimper rather than a bang. There is no real distinction between pretrial and trial; investigation, research, and decision making all occur at the same time.

That litigation structure is virtually impossible with juries. The first obstacle concerns historical expectations. Over the centuries, juries and the single climactic trial were woven together. The climactic trial — the bang rather than the whimper — is a part of our cultural expectation. A second obstacle that juries pose for the continuous trial is the question of efficiency: To ask jury members to give a week to a trial is one thing, but to ask them to interrupt their lives on a regular and periodic basis to render perhaps dozens of factual findings is quite another. A third obstacle is constitutional. In the last section, we looked at the first half of the Seventh Amendment. The Seventh Amendment also contains a second clause, known as the Reexamination Clause, which prevents the reexamination of any "fact tried by a jury . . . [except] according to the rules of the common law." As seemingly opaque as the right-to-jury-trial clause, this clause stakes out the jury's supremacy in matters of fact finding. At common law, judges had limited powers to set aside a jury's verdict, but they were just that — limited. Therefore, if we employed periodic hearings as in the European system, juries used for the later hearings could not constitutionally redetermine facts found in earlier jury proceedings. As a practical matter, the Reexamination Clause makes it far simpler to hold a single trial in which all factual issues are placed before a single jury once and for all.

Thus, juries determine one of the core features of American litigation: a culminating trial. They also determine another core feature: a concentrated and comprehensive pretrial process to deal with the need for investigation, research, and issue-narrowing. The pretrial process must adequately equip the parties with a sufficient sense of the legal and factual issues that they can present the case to 12 ordinary people.

The judge has some power to alter this structure by splitting up the case into segments. This process is usually called *bifurcation*, and Federal Rule 42(b) authorizes it when it would be convenient, avoid prejudice, or expedite and achieve economy in the case. By its terms, Rule 42(b) contemplates only separate trials, but the broad *case management* authority of Rule 16(c) also appears to give judges the ability to bifurcate the pretrial process. Bifurcation can be useful when a distinct and severable issue that is likely to terminate the case exists. For instance, suppose that, in a car accident, the question of liability revolves around whether the defendant ran a red light, but other issues also exist (for example, the extent of the plaintiff's damages). If the preliminary evidence strongly suggests that the plaintiff ran the light, it might be more efficient to bifurcate the case and decide only the question of who ran the light. If the jury finds that the plaintiff did so, the case can be terminated without the need to explore the fact-intensive damages issue. If the jury finds that the defendant ran the red light, that finding will not need to be reexamined by a second jury that will hear the damages issue.

Nonetheless, bifurcation remains the exception rather than the rule. One reason is the inefficiency that bifurcation can cause: If the jury determines that the plaintiff and not the defendant ran the red light, the parties must restart the pretrial process to examine the other issues. It is sometimes cheaper and faster in the long run to get all the pretrial issues out of the way at once. Another reason is the pesky Reexamination Clause, which limits the ability of the court to divvy up a case in the most efficient way. Third, empirical evidence suggests that, in some situations, bifurcating a case significantly increases the chances for a verdict for the defendant; and on the theory that cases should be treated alike, bifurcating some but not all cases is problematic. The final reason is tradition. Thanks to juries, a single culminating trial is the default setting in our civil justice system.

Jury Control

Once we opt for a jury system, we must next consider whether to place controls on the jury to make sure that it remains faithful to its responsibility to find the facts according to the evidence and the law rather than according to the prejudices or irrational influences of its members. One possible response, to place no controls on the jury whatsoever, has never garnered much support. Indeed, even in medieval times, lawyers and judges knew that, as a human institution, the jury was fallible. The desire to constrain the error-prone ways of the jury led to both the draconian system of common-law pleading and the jury-free system of equity. In modern times, most of the law of evidence has developed to keep certain types of information away from the impressionable lay people on the jury. Likewise, jury instructions not only communicate the law; they also check the jury's ability to decide a case as it would like.

In this section, we focus on three jury control devices that you are likely to study in Civil Procedure: *summary judgment, judgment as a matter of law,* and *new trial.* Of the three, judgment as a matter of law applies only to jury trials; summary judgment and new trial can also be awarded in bench trials. To lay out the issues concerning these devices in the most logical way, we take them in the reverse of the order in which they will arise in litigation: new trial, judgment as a matter of law, and summary judgment.

The Motion for a New Trial An order for a new trial does exactly what it says: After the first trial has concluded and a judgment has been rendered, it reopens the case and orders a new trial to take place. Any party who believes that an error in the first trial created a result that was less favorable than it should have been can ask for a new trial. Most often, the person who requests a new trial is the person who lost at the first trial. As you might expect, judges are not eager to retry cases on which considerable resources have already been spent, but new trials are granted in certain situations. In the federal system, Rule 59 specifies only two circumstances for granting new trials. In jury-tried cases, a new trial is proper "for any of the reasons for which new trials have heretofore been granted in actions at law."[13] In bench trials, a new trial is proper "for any reasons for which rehearings have heretofore been granted in suits in equity."[14] Making sense of these unilluminating standards requires some knowledge of the history of common law and equity.

Generally, the common law allowed a new trial in two situations. The first involved some defect in the trial process. Perhaps the judge made a wrong ruling on the evidence, and admitted evidence the jury should not have heard (or refused to admit evidence the jury should have heard). Maybe the judge incorrectly instructed the jury about the law, or the judge permitted a lawyer to make an unfairly prejudicial remark during argument. Once the heat of battle cooled, the judge realized the error, and also realized that the error might have had an influence on the outcome of the trial. The only remedy to correct the judge's error was a new trial. Similarly, a judge could sometimes grant a new trial if newly discovered evidence that would have changed the outcome came to light only after trial.

The second situation involved a defect in the verdict itself. Simply put, the judge believed that the jury was wrong—either that the evidence did not support the jury's verdict on liability, or that the evidence did not support the size of the damage award. Again, the remedy that the common law provided in these situations was a new trial.

The first situation in which new trials were ordered is not especially controversial, at least if we think that getting the result right matters more than getting the case over and done with. But the second situation creates friction between judge and jury. The jury is supposed to be the fact finder. If a judge has the power to reject the jury's factual findings and order a new trial at which (with luck) a more acceptable verdict might be achieved, can't the judge just keep ordering new trials until some jury finally delivers the result the judge wants? If so, isn't the right to trial by jury a charade? A partial answer to these well-founded criticisms is that a judge cannot order a new trial willy-nilly. The usual formula permits a judge to order a new trial only when the verdict is "against the weight of the evidence" or the verdict is so monstrously large as to "shock the conscience."* The "against the weight" standard

---

* In cases involving excessive damages, judges developed a power known as *remittitur*. For instance, if the verdict was $200,000 and the judge thought that $50,000 was the highest supportable award, the judge could tell the plaintiff that a new trial would be ordered unless the plaintiff agreed to accept $50,000. If the plaintiff accepted the remittitur, a new trial would be avoided. The Supreme Court has held that a judge's power of remittitur passes muster under the Seventh Amendment. A separate power, called *additur*, permits a judge to increase the verdict if the judge believes the award is shockingly small. The Supreme Court

has been understood to mean, in effect, against the *great* weight of the evidence, so it operates much like the "shock the conscience" standard in practice. In other words, only when a jury is way off base in its findings can a judge order a new trial. A judge who merely disagrees with a plausible jury verdict cannot do anything.

Is this power to order new trials consonant with the Seventh Amendment? Because the Seventh Amendment "preserved" the right to jury trial as it existed in 1791, and because judges could order new trials in 1791, the new-trial power has never been thought to violate the jury trial right guaranteed by the first clause of the Seventh Amendment. Nor does it offend the second clause of the Seventh Amendment, the Reexamination Clause. Although a new trial requires a second jury to reexamine the factual findings made by a prior jury, the closing words of the Reexamination Clause allow reexamination "according to the rules of the common law." Because the common law permitted new trials when the verdict was against the weight of the evidence or shocked the conscience, a modern judge who hews to the common law's limits creates no Seventh Amendment problem.

The extent to which the judge can control the jury hinges on exactly what "against the weight of the evidence" means in practice. Suppose that 20 bishops who witnessed the car accident all say the plaintiff ran the red light, and a video shows exactly the same thing on tape. The only witness who claims that the defendant ran the red light is the plaintiff, a thrice-convicted perjurer. But the jury comes back with a verdict in favor of the plaintiff. Would this verdict be against the weight of the evidence? Now suppose that the defendant was also a bishop, and a good friend of the 20 witnesses. Is the verdict still against the weight of the evidence? Now suppose that, in addition, no videotape exists. As a judge, would you now let the jury's verdict stand or would you order a new trial?

It would be nice if we could give clear answers to these hypotheticals. Unfortunately, we can't. By reading lots of cases in which judges grant or deny motions for a new trial, a lawyer can begin to get some sense of where the "against the weight" line lies, but each case still presents a unique set of facts. It is hard to distill any general rules. The best you can do for now is to rely on basic principles about the value of juries in comparison to the value of getting the right answer in each trial. If you still do not know exactly where the line is, you are in good company. The line probably lies in a slightly different place in every courtroom in the country. Some judges have more respect for jury fact finding than others, and thus allow the jury a bit more leeway. We do not mean to suggest that a judge can do whatever he or she wants. But granting a motion for a new trial lies within the trial judge's discretion, and at the margins different judges will exercise their judgment in different ways.

In bench trials, judges use the same grounds for granting new trials: either errors in the trial itself or an erroneous result. Because the judge is the fact finder in a bench trial, trying to convince the judge that the result was erroneous is no easy task. If the judge grants a motion for a new trial in a bench trial, the judge often does not need to retry the entire case, but limits the new trial to the taking of additional evidence in those parts of the trial infected with error.

The Motion for Judgment as a Matter of Law and the Renewed Motion for Judgment as a Matter of Law A second jury control device is judgment as a matter of law. Found in Rule 50, judgment as a matter of law merges two related devices. The first device, which used to be called a motion for *directed verdict*, is now called a motion for judgment as a matter of law; it is used during the trial when one party claims that a reasonable jury could only find the facts in that party's favor, so the judge might as well stop the trial and direct the jury to return a verdict in the party's favor. The second device, which used to be called a motion for *judgment notwithstanding the verdict* (or *j.n.o.v.*, an abbreviation from *judgment non obstante veredicto*), is now called a *renewed motion for judgment as a matter of law*; it is used after the jury has announced its verdict. The idea of the renewed motion is the same as the original motion, but now the moving party has lost the verdict. The moving party asks the court to enter judgment in its favor despite the contrary verdict because the evidence is so strong that no reasonable jury could have decided the case as this jury did. In both cases, the standard that the judge applies — the "reasonable jury" standard — is identical. Rule 50(a) describes the procedures for making the motion for judgment as a matter of law during trial. Rule 50(b) describes how a party can renew that motion within ten days after the jury's verdict.* Because they differ only in their timing, we analyze both the original motion and the renewed motion for judgment as a matter of law together.

Judgment as a matter of law invites a comparison to new trial. An obvious difference is the remedy for each. A successful motion for a new trial leads to a new trial before a new jury, which might end up with the same verdict as the first jury. A successful motion for judgment as a matter of law ends the case in the trial court; the judge steps into the jury's shoes, decides the case, and enters judgment. No trial before another

---

* The word "renew" is critical: A judge can grant a *renewed* motion only if the same motion for judgment as a matter of law was first made *during* the trial. Fed. R. Civ. P. 50(b). Because the standards for the motion for judgment as a matter of law and the renewed motion for judgment as a matter of law are identical — the "reasonable jury" standard — you might wonder why we need the renewed motion. After all, if the evidence is so clearly one-sided during trial, won't the judge grant the motion at that point? In theory, yes, but judges often deny motions for judgment as a matter of law during trial in the hope that the jury will decide the case the "reasonable" way. The party opposing the motion cannot then complain on appeal that its right to a jury trial was infringed by unwarranted judicial action.

jury will occur. Thus, judgment as a matter of law provides the judge with stronger control over jury fact finding than new trial.

Second, and relatedly, the standard under which judgment as a matter of law is granted is more stringent. Recall that a new trial can be ordered either for defects in the first trial (erroneous rulings on evidence, and so on) or for an erroneous verdict. Judgment as a matter of law is not meant to address trial defects; it addresses only the problem of an erroneous verdict. With regard to erroneous verdicts, the standard for judgment as a matter of law is higher than the "against the weight" standard. To use the exact language of Rule 50, judgment as a matter of law can be granted when "the court finds that a reasonable jury would not have a legally sufficient evidentiary basis to find for the party on that issue" and "under the controlling law, [that party's claim or defense] can be maintained or defeated only with a favorable finding on that issue."[15] So we have two standards: the "against the weight" standard for new trial and the "reasonable jury" standard for judgment as a matter of law.

Like "against the weight," the words "reasonable jury" are not self-defining and not easily susceptible to any sweeping legal principle. When absolutely no evidence supports a finding critical to the jury's verdict, judgment as a matter of law is clearly appropriate. But the "reasonable jury" standard also allows the judge to enter judgment in the case of lopsided evidence, when weighty evidence on one side overwhelms insubstantial evidence on the other.* The hard question is exactly how lopsided the evidence must be. To aid judges trying to find the "reasonable jury" line, the Supreme Court has established some guiding principles. First, a judge must look at all the evidence, not just the evidence favoring the party opposing the motion, to determine what a reasonable jury could

---

* At one time, in some states, the "reasonable jury" standard was determined by the *scintilla rule* — in other words, that a jury's verdict could not be overturned if one scrap, or scintilla, of evidence supported its verdict. The scintilla rule has been rejected in modern federal practice.

permissibly find. Next, a court must draw all reasonable inferences from the evidence in favor of the party opposing the
motion. Relatedly, the court must disregard all evidence favorable to the moving party if the jury is not required to believe
that evidence. This means, in essence, that only uncontra-
dicted, unimpeached evidence from disinterested sources
can be credited. Likewise, the judge cannot make credibility
determinations about the witnesses; it is up to the jury to
decide whether a witness is telling the truth, and a judge cannot ignore a witness's testimony simply by deciding that the
witness is lying. Finally, the judge is not to weigh the
evidence.[16]

We can apply these principles to the car accident hypothetical. Suppose that the testimony of 20 disinterested bishops
and a videotape all show that the plaintiff ran the red light; the
only evidence to the contrary is the testimony of the plaintiff, a
thrice-convicted perjurer. It might seem that the principles
that the Supreme Court articulated would not permit the
judge to credit the testimony of the 20 bishops because the
plaintiff's testimony contradicts this evidence, and credibility
issues are supposed to be left to the jury. Nor is the judge
supposed to weigh the evidence, regardless of how lopsided
the evidence of 20 disinterested witnesses and a videotape is in
comparison to the evidence of one interested witness with
some prior problems telling the truth. So you might think
that under a "reasonable jury" standard, the judge could not
enter judgment as a matter of law either during the trial or, if
the jury finds for the plaintiff, afterward. Nonetheless, on these
facts, we believe that nearly every federal judge would enter
judgment as a matter of law.

Why? The precise reason is hard to articulate, but we will
try. At the time of the accident, either the defendant's signal
was red or it was not. The lawsuit is trying to determine the state
of the world at a particular time, but that state of the world is not
knowable, so we apply human reason to figure out what that

world must be. When different possible worlds (here, that either the plaintiff or the defendant ran the red light) are consistent with reason, we let the jury choose which world is the "right" one. In other words, despite the rubric of the reasonable jury, we actually use juries to answer factual questions that reason and logic alone cannot answer. We let the jury, using a combination of logic, experience, and values, make a prudential judgment about what must have happened. When reason and logic lead to only one possible state of the world, and when the alternative to that conclusion seems so unlikely that it offends reason, judgment as a matter of law is appropriate.

In the hypothetical, when a judge stacks the evidence of a videotape and 20 disinterested witnesses against the testimony of a self-interested perjurer, it defies logic and reason to believe that the defendant's light was red. So a judge can properly enter judgment for the defendant. But then we can play the usual law-school game and start changing the hypothetical's facts:

- What if no videotape existed?
- What if the plaintiff was not a perjurer?
- What if only 1 bishop saw the accident, not 20?
- What if the one eyewitness was a fellow bishop and a friend of the defendant?

Without doubt, by the time we get to the last hypothetical (no videotape, no perjury convictions for the plaintiff, only one eyewitness bishop who is friendly with the defendant), logic and reason alone cannot tell us if the plaintiff's or the defendant's light was red. Thus, a reasonable jury must make a prudential judgment. At exactly what point along the trail of hypotheticals is the line crossed, so that the judge can no longer interfere with the jury's fact finding? At the point when the videotape no longer exists? At the point when the testimony drops from 20 bishops to 1? The answer, unfortunately, is not perfectly clear.

What is clearer, however, is that a sliver of a window exists in which a judge can order a new trial but cannot order judgment as a matter of law. On a motion (or renewed motion) for judgment as a matter of law, a judge is not to weigh the evidence; on a motion for a new trial, the judge can do so. To return to the hypothetical, suppose that no videotape existed, so the case involved the testimony of 20 disinterested bishops against the testimony of an interested and truth-challenged plaintiff. At this point, even though the evidence is lopsided, the case is largely one of credibility; logic alone cannot provide us with an answer. Arguably, judgment as a matter of law is no longer appropriate.* Nonetheless, the great weight of the evidence favors the defendant, so a judge might still order a new trial if the jury returns a verdict for the plaintiff. In short, in some cases the evidence is so lopsided that both a new trial and judgment as a matter of law would be appropriate to guard against the jury's contrary fact finding. In other cases, the evidence is such a horse race that neither a new trial nor judgment as a matter of law would be appropriate as a jury control. And in a sliver of cases in the middle, the evidence is lopsided enough that a new trial is appropriate, but not so lopsided that a judgment as a matter of law is appropriate.

It is common for a party who loses the verdict to file both a renewed motion for judgment as a matter of law and a motion for new trial at the same time — the one seeks the entry of judgment in the moving party's favor, and the other seeks a new trial. Obviously a moving party prefers to win the former motion, but in some cases (involving defects in the trial process, excessive damages, or the sliver of cases in which the jury's fact finding is against the weight but not

---

* We say "arguably" because we believe that, if a jury were to come back with a verdict for the plaintiff, many federal judges would grant a renewed motion for a judgment as a matter of law. In close cases, the point at which a judge takes a case away from a jury is to some extent a matter of individual judgment. No precise, mechanical line between permissible and impermissible jury fact finding exists.

unreasonable), the motion for a new trial can succeed even when the renewed motion for judgment as a matter of law fails.

As we described, an order granting a new trial is consistent with the Seventh Amendment. Is an order granting judgment as a matter of law also constitutional? A motion for judgment as a matter of law makes the judge, not the jury, the ultimate fact finder; in the case of a renewed motion for judgment as a matter of law, it also requires the judge to reexamine facts found by the jury. Moreover, unlike the power to order a new trial, which existed in 1791, the power to enter judgment as a matter of law developed in the nineteenth century, and thus was not a power known to the common law when the Seventh Amendment was ratified. Despite these facts, the Supreme Court has upheld the constitutionality of the motion for judgment as a matter of law (and, presumably, the renewed motion as well).[17]

Judgment as a matter of law is a procedure peculiar to jury trial, invented to create a judicial control over the fact-finding function of the civil jury. In bench trials, an equivalent rule allows the judge to enter a *judgment on partial findings*.[18] After one party has been fully heard on a factual issue essential to that party's case, the other party can ask the judge to find against the first party on that issue and enter an immediate judgment. Because the judge is the fact finder, the "reasonable jury" overlay does not exist. The judge can make the findings of fact, and enter judgment if it is appropriate to do so. The simplicity of this process might be relevant as you consider the benefits and costs of jury trial.

The Motion for Summary Judgment The idea of summary judgment is simple. If it can be shown *before* trial that no legitimate factual disputes exist, there is no need to conduct a trial. The judge can enter judgment in a summary fashion. In this sense, summary judgment is a jury control device. Even though the jury has not even come into existence when the motion is made, summary judgment allows the judge to act as fact finder, thus depriving the jury of its role at trial.

Summary judgment first developed in nineteenth-century England as a swift procedure to handle commercial disputes in which a defendant had clearly failed to pay a debt. It moved across the ocean soon afterward, and found a home in the Federal Rules of Civil Procedure in 1938. Today it is the single most important rule in American civil litigation. A successful summary judgment motion terminates some or all of the claims or defenses in a case, thus narrowing the trial or obviating it altogether. Even if it does not eliminate claims or defenses, parties often make important factual concessions that also narrow the trial. From the parties' viewpoint, the motion also serves a very different purpose: It gives the parties an opportunity to influence the judge in advance of the trial, and it helps them to understand both the risks of continuing to trial and the likely value of a settlement.

Rule 56 authorizes a judge to enter summary judgment when the evidence obtained from *discovery* or from other sources "show[s] that there is no genuine issue as to any material fact and that the moving party is entitled to judgment as a matter of law." Both elements are important: There must be no genuine issue of material fact, *and* the consequence of the lack of factual dispute is that the party moving for summary judgment is entitled to prevail on a claim or defense.

Start with the second element. In the hypothetical car accident that we have been discussing, suppose that all the evidence agrees that the defendant ran the red light, but there is legitimate disagreement about whether the accident caused any injury to the plaintiff: The plaintiff says the injuries are severe, and the defendant says that the plaintiff is faking it. Summary judgment in favor of the plaintiff is not appropriate. There may be no genuine issue whether the defendant ran the red light, but the factual dispute concerning the extent of the plaintiff's injuries means that the plaintiff is not yet entitled to judgment. Conversely, suppose that all the evidence shows that the plaintiff, not the defendant, ran the red light. Summary judgment in favor of the defendant is appropriate. Even though there is a still a dispute about the extent of the plaintiff's injuries, that dispute doesn't matter.

The first requirement for summary judgment — "no genuine issue as to any material fact" — is the one that occupies most of a court's attention. "Material" simply means *relevant*. The meaning of "genuine issue" is less evident, but the phrase has an obvious analogue. In effect, in cases that would be tried to a jury, summary judgment acts exactly like a motion for judgment as a matter of law, except that the judge is taking the fact-finding function away from the jury *before* the trial, rather than during or after the trial. Therefore, it seems logical to equate the genuine issue for summary judgment with the "reasonable jury" standard for judgment as a matter of law: An issue of material fact is "genuine" (and thus summary judgment is inappropriate) if and only if the evidence would allow a reasonable jury at trial to find either for or against the moving party.* Indeed, the Supreme Court has made precisely this equation.[19] Therefore, everything that we have just learned about when judgment as a matter of law should and should not be granted applies in equal force in the summary judgment context.

In some cases, applying the genuine issue standard is easy. For instance, in *Celotex Corp. v. Catrett*,[20] the Court held that, as long as the opponent has been afforded an adequate opportunity to obtain evidence, a party who will not bear the burden

---

* Although the convergence of the "genuine issue" and the "reasonable jury" standards is logical, it is not logically required. On a motion for summary judgment, most of the evidence and testimony of witnesses is introduced on paper. If you strongly believe that a better result can be obtained by hearing eyewitness testimony in open court, rather than simply reading their testimony on a page, then you might wish to make the genuine issue standard more stringent than the reasonable jury standard. Some older decisions of the Supreme Court could be read to suggest such greater stringency, but the Court's more recent cases have conflated the two standards.

of proof at trial on a factual issue that is essential to the opponent's case can obtain summary judgment by showing that the opponent has no evidence whatsoever to support that factual assertion. When an opponent presents absolutely no evidence at trial on a factual issue that the opponent must prove to win, then judgment as a matter of law is appropriate. *Celotex* simply accelerates that result to the pretrial process.

Other cases are hard. When one party has some evidence on an essential factual issue, but that evidence is weak, drawing the line between cases that a jury must hear and those proper for summary judgment is tricky. Recall the car accident hypothetical. When we discussed judgment as a matter of law, we added or subtracted various facts — the videotape, the plaintiff's prior perjury, the number of eyewitness bishops, the friendship with the defendant — to determine the line at which a judge must let the jury decide the facts. We also discussed a series of guiding principles — for instance, do not make credibility judgments, do not weigh the evidence, draw reasonable inferences against the moving party — that help the judge to draw the proper line. Equating summary judgment with judgment as a matter of law means that exactly the same line and exactly the same principles apply to give the phrase "genuine issue" its meaning. As we saw, discerning the exact fact-finding line between a judge and jury is not always an easy task.

Because the Supreme Court has decided that judgment as a matter of law passes muster under the Seventh Amendment, and because the Court's interpretation of Rule 56 gives a judge on summary judgment no greater fact-finding powers than judgment as a matter of law, the general assumption is that summary judgment in jury-tried cases is constitutional.*

---

* Comparable concerns do not affect the use of summary judgment in bench trials. When the judge is going to be the fact finder in any event, the "reasonable jury" overlay does not affect the meaning of "genuine issue".

Surprisingly, the Supreme Court has never squarely said so, although a number of its cases leave little doubt about its view of the constitutionality of Rule 56.

Nonetheless, a broad use of summary judgment might, in Justice Brennan's words, "erode the constitutionally enshrined role of the jury." Balanced against that concern is the utility of summary judgment, which is, in Justice Rehnquist's words, "properly regarded not as a disfavored procedural shortcut, but rather as an integral part of the Federal Rules as a whole, which are designed 'to secure the just, speedy and inexpensive determination of every action.'" In the tension between those two statements lies courts' struggle with the scope and meaning of summary judgment. We must protect the jury's constitutional role in fact finding. But we also want accurate, efficiently rendered outcomes.

Celotex has been widely understood to place emphasis on the latter concern. Many observers believe that, in the two decades since *Celotex*, courts have been granting summary judgment with more enthusiasm than in they did the decades before *Celotex*. A recent study suggests that the increased use of summary judgment actually began in the decade before *Celotex* and has leveled off since, so that *Celotex* confirmed rather than initiated the trend. Other empirical work suggests that judges grant summary judgment more frequently against certain classes of litigants such as civil rights plaintiffs. (Of course, we have no way of knowing whether juries would have been any more sympathetic to these litigants than judges were.) These data might help to give you some context for thinking about the consequences of an invigorated summary judgment rule in American litigation. Another thing to keep in mind as you do so is that these same decades have seen the rise of case management. We suggest that the two phenomena are linked. If it works, case management should bring more cases into clear focus, thus making them more susceptible to summary judgment. At another level, the adversarial system and jury trial share the common bond of diffusing adjudicatory power away from the judge. Case management and summary judgment have as a common element the recapture of some of that power by the judge.

As you can see, summary judgment is a wonderful vehicle for exploring how such bedrock principles as the adversarial system, jury trial, *accuracy*, and *efficiency* should be balanced against each other.

THE CONTROVERSIAL JURY

The American jury is as controversial as it is important. You have heard the debate: The jury reflects the community's values, or it is a rag-tag collection of the riff-raff, the under-employed, and the aged. It is the palladium of American liberty, or it undermines American enterprise and business competitiveness. It is essential to American democracy, or it reaches unpredictable and crazy results that make McDonald's liable for selling hot coffee. Sound familiar? Until now, we have tried to avoid the issue of whether juries are a good or a bad thing. Instead, we have focused on the effect of juries on the law, thus trying to give you information that sidesteps the cluttering of emotions and beliefs that jury trial often provokes.

Inevitably, however, answers to questions such as what the Seventh Amendment means and where we should draw the reasonable jury line pull us toward the question of the jury's value. To some extent, that value depends on political preferences, such as the role that citizens should play in democratically established institutions or the amount of power that you wish federal judges or plaintiffs' lawyers to possess. To some extent, the value of the jury is an empirically testable matter. Although we cannot pretend to end the controversy over the American civil jury, let us bring into the discussion two ideas that you might not have considered. We do not suggest that these ideas will make the controversy surrounding the jury go away, but we hope that they give you a fuller picture of the American jury and its future.

The first point is the empirical one. As you might expect, psychologists, social scientists, and lawyers have studied juries in great detail over the years. We cannot provide all of these studies' many findings here, but let us highlight a few.

- Juries do a reasonably good job of finding the facts. As a general rule, 12 heads are better than 1; a jury will not make as good a decision as its best member would make, but it will make a better decision than its average member would make.
- Juries treat their fact-finding job with seriousness and diligence; they are not renegades flipping coins. But legally extraneous factors such as the wealth, age, or status of parties can have some effect on a jury's verdict.
- Judges and juries actually agree on the outcome in a high percentage of cases, from about 63 percent in some complex cases, to 80 percent or more in routine matters. When they disagree, judges, not juries, tend to be slightly more sympathetic to plaintiffs. On the other hand, when they do find for the plaintiff, juries tend to award higher damages than judges.
- The clear deficiencies in jury trials are the jury instructions. Instructions are written in such complex legalese that in some cases juries understand only about half of them. (Pick up a jury instruction book some day. You're trained in the law: How many of them do you understand perfectly well?) Indeed, the most likely error a jury will make is misunderstanding the instructions. This fact, of course, might argue for clearer instructions rather than fewer juries.

The second idea is a comparative point. Americans stand alone in the world in their commitment to the civil jury.

Although the jury rose to maturity in the English legal system, Britain has essentially weaned itself of its invention. Today British courts employ juries only in a very limited array of civil disputes. The same is true of the other legal systems descended from the English. The rest of the world never used civil juries to begin with, so the jury is not even a fond memory. In most of the world, the idea of having untrained lay people decide legal disputes is nonsensical and irrational. Absolutely no momentum exists in other procedural systems to import the civil jury or to increase its use. Indeed, the trend is running in the other direction. Trial by jury in civil cases is perhaps the clearest single example of "American exceptionalism" in procedure.

At the same time, pressure is building to create transnational procedural systems that are capable of handling the increasing volume of transnational litigation occasioned by transnational commerce. A globalizing world might mean, some day down the road, a globalized legal process. In that world, the fate of the American civil jury is uncertain.

THE VANISHING JURY

A final note on juries: They are vanishing. The term "vanishing jury" has been coined to describe an accelerating phenomenon in American litigation: Fewer and fewer cases go to trial. The most recent data from the federal courts indicate that 1.44 percent of civil cases filed in federal court are tried. Of that number, about 0.96 percent are jury trials and 0.48 percent are bench trials. The rest of the cases end at earlier points in the process. Some end either on a *motion to dismiss* or a motion for summary judgment. Most cases settle. Even more disputes never enter the litigation system to begin with; parties settle, mediate, or arbitrate them without ever seeking redress in court. Among modern litigants, alternative methods of dispute resolution are far more popular than jury trial.

From an ADR perspective, litigation is only one option among numerous dispute resolution possibilities. This view has consequences for how we should design litigation processes. One logical consequence is to tailor litigation processes to the most likely dispute resolution outcomes. Thus, if most cases settle, we should choose procedural rules that promote settlement. We are not doing that at the present time. Even though jury trial is one of the least likely ways in which a case will be resolved, the jury has an enormous influence over the current structure of the procedural system. Whether the jury should continue to have that degree of influence as it vanishes from the American scene is a critical issue for the future direction of the American legal system.

⁓ 4 ⁓

Accuracy

Fundamental choices like the *adversary system* and *jury trial* rough-in the structure of a procedural system. They do not, however, deliver a fully specified set of rules, with each and every detail accounted for. Over the course of the next three chapters, we discuss three values that supply many of the details of the American procedural system: *accuracy, procedural fairness*, and *efficiency*.

These principles are the goals of nearly every procedural system in the world. Attaining these goals, however, is not a simple task—a fact to which the plethora of procedural systems attests. Part of the difficulty is the present limit of human institutions; we have not yet been able to develop (and probably never will) absolutely accurate, scrupulously fair, and utterly costless legal procedure. Another part of the difficulty in implementing these goals is that they must coexist with other goals, such as the use of juries or the adversarial system, that vary from society to society. And part of the difficulty is that the goals of deciding cases accurately, fairly, and efficiently can conflict with each other. In any procedural system, compromise among procedural values is necessary, and the emphases that different societies have historically placed on different procedural values have led to a vast variation in procedure.

In this chapter, we examine how we have balanced the goal of deciding cases accurately with other values such as the adversarial system and jury trial.

THE MEANING OF "ACCURACY"

The word "accuracy" has a more complicated meaning in American law than it might seem. On the surface, the word seems to mean that adjudicatory decisions should correspond to some objective truth about the world. Correct decision making is a part of the meaning of accuracy. Obviously, we want to get the facts and the law right, and apply the facts to the law correctly.

As you think about adjudication, however, you begin to realize that the goal of accuracy is an ideal at best. To begin with, it implies that a single right answer exists for every dispute. Is that a correct view of the world? Consider the law. You are already far enough into law school to know that different jurisdictions take different views on a host of legal rules. Is one and only one of those substantive rules the authentically "correct" rule in each circumstance? Most of us would say no. From a given set of arguments, and with the present limits of human knowledge and foresight, any of a range of legal rules can be deemed "acceptable," if not "accurate."

Factual decision making seems a more likely place to speak about accuracy: Either the defendant ran the red light, or he did not. But even here, in the absence of some conclusive evidence like a videotape, the limits of human knowledge make it impossible for us to know with absolute certainty what happened at the intersection. Moreover, adjudication sometimes involves determining "facts" that are more predictive than historical; for instance, deciding if the plaintiff needs to be compensated for some possible future surgery or if the defendant is likely to be dangerous in the future. In many cases, therefore, speaking of a single "correct" factual answer is insisting on a kind of accuracy that no procedural system can deliver. Indeed, in the civil system, we usually require a plaintiff to prove his or her case by a preponderance of the evidence (or "more likely than not") standard; in other words, the fact finder must believe that there is more than a 50 percent chance that the plaintiff's version of the events is correct. The system is willing to tolerate a large risk that the fact finder will be inaccurate in close cases.

So the idea of accuracy in adjudication is more elusive than it might seem. But it is still important. If a legal system makes no effort to achieve accurate results, people have less incentive to invest, to accumulate wealth, or to engage in behavior that might be beneficial to others in society. Therefore, whether or not the legal system can ever obtain a single "correct" answer, it needs to deliver an answer that is comfortably within the range of answers that the society deems acceptable. In our country, acceptability requires that the legal system must neither systematically exclude information or arguments that bear on the outcome nor systematically include information or arguments that do not bear on that outcome.

To take an example we mentioned in Chapter 1, in the days before jury trial, trials in medieval England were sometimes conducted by ordeal. An alleged wrongdoer was thrown into the water. If the person floated, then he or she was pronounced guilty on the theory that the water rejected the wrongdoer; if the alleged wrongdoer sank, he or she was pronounced innocent on the theory that the water received the guiltless. (Of course, the "innocent" person might also drown, an inconvenient side effect of winning the case.) Today we recoil from such a process in horror. Why? Because it does not allow the defendant to provide evidence and arguments to prove the lack of wrongdoing, and because it entertains information (the defendant's buoyancy) that we regard as extraneous to the question of liability.

Thus, deciding a case "accurately" has as much of a procedural quality (making sure that the system entertains *all* the relevant information and arguments, and *only* the relevant information and arguments) as a substantive quality (making sure that the answer itself is correct). It also has a particular historical meaning for the American legal system. As we described in Chapter 1, at one point the English, and ultimately the American, legal system was divided between *common law* and *equity*. The common law was known for its procedural rigor. If a plaintiff obtained one *writ* to commence a case but should have used another writ, the case was thrown out. If a defendant responded to the plaintiff's correct plea with a wrong plea, the defendant lost the case, even if the defendant could have won with a different plea. So much energy was concentrated on getting the case procedurally in order, with so little mercy shown to those who did not, that the legal and factual merits of the dispute often became a casualty. Equity arose as an alternative to the common law system. The watchwords of equity were procedural flexibility; the motto of equity was "to do complete justice between the parties." Procedural niceties were never supposed to get in the way of resolving the case on the evidence and the arguments. As equity matured, it too calcified, and became as caught up in the observance of procedural detail as the common law. But the equitable ideal of judicial *discretion* wielded to ensure that cases were decided on their substantive merits endured as a counterweight to the rigidity of the common law system.

Therefore, procedural "accuracy" has multiple meanings: correctness of the outcome, acceptability of the outcome, and avoidance of procedural traps that prevent a court from reaching the factual and legal heart of the case. These meanings are in some tension with each other. Among them, however, they explain major features of our procedural system.

DESIGNING A PRETRIAL PROCESS TO RESOLVE CASES ACCURATELY

The interaction of jury trial, the adversarial system, and the desire to determine cases accurately establishes one of the most distinctive features of American litigation: the *pretrial process*. Because of the difficulty of bringing together the jury, the trial must be concentrated in a way that all legal and factual issues can typically be resolved at one time. Because we want this trial to result in an accurate judgment, we therefore need to provide a process before the trial — a pretrial process — that permits sufficient investigation, research, and formulation of legal and factual issues to give us some confidence in the quality of the trial. Furthermore, at trial the adversarial system expects the lawyers to present the evidence and arguments to the fact finder. Although the choice is not logically compelled, it makes sense to place the lawyers in charge of the formulation, investigation, and research of issues during the pretrial process as well.

We want the pretrial process to accomplish two things. The first is to allow the full development of all legal and factual issues — to surface all the legal and factual claims that the parties might wish to make at trial. The second is to narrow the issues down for trial. If every tiny legal or factual dispute that surfaced during pretrial became the subject of a full-blown trial, trials would be very long, and the decision maker at trial, whether judge or jury, would be distracted by peripheral matters. An ideal pretrial process explores all issues and then narrows the case down to the disputes that are truly central, so the trial can run as effectively as possible.

Unfortunately, the desire to fully develop the issues conflicts with the desire to narrow the issues. The develop-and-narrow process has a chicken-and-egg quality: Do we narrow the issues first (with the risk that, not knowing all the facts, we will fail to develop important and possibly winning lines of attack or defense), or do we fully develop all the issues first (with the risk that so many peripheral disputes will erupt that we cannot narrow the case to the central questions)? In the real world of limited time and resources, it is not possible to do both jobs equally well. A procedural designer writing on a clean slate must establish an orientation for the system — either to develop the facts and the law first or to narrow the issues first — and then to build in some features from the other orientation as well.

In the case of the American system, we are not writing on a clean slate, and the failed choices of our procedural ancestors have had a heavy influence on our present system's orientation toward full factual and legal development. The common-law pleading system was essentially a series of issue-narrowing steps. Common-law pleading did not require the pleaders to provide many details about the dispute, nor was there any development of the factual or legal issues after the close of the pleadings. Rather, the point of the system was to boil the case down to a single issue a jury or judge could resolve. But the rigor of the common law process often interfered with substantive justice. Equity went entirely the other way; in its ancient form, its motto of "doing complete justice" led equity to reject rigorous issue narrowing in favor of a full exploration of the factual and legal issues. Equity, however, was slow and expensive. The *code pleading* that arose in the nineteenth century sought to provide more legal and factual detail than the common law while still defining the issues with more precision than ancient equity; but like the common law, it provided no mechanism for developing the facts and the law other than the *pleadings*. Unfortunately, code pleading turned out to be as intricate, as arcane, and as unforgiving of procedural miscues as common-law pleading had been.

Our most recent effort at reform, the Federal Rules of Civil Procedure, returned to the ancient spirit of equity. Avoiding one of the major breeding grounds of procedural rigor and technicality, the Rules are *trans-substantive* — in other words, uniform across all substantive doctrinal fields, such as torts and contract.[1] The judge has considerable discretion, especially during pretrial, to tailor the procedures to assure the accurate determination of each case. Procedural traps are few.

Issue-narrowing devices are few. In an utter rejection of common law procedure, the Federal Rules of Civil Procedure are dedicated, perhaps as much as any procedural code in the history of the world, to the full factual and legal development of every claim.

The principal components that give effect to this particular vision of procedural accuracy are a generous pleading system, a liberal *disclosure* and *discovery* system, a dearth of devices to narrow the issues before trial, judicial discretion, and broad rights of *claim joinder* and *party joinder*. Because claim and party joinder raises unique concerns, we defer examination of this topic to Chapter 7. In this chapter, we examine the benefits and costs of the remaining aspects of the pretrial system — pleading, disclosure and discovery, issue narrowing, and judicial discretion. Not surprisingly, both the benefits and the costs of this system echo back to the ancient days of equity.

THE AMERICAN PRETRIAL PROCESS

In the United States, as in most countries, the lawsuit commences with the pleadings. A *pleading* is a written document in which a party states factual and legal grounds for the court to enter a judgment in the party's favor.* That definition conceals as much as it reveals. Must the pleadings state each and every factual detail, right down to the specific pieces of evidence a party intends to use as proof? Must they provide each and every legal theory or authority that might be used to argue for a favorable judgment? Or can they be more cursory summaries of the parties' factual and legal positions? If so, how cursory?

The answers to these questions depend a great deal on the purpose or purposes that a system of pleading is expected to

---

* You should distinguish *pleadings* from *motions*, in which a party asks, or "moves," the court to take a specific action or enter a specific order. *See* Fed. R. Civ. P. 7(a), (b).

fulfill in the overall procedural regime. In the end, we need the pretrial regime to accomplish a number of functions. The first is to notify other parties about the outline of the case that a party will present at trial. Another function is to provide all of the factual details of a party's case. A third is to provide all of the legal grounds. A fourth function is to winnow out the factual and legal issues that will not be disputed at the trial. In an ideal world in which we want cases to be decided accurately, the pretrial process would perfectly address all of these tasks.

Of course, that ideal world does not exist. For instance, consider the pleadings. In most cases, no one has full knowledge about the case when the initial pleadings are filed. The plaintiff has some information, the defendant probably has other information, and third parties possess still more. Hence, it is unrealistic to expect that the initial pleadings can fully detail the facts; without that, it is unrealistic to expect that the parties can fully specify the legal theories either. Nor is it realistic to expect that the initial pleadings will perfectly narrow the case down to the issues that deserve a trial.

If it is impossible for the initial pleadings to fulfill all of the desired goals of a pretrial system, the next question is what we should do about it. One response is to accept the imperfection of pleadings, and to create a pleading system that emphasizes one of the pretrial tasks at the expense of others. For instance, common-law pleading concentrated on stating the legal issues, and code pleading concentrated on stating the factual issues. A different response is to design additional processes, after the pleadings but before trial, to accomplish the tasks that the initial pleadings neglect. For instance, if we could design a post-pleading process that did an excellent job of developing and narrowing the issues, the only function for the pleadings would be to give each side sufficient notice to kick off the case. In other words, the need for extensive pleading is inversely proportional to the availability of inexpensive and effective post-pleading mechanisms for discovering the facts and the law and then narrowing the case for trial.

Against this backdrop, we can critique the pleading and pretrial system established by the Federal Rules of Civil Procedure. The Rules expect the pleadings to perform only the function of providing notice. The Rules have created a wonderful post-pleading system of disclosure and discovery to develop fully the factual and legal issues, although it is expensive, slow, disruptive of privacy, and subject to abuse. But the Rules contain very limited mechanisms to narrow the issues. The following three sections explore in more detail the pleading, disclosure and discovery, and issue-narrowing processes used in the Federal Rules. As we study each of these components, keep in mind that they have a symbiotic relationship. The less that we expect of one part to fulfill a particular function, the greater is the demand that we place on other components of the pretrial process to take up the slack. Granting that no system can handle all of the pretrial functions perfectly, the ultimate question is whether we have struck the right balance.

Pleading: Giving Notice

The basic pleading Rules are found between Rules 7 and 12. Rule 7(a) states that, in most cases, the basic pleadings are the *complaint* and the *answer* to that complaint.* The intricate back-and-forth pleading of the common law is gone, but the old adversarial spirit of the common law remains alive in another way. One of the inveterate features of American pleading is the *master of the complaint* rule — the plaintiff determines the

---

* Aside from the plaintiff's initial complaint and the defendant's initial answer, Rule 7(a) also describes the need to file complaints and answers for counterclaims, cross-claims, or third-party claims. We discuss these devices in Chapter 7. For now, it is important to know only that in using these devices, the parties follow the standard pleading regime of filing complaints and answers. In addition to complaints and answers, Rule 7(a) allows a court to order a plaintiff to file a *reply* to an answer. In the real world, judges almost never order a reply.

content of the complaint, including choosing the claims to assert, the parties to sue, and the court in which to sue. The defendant has less control over the party structure or the chosen court, but the defendant does decide which defenses to raise in the answer. It is not the court's job to rewrite the complaint or the answer to assert more or different claims or defenses.

Rule 8(a) describes the requirements that the plaintiff's complaint must meet, and Rules 8(b) and (c) describe the pleading requirements for the defendant's answer. Taken as a whole, these Rules evince one of the most lax attitudes toward pleading in the world.

The Complaint   Rule 8(a) requires that a complaint contain three elements: "a short and plain statement" of the grounds of the court's jurisdiction, "a short and plain statement of the claim showing that the pleader is entitled to relief," and a demand for the relief the pleader seeks. These requirements do not sound onerous, but exactly how "short and plain" is a short and plain statement supposed to be? The answer to that question requires us to engage in the lawyerly exercise of interpreting language.

We can use three interpretive tools to better understand the meaning of "short and plain": the history and purpose of the Rule, the context of the Rule, and cases that have interpreted the Rule. All three sources confirm the minimal expectations that Rule 8(a) imposes on a plaintiff. With respect to history and purpose, the drafters of the Federal Rules were well aware of the failings of the common law's *issue pleading* and the codes' *fact pleading*. They rejected the view that the pleadings should be the principal means either for developing the facts and law, or for narrowing the issues; they created the discovery system to handle the former task, and summary judgment and a few other techniques to handle the latter. The Federal Rules adopt a system of *notice pleading*. All that the drafters expected of the pleadings was to supply enough information for the parties to kick off the rest of the pretrial process — in other words, to give opponents notice of a party's case, and no more.

The context of Rule 8(a) supports the minimalist role of the complaint. As we have said, other Rules handle the develop-and-narrow functions during pretrial. Another Rule that lends important support to the modest expectations of the "short and plain" requirement is Rule 9(b). Rule 9(b) states that allegations of fraud and mistake must be pleaded "with particularity," while other allegations of a state of mind "may be averred generally." We can draw the inference that the lack of any comparable "particularity" language in Rule 8(a) means that something less than particular allegations are expected. Even more helpful context is supplied by Rule 84, which says that the forms in the Rules' Appendix of Forms "indicate the simplicity and brevity of statement which the rules contemplate." A perusal of these model forms reveals that complaints are supposed to be brief indeed.

The third interpretive tool, precedent, is the final confirmation of this approach to pleading. The Supreme Court has decided a number of Rule 8(a) cases, the most significant of which are *Conley v. Gibson*,[2] *Leatherman v. Tarrant County Narcotics Intelligence and Coordination Unit*,[3] and *Swierkiewicz v. Sorema N.A.*[4] All three cases have some common features. First, the defendants found a common fault in the complaints in all three cases: a failure to allege specific facts that the plaintiff would ultimately need to prove at trial to win the case. Second, all three cases involved claims that might be described as unpopular in their day: *Conley* involved a claim of racial discrimination within a union; *Leatherman* involved a civil rights complaint against police officers at a time when such complaints, many ultimately without merit, were thought to be clogging the federal courts; and *Swierkiewicz* involved a race and age discrimination claim by a 49-year-old Hungarian employee at a time when employment discrimination claims were also thought to be clogging the courts. In each case, however, the Supreme Court made clear that the plaintiff's allegations were sufficient. In particular, the plaintiff did not need to allege facts sufficient to prove each and every element that the plaintiff would eventually have to prove at trial. The Supreme Court also made clear that the desire of lower federal courts to heighten pleading requirements as a means of weeding out unmeritorious and unpopular claims, even if laudable in theory, was irreconcilable with the minimal requirements of Rule 8(a). The famous language from *Conley*, repeated in *Leatherman* and *Swierkiewicz*, is this:

> [T]he Federal Rules of Civil Procedure do not require a claimant to set out in detail the facts upon which he bases his claim. To the contrary, all the Rules require is "a short and plain statement of the claim" that will give the defendant fair notice of what the plaintiff's claim is and the grounds upon which it rests.[5]

In a separate holding, *Conley* indicated that a complaint must clear a second low hurdle: Aside from giving notice of the claim and the grounds on which it rests, the complaint must demonstrate a legal theory plausible enough to believe that the plaintiff might recover from the defendant. Suppose that, after alleging jurisdiction, the complaint said: "On September 12, 2006, it was rainy in Chicago. As a result, plaintiff's clothes got wet. Therefore, defendant is liable to the plaintiff." The problem with this complaint is not that it fails to give notice of the factual nature of the plaintiff's beef; rather, it is that the complaint seems to state no legal theory of recovery against the defendant. Just as a pleading must adumbrate a few (albeit not many) facts, it must provide some clue about the legal grounds for the case. In judging the sufficiency of the complaint's statement of the legal claim, *Conley* established a different, but equally famous and equally quoted standard:

> A complaint should not be dismissed for failure to state a claim unless it appears beyond doubt that the plaintiff can

prove no set of facts in support of his claim which would entitle him to relief.[6]

In applying the standard to the complaint of the wet plaintiff, assume that the plaintiff is suing you. It would be hard to imagine a set of facts on which the plaintiff might prevail, so the complaint is likely to be deemed insufficient. On the other hand, suppose that the defendant named in the complaint is a major manufacturer of umbrellas. Now a judge might be less willing to *dismiss* the case. It is not beyond doubt that a product-liability claim for some defect in the umbrella might exist.

But wait, you might object, that's too much extrapolation. The complaint doesn't say anything about the plaintiff's purchase or use of the defendant's umbrella, or about a product-liability claim. That's a good point, but it misses the mark slightly. Your argument is that the complaint failed to meet the first *Conley* standard — that it didn't give enough facts to provide even minimal notice of the nature of the plaintiff's complaint. The second standard asks a different question: Is this the type of harm that the law might redress? These two standards judge different aspects of the complaint. The first is the *formal sufficiency* of the complaint: Does the complaint provide enough factual information to give the defendant notice of the case and the grounds on which it rests? The second is the *substantive sufficiency* of the complaint: Assuming that the factual allegations are true, does the complaint show a possibility of a legal violation for which some remedy exists?

The one thing that unites the two standards is their lack of bite. The Federal Rules do not expect much of the complaint. Bare-bones statements of fact out of which an imaginative legal mind might craft a theory of the defendant's liability are all that a complaint must contain. Procedural miscues in failing to provide a lot of factual and legal detail or in failing to say exactly the right thing will almost never keep a court from moving the case along toward a decision on the merits of the dispute.

The Answer   After filing the complaint with the court, the plaintiff must serve it on the defendant.* After receiving the complaint, the defendant has a short period of time (20 days for most defendants, 60 days for the United States) within which to respond.[7] The response can take one of two forms. One response is to file a motion, which typically seeks to dismiss the complaint because the complaint is deficient in one of the ways listed in Rule 12(b). (We examine Rule 12(b) motions later in the chapter.) The second response is to file an answer. Rules 8(b) and (c) provide the requirements that an answer must meet. First, the answer must address the plaintiff's allegations. Second, the defendant must "state in short and plain terms" any defenses to the complaint.

Like the complaint, the answer is not intended to be a high hurdle that trips a defendant before reaching the merits. But a couple of minor traps exist. First, Rule 8(b) requires the defendant to respond to each allegation in the complaint by either admitting it or denying it. If the defendant lacks knowledge or information about an allegation, the defendant can so plead; a plea of a lack of knowledge or information is treated as a denial. In essence, Rule 8(b) acts as a modest issue-narrowing device; a defendant's admission of an allegation removes that issue from the case and limits the litigation only to the matters that the parties still dispute. The trap arises when the defendant fails to respond to an allegation with an admission, a denial, or a claim of lack of knowledge or information. Rule 8(d) states that allegations in the complaint "are admitted when not denied in the responsive pleading."[8] Occasionally a court will stick a defendant who tries to deny an allegation, but does not quite get the job done, with an admission.[9] The argument for this result is the flip side of the plaintiff's obligation: As the plaintiff must put the defendant on notice of the nature of the claim, the defendant must put the plaintiff on notice of the nature of the

---

* We examine *service of process* in Chapter 5.

defense. But this result also frustrates resolutions on the merits and seems a harsh penalty for a modest pleading miscue. Crediting the spirit of notice pleading rather than the letter of Rule 8(d), most courts have shown more mercy.

A second trap arises from the defendant's Rule 8(c) obligation to plead *affirmative defenses*. A legal claim consists of two aspects. The first aspect concerns the elements that a plaintiff must prove to win the case. For instance, in a standard negligence claim, the plaintiff must prove the elements of duty, breach, causation, and damages. If the plaintiff fails to prove any one of these elements, the plaintiff loses. If the plaintiff proves all four, he or she has proven what is usually called the *prima facie case*. But that does not automatically mean that the plaintiff will win. The defendant can still win if he or she proves an affirmative defense to the prima facie case. For instance, at common law and still in a few states today, a defendant who has breached a duty of care and caused damage can still prevail by proving that the plaintiff was contributorily negligent or assumed the risk of injury. The elements of the prima facie case and the elements of the affirmative defenses to that case are a matter of substantive law, which you study in your substantive courses. Rule 8(c) does not create these defenses, but it does make one very important demand on the defendant: Plead the affirmative defenses you have. Again, this obligation amounts to the flip side of the plaintiff's notice-pleading obligation. The defendant must give notice of the grounds on which he or she intends to defend the case.

Rule 8(c) contains a list of 19 affirmative defenses, and Rule 12(b) contains 7 other defenses that a defendant can assert in the answer. Rule 8(c) makes clear that these two lists are not exhaustive; a defendant must also plead any other "avoidance or affirmative defense." Cases have recognized at least two dozen off-book affirmative defenses. A rough rule of thumb that courts have applied is to ask whether a defendant will bear the burden of proving the elements of a particular defense at trial. A less legalistic description is that an affirmative defense is any issue that lets the defendant win even if all the plaintiff's allegations are true.

Rule 8(c) is silent about the consequences to the defendant of failing to plead an affirmative defense. Cases have filled in the gap. Not surprisingly, the usual rule is that the failure to plead an affirmative defense in an answer amounts to a waiver of that defense.[10] As with Rule 8(d), this result might seem harsh in a system designed to prevent procedural miscues from frustrating accurate decision making. But other considerations are also at work. To some extent, the waiver rule meets a different pretrial goal: It is an issue-narrowing device. Moreover, most courts have created exceptions to the waiver rule. The principal exception involves a lack of prejudice: When the plaintiff suffers no harm from the defendant's failure to plead an affirmative defense, then the defense can still be raised. Finally, defendants who fail to plead correctly can often amend their pleadings to include the omitted defense. We turn to the issue of amendments in the next section.

Amendments   In our pretrial system, which permits extensive investigation and research between pleading and trial, new factual and legal theories of which the parties were initially unaware often emerge after the close of the pleadings. In other cases, a party wishes to add a new party to the case, or perhaps drop a theory or party mentioned in the initial pleading. Any procedural system needs to decide whether to permit the addition or subtraction of new theories or parties, and, if changes are permissible, to determine the standards and procedures for making the amendment. This question is especially critical in a system such as ours.

Returning to first principles, a procedural system that is dedicated to resolving cases accurately should in theory impose no significant roadblocks when the plaintiff or defendant wishes to add or remove theories or parties from the case.

The party should be able to simply file a new complaint or answer, and the amended pleading should be judged under the same standard as the initial pleading: Does it give enough notice that the merits can be more fully developed during the pretrial process?

For the most part, this approach is precisely how the Federal Rules of Civil Procedure handle amendments. The principal rule governing the amendment process is Rule 15. Rule 15(a) provides that each party has a small window to amend the pleading once *as a matter of course* (that is, without seeking permission from the other party or the court); that window closes either when the opposing party files a responsive pleading, or after 20 days if the pleading is one to which no responsive pleading is permitted. Beyond that window, Rule 15(a) requires a party seeking an amendment to obtain either the other party's written consent or *leave of court* (that is, approval from the court). True to first principles, Rule 15(a) states that a court should "freely" give leave "when justice so requires."

Courts have interpreted this phrase with all the liberality that it suggests. The leading case is *Foman v. Davis*.[11] *Foman* defined "justice" in negative terms; in other words, a court should grant leave to amend unless it is unjust to do so. The specific types of injustice that *Foman* listed were "undue delay, bad faith or dilatory motive on the part of the movant, repeated failure to cure deficiencies by amendments previously allowed, undue prejudice to the opposing party by virtue of allowance of the amendment, futility of amendment, etc." Despite the "etc." at the end, courts have usually treated the list of five circumstances as exhaustive; if an amendment suffers from none of the five defects, the trial judge will grant leave to amend.

Two circumstances limit the generosity of the amendment process. The first is the confusing Rule 15(c), which describes the *relation back* doctrine. The problem that Rule 15(c) addresses is this: Every civil claim has a statute of limitations associated with it. Statutes of limitations require that a case be filed (or sometimes served) within a certain number of years of a specified event (typically either the date of the act that caused the injury or the date of the injury itself). When the original complaint is filed before the end of the statute of limitations, but an amendment adding a new claim is not filed until after the statute of limitations has expired, the court faces a critical question: Should the new claim be treated as if it had been pleaded in the original complaint (in other words, should it "relate back" to the original filing), so that the statute of limitations has been satisfied?

To take a concrete example, suppose that a plaintiff sues a defendant for failing to stop at a red light. The injury happened on January 2, 2005, and the relevant statute of limitations is two years. The plaintiff files and serves the complaint on December 31, 2006. So far, so good; the plaintiff has satisfied the statute of limitations. Now, suppose that, after some discovery, it begins to appear that the defendant was a hitman who actually tried to kill the plaintiff. Suppose as well that the statute of limitations for a battery claim is the same as for a negligence claim. On January 9, 2008, the plaintiff moves to amend the complaint to add a claim for battery, along with a request for punitive damages. Had the plaintiff filed the battery claim as a new case on that date, the statute of limitations (an affirmative defense under Rule 8(c)) would have barred the case. But the plaintiff is instead seeking to amend the original complaint, which was filed within the statute of limitations. The question is whether the battery claim relates back — in other words, whether it should be treated as if it had been filed on December 31, 2006. (Relation back is a legal fiction; obviously the battery claim was not really filed on December 31, 2006, but the doctrine treats the claim as if it had been.) If the battery claim relates back, then the statute of limitations acts as no bar.

Rule 15(c) states three circumstances under which relation back is permitted. The most common situation occurs when the claim or defense added by the amendment "arose out of the conduct, transaction, or occurrence" described in the original pleading. It has been difficult for courts to lay down a general principle for determining when the original and the amended theories involve the same conduct, transaction, or occurrence. (As we see in Chapter 7, the phrase "transaction or occurrence" is used in a number of the Federal Rules of Civil Procedure, and its meaning changes somewhat with the context in which it is used.) On the one hand, courts want to decide the case accurately, and not allow procedural technicalities to deprive parties of the opportunity to present their cases. On the other hand, the statute of limitations serves important policies, such as giving *repose* to defendants and avoiding trials that are based on stale evidence. In hard cases, courts tend to fall back on these two sets of concerns, and decide the relation-back issue in accordance with the policies that seem the strongest on the particular facts. This balancing act is a good reminder that the accuracy principle is not absolute, and must be compromised against other policies.

The second situation that limits the generosity of Rule 15(a) is Rule 16(b). As the principal *case management* rule, Rule 16 gives trial judges broad powers, especially during the pretrial process, to expedite the litigation. Rule 16(b) requires the judge, in most cases, to enter a *scheduling order* that establishes certain pretrial deadlines. One of the deadlines that a scheduling order must contain is a deadline to "amend the pleadings." Once established, deadlines can be modified only for "good cause," a phrase that courts have tended to interpret strictly.

When a party seeks to amend a pleading after the expiration of the Rule 16(b) deadline, cases have uniformly held that the liberal "when justice so requires" standard of Rule 15(a) gives way to the more stringent "good cause" standard of Rule 16(b). These holdings are a logical way to reconcile the language of the two different Rules, but they are also inconsistent with the usual orientation of the notice-pleading system. Once again, the accuracy principle must accommodate itself to other important principles, such as efficiency.

Disclosure and Discovery: Developing the Facts and the Law

If the primary purpose of the pleadings is to provide an opponent and the court with notice of only the legal and factual skeleton of the case, the purpose of the disclosure-and-discovery process is to add the muscle and flesh. The discovery system that the Federal Rules established in 1938 was a great experiment. At common law, there was virtually no discovery. Equity permitted broader discovery, but equity was a small percentage of the work of the federal courts. Today, the disclosure-and-discovery process is the most important feature in American litigation, the meat and potatoes of American litigators. Pleadings are not difficult to draft; trials are rare. Disclosure and discovery are where the action is.

Ideally, disclosure and discovery permit both sides to obtain the factual information necessary to present their cases at trial and to uncover the outline of the legal theories that the other side will pursue. Once the parties arm themselves with the facts and the legal theories, the trial can proceed, without trickery or surprise, to render an accurate decision. Knowledge of the evidence and the legal claims should also have a beneficial side effect: Parties with full information are more likely to settle their differences before trial.

Put in this way, it is hard to oppose the idea of disclosure and discovery, and equally hard to imagine why every legal system does not employ this approach. But the disclosure-and-discovery process is perhaps the single most controversial feature in American litigation. The fundamental problems with discovery are four: expense, delay, infringement on privacy, and abuse. The best way to understand these concerns is to examine the mechanics of discovery (exactly what devices can be used to discover information) and the scope of discovery (exactly how much information can be discovered).

The Mechanics of Disclosure and Discovery The first process by which parties can obtain information about the case is *mandatory disclosure,* involving information that one party must automatically give to the other party without the other party requesting it. The second is party-initiated *discovery,* involving information that a party can obtain only on request.

Mandatory Disclosure. Rule 26(a) requires the parties to disclose three types of information to their opponents, at three different times before trial. The first round, known as *initial mandatory disclosure,* requires, among other things, that each party supply a list of the witnesses and documents that the party may use to support the party's claims or defenses. Initial mandatory disclosure occurs early in the case, typically before the scheduling conference with the judge. Two later rounds require the parties to disclose their expert witnesses, and then to disclose the witnesses, documents, and deposition transcripts that they expect to use at trial.

The mandatory disclosure provisions were adopted in 1993 and significantly amended in 2000. When they were proposed, they were controversial. Most of the controversy surrounded initial mandatory disclosure. One argument against mandatory disclosure was the fear that disclosure would front-load the parties' discovery costs, thus discouraging some plaintiffs from filing. Another argument was that a plaintiff could extract vast quantities of sensitive information from a defendant simply by filing a bare-bones complaint, thus raising expenses and violating the privacy interests of defendants. A third concern was that mandatory disclosure offended the adversarial ideal. On this last concern, some opponents, already believing that case management was the start of a move toward court-initiated, inquisitorial justice, saw initial mandatory disclosure as another large step in this direction. But the information disclosed under Rule 26(a) was already the type of information that good lawyers asked for routinely in the discovery process. It is fair to say that, so far, the worst fears about mandatory disclosure have not come to pass, and it is now an established feature of the pretrial process.

Party-Initiated Discovery Devices. Unlike the disclosure process, the discovery process is party-initiated and party-controlled: A person has no obligation to provide discoverable information unless a party asks for it. Depending on how you count them, the Federal Rules contain either four or five discovery devices. The four clear devices are *depositions* (Rules 30-32 and 45), *interrogatories* (Rule 33), requests for production of documents or other tangible things (Rules 34 and 45), and requests for a physical or mental examination (Rule 35). Depositions solicit the sworn oral testimony of individuals with relevant information.* Requests for production permit the gathering of documents and physical or tangible evidence. Interrogatories are written questions that one party can propound to another. Requests for a physical or mental examination are useful when a party's health is an issue in the case.

The fifth "discovery" device is the request for admission (Rule 36). Requests for admission ask an opponent to admit the truth of a particular factual or legal point. As such, the request for admission is an issue-narrowing rather than a discovery device, although it is more useful to eliminate non-controversial matters like the authenticity of documents than to narrow issues truly in dispute. But it is also a handy adjunct to discovery; when an opponent refuses to admit a request, a party can follow up with interrogatories or other devices to discover the basis for that denial.

---

* Depositions differ from courtroom testimony in two ways. First, they are not usually conducted in a courtroom, but rather in an office. Second, the judge is not usually present to make immediate rulings on objections to questions.

Rules 30-36 and 45 are lengthy, and in some places intricate. Rather than focusing on their details, we make five thematic points that should help you to keep your eyes on the forest instead of the trees.

First, in conjunction with disclosure, the discovery devices seem to allow access to any kind of factual information imaginable. Some of these devices (interrogatories, requests for admission, and in most cases requests for an examination) can be employed only against other parties in the case, but a deposition and production of documents or other tangible information can be sought from anyone. (Rule 45 is the vehicle through which nonparties can be forced to provide a deposition or produce documents or other tangible things.) Among them, however, it is difficult to imagine any information related to the case that cannot be unearthed during pretrial. Such broad discovery seems to vindicate fully the ideal of deciding cases on their merits.

Second, real-world constraints limit the ability of the discovery devices to vindicate this ideal perfectly. For one thing, discovery is expensive. When the attorneys' fees for both sides and the court reporter's fees are combined, a single six-hour deposition can cost $2,000 to $5,000. If the parties have a significant number of documents or electronic files to search, the costs of locating requested material can run into the thousands of dollars, and the requesting party's costs in reviewing those documents can amount to thousands more. Unless the parties are very well funded and the stakes in the case are high, the economics of discovery impose a limit on how much information each party can get about the merits.

Third, two types of asymmetries related to cost can skew the discovery system. The first asymmetry is wealth. If one party is well funded and the other is not, one side will have greater opportunities to uncover the merits of the dispute than the other. A second asymmetry is informational. In general, each party bears its own costs in discovery: One side bears the costs in asking, and the other party bears the costs in responding. If one party has significantly more information than the other side, the second party can impose significant nonreciprocal costs on the first. These asymmetries raise a concern that discovery will be used for purposes other than determining the merits — to browbeat an impoverished opponent to drop a meritorious case, or to browbeat an information-rich opponent into settling a meritless case to avoid the expense of discovery.

Fourth, the adversarial system is a principal source of the friction between the ideal of discovery and its reality. As we have seen, the adversarial approach to litigation can induce lawyers to use rules that are intended to achieve a public good to achieve private advantage instead. Have American litigators ever exploited asymmetries to their clients' advantage? Of course. Moreover, in an adversarial competition, having exclusive access to information is often a good thing. (Put differently, a party wants an opponent to have access to private information within the party's control only when the party benefits more from the disclosure than from the secrecy.) So have lawyers ever resisted full discovery by construing an opponent's requests as literally and narrowly as possible? Yes, every day of the week. A good civil litigator must be dogged, creative, and precise if he or she hopes to obtain a fairly full picture of the case's merits.

Fifth, these concerns about expense, abuse, and noncompliance have driven numerous recent amendments to the discovery process. Mandatory disclosure is one example. Another is the recent spate of limitations on the use of various discovery devices. Today a party may take no more than ten depositions, and no deposition may last longer than seven hours.[12] Likewise, a party can ask no more than 25 interrogatories.[13] A court (or the parties by agreement) can expand these limits when the case requires it, but the limits seek to force the parties to "go for the jugular" rather than to track down every detail in the case.

The Scope of Discovery To obtain information through one of the discovery devices, a party must clear three hurdles contained in Rule 26(b)(1) and (2): The requested information must be relevant, it must be proportional to the needs of the case, and it must not be privileged. Together, these three doctrines limit the *scope of discovery,* and, in theory, the ability of the parties to develop the full merits of their cases. Of the three, *relevance* is the least significant limit. Under Rule 26(b)(1), parties are entitled to obtain discovery of any matter "relevant" to any "claim or defense." In addition, parties can get discovery of any matter "relevant to the subject matter" of the case on a showing of "good cause."* Although the Federal Rules of Civil Procedure contain no definition of relevance, courts often borrow the definition from the Federal Rules of Evidence, which define relevant evidence as "evidence having any tendency to make the existence of any fact that is of consequence . . . more probable or less probable than it would be without the evidence."[14] This definition is capacious, exactly in line with a broad investigation designed to produce an accurate decision.

Proportionality imposes a somewhat more significant limitation on discovery. Now found in Rule 26(b)(2)(C),** proportionality was ushered into the Rules in the same 1983 amendments that created Rule 16's case management orientation and Rule 11's frivolous filings *sanctions.* Like those provisions, proportionality responds to increased concerns about cost

---

* To understand the difference between "claim or defense" relevance and "subject matter" relevance, suppose the plaintiff files a lawsuit alleging that the defendant negligently injured him or her. The plaintiff would like to conduct discovery to decide whether to pursue a new theory — that the defendant also committed a battery. This discovery is not relevant to a claim or defense, but it is relevant to the subject matter. Before 2000, parties could discover any information relevant to the subject matter; Rule 26(b)(1) was amended in 2000 to prevent access to "subject matter" discovery without a showing of good cause.

**Rule 26(b)(2)(B) contains a separate proportionality rule applicable only to the disclosure or discovery of electronically stored information.

and abuse in the pretrial process. Specifically, proportionality asks whether particular discovery is worth it — whether the expected benefits of particular discovery justify its expense. Thus far, Rule 26(b)(2) has not been interpreted in a ruthlessly economic way, with precise calculations of the marginal utility of potential evidence balanced against its marginal cost. For the most part, the proportionality limitation has blocked only discovery that is expensive to obtain and has little chance of yielding useful information — in other words, discovery for which the potential for abuse is high. It, too, is a fairly weak check on discovery.

The third limit, *privilege*, is the strongest, but also the least likely to be applicable. Privileges prevent the disclosure of certain types of evidence in court. Many evidentiary privileges have developed over the centuries. The establishment of a privilege represents a policy judgment that the protection of communications within a certain relationship outweighs the additional accuracy that the protected information might lend to judicial decisions. For instance, we have the *attorney-client privilege*, which bars disclosure of communications between an attorney and his or her client, because we believe that, in the long run, society benefits more from fostering trust and confidentiality between attorneys and clients than it does from getting the results in particular cases right. The refusal in Rule 26(b)(1) to permit the discovery of privileged information constitutes a classic limitation on the accuracy principle.

One "privilege" that often confounds students is the *work-product doctrine*. The work-product doctrine is not a true privilege, because it does not necessarily protect communications between people. Rather, the doctrine protects a lawyer's work product — in other words, the material that a lawyer prepares "in anticipation of litigation or for trial." Because the lawyer's work product (interviews, research, notes, and so on) is often not communicated to the client, it may not qualify for protection under the traditional attorney-client privilege.* In *Hickman v. Taylor*,[15] however, the Supreme Court recognized that disclosure of this information is inconsistent with a well-functioning adversarial system. In the famous words of Justice Jackson's concurrence, discovery "was hardly intended to enable a learned profession to perform its functions either without wits or on wits borrowed from the adversary."

Rule 26(b)(3), which was written in 1970 to codify *Hickman*'s common law doctrine, creates two tiers of work product. The first tier of work product is protected from disclosure unless the opposing party can show "substantial need" for the information found in the attorney's work product, as well as "undue hardship" in obtaining the information by other means. The second tier is sometimes called *core work product*: "the mental impressions, conclusions, opinions, or legal theories" of a party's attorney or other representative. The usual view is that core work product is absolutely protected from disclosure, although this view rests more on an inference from Rule 26(b)(3) than its explicit language.[16]

Rules 26(a)(2) and (b)(4) create an important exception to the work-product doctrine. These Rules require disclosure and discovery of the opinions of those experts a party may call at trial. Expert witnesses are usually not eyewitnesses to the events, but they have an expertise that allows them to form opinions on issues that are often crucial to the case. For instance, an accident reconstruction expert can form an opinion about the speed of the defendant's car by examining skid marks and the damage to the car. Because the opinions of experts are classic work product (they are created in anticipation of litigation or for trial), they would seem undiscoverable without a showing of substantial need and undue hardship. Nevertheless, protecting expert testimony would thwart

---

* Sometimes, however, work product is communicated between attorney and client. If this occurs, the communication is eligible for protection under both doctrines.

the desire to have trials determined accurately, without rabbit-out-of-the-hat testimony. The work-product doctrine and its exception for expert testimony present an excellent example of how the fundamental values in American procedure can come into conflict — in this case, the conflict is between the adversarial system and accurate resolutions — and how the system seeks to accommodate these competing interests.

Another excellent example of this accommodation is the sanctioning process in discovery. When one party asks for discovery, the party or other person from whom discovery is sought must respond. The response takes one of two forms: Either the information is provided, or the person *objects* to providing it. For the most part, the only legitimate grounds for objection are lack of relevance, disproportionality, or privilege. Ultimately, the discovery system relies on the parties and their lawyers to use good faith in seeking only the information that each side truly needs, in providing all of the discovery the other party legitimately requests, and in objecting to discovery only when legitimate grounds for objection exist. At the same time, adversaries are competitors, and they have little incentive to build their opponents' cases. Thus, the discovery system must create incentives to induce adversaries not to tax the other side with unnecessary requests or to refuse to provide legitimate discovery. The incentives must be effective, but they must not be so stringent that they frustrate resolutions on the merits.

This balance works itself out in two rules: Rule 26(g) — the equivalent of Rule 11 for discovery requests and responses — and Rule 37. Especially in Rule 37, we see the effort to adjust competing interests. As a general matter, a party's failure to provide discovery is handled initially under Rule 37(a). A party faced with an opponent's objection to providing discovery must file a *motion to compel*. The judge then issues an order either granting or denying the motion to compel, and can in some circumstances impose modest sanctions under Rule 37(a) against the losing party. If the judge orders the discovery and the opponent provides it, then the matter is over. If the opponent refuses to comply with a Rule 37(a) order to provide discovery, however, the far more serious sanctions of Rule 37(b) — including the "death penalty" sanction of dismissing a case for a willful violation of the order — come into play. At this point, accurate decision making takes a back seat to disciplining a recalcitrant adversary.

Issue-Narrowing Devices

The pleading and disclosure-and-discovery systems develop the legal and factual issues for trial. For the most part, however, they do nothing to narrow these issues before trial. Indeed, the minimalism of pleading, the ease of amendment, and the breadth of discovery encourage the proliferation, rather than narrowing, of issues during pretrial. Unless significant issue-narrowing devices also exist, the pretrial balance between developing and narrowing issues is lopsided indeed.

And that is precisely the case. The American system is far better at developing factual and legal issues than at narrowing them. There are four principal issue-narrowing devices, most of which we have already encountered. The first is the answer. Under Rule 8(b), a defendant can affirmatively or by silence admit one or more allegations of the complaint, and under Rule 8(c), a defendant's silence waives any unasserted defenses. Second, under Rule 36, a party can admit one or more of another party's requests for admission, again eliminating the need for further proof. Third, Rule 12(b) allows a court to dismiss a claim that runs afoul of one of seven enumerated defenses. Most of these defenses — lack of subject matter jurisdiction (Rule 12(b)(1)), lack of personal jurisdiction (Rule 12(b)(2)), lack of proper venue (Rule 12(b)(3)), defects in the summons or the service of the complaint (Rules 12(b)(4) and (b)(5)), and failure to join a Rule 19 party (Rule 12(b)(7)) — concern defects that are unrelated to the merits of the dispute.* The Rule 12(b)(6) motion to dismiss is the one device that narrows cases on their merits.[17] As we have seen, however, it is also a modest issue-narrowing device. Dismissal under Rule 12(b)(6) is appropriate only when a complaint fails to meet the criteria for formal and substantive sufficiency that *Conley v. Gibson* established. These standards eliminate only the most egregiously inadequate claims. As an issue-narrowing device, Rule 12(b)(6) is more of a broadaxe than the necessary scalpel.

The fourth issue-narrowing device is the most significant: the Rule 56 motion for summary judgment. As we saw in Chapter 3, summary judgment on a claim or defense is proper when the lack of a "genuine issue as to any material fact" entitles the moving party judgment as a matter of law. Perhaps you can now see the motion for summary judgment in a new light. The other issue-narrowing devices are fairly ineffective or limited in their scope. An answer's frivolous failure to admit an allegation might draw sanctions under Rule 11, and a frivolous failure to admit a request for admission might require a party to pay limited trial expenses under Rule 37(c)(2). But neither of these sanctions is a significant deterrent to a party who refuses to engage in issue narrowing. Likewise, the Rule 12(b)(6) motion to dismiss imposes such a high bar that it screens out few claims. The one device that effectively examines the evidence generated during pretrial and seeks to resolve claims and defenses on their merits is summary judgment.

Summary judgment is in fact quite effective. In the federal system, more than ten times as many cases are resolved on summary judgment as are resolved by trial. Indeed, the Supreme Court has explicitly acknowledged summary judgment's

---

* They do, however, vindicate other values, such as *federalism*, *notice* and *opportunity to be heard*, *efficiency*, and *transactionalism*, which we discuss in other chapters of this book.

central issue-narrowing role. As the Court said in *Celotex Corp. v. Catrett*,[18] "with the advent of 'notice pleading,'" summary judgment "is properly regarded not as a disfavored procedural shortcut, but rather as an integral part of the Federal Rules as a whole."

Nonetheless, summary judgment suffers from several flaws as an issue-narrowing device. One problem is summary judgment's ineffectiveness when a genuine factual issue remains for trial. Another is the question of timing. In *Celotex*, the Supreme Court made clear that summary judgment could be granted only "after adequate time for discovery." Courts are often reluctant to entertain a motion for summary judgment until discovery is completed. A more thoroughgoing commitment to issue narrowing would integrate summary judgment into discovery to pretermit some factual and legal development, much as the civil law system integrates trial hearings with factual investigation. At present, summary judgment is more a substitute for trial than a true pretrial issue-narrowing technique.

Summary judgment is also an all-or-nothing device. It can eliminate entire claims or defenses, but it is not capable of surgically removing discrete factual or legal issues. For instance, if the evidence overwhelmingly proves the defendant's negligence but a genuine issue remains about whether the negligence caused the plaintiff's injury, the plaintiff cannot move for summary judgment; even though the negligence is clear, the plaintiff is not entitled to judgment because of the disputed issue of causation. Summary judgment is not a broadaxe, but it is more of a meat cleaver than the scalpel that an effective issue-narrowing device should be.

Summary judgment's final flaw is that it is almost always party-initiated. In an adversarial system, a party's private agenda for whether and when to narrow the issues might diverge from the socially optimal approach. To some extent, judges' case management powers under Rule 16 can overcome this problem. In particular, Rule 16(c)(1) authorizes a judge to "take appropriate action" regarding "the formulation and simplification of the issues, including the elimination of frivolous claims or defenses."[19] This intriguing language does not, however, give the judge an issue-narrowing carte blanche. Although a judge can dismiss a case or enter a summary judgment without waiting for a motion from a party, the standard that the judge must apply is identical to that for a party-initiated motion. Rule 16(c) has also been interpreted to authorize a few other issue-narrowing devices that are useful in specific circumstances,[20] but as a general principle, issue narrowing takes a back seat to factual and legal development in the American pretrial system.

Judicial Discretion

A central feature of the Federal Rules' approach to accurate decision making is judicial discretion. Discretion courses through the Federal Rules of Civil Procedure. The Rules contain few "musts" and many "mays." By one count, approximately one-third of all the Federal Rules, including most of the significant rules, vest discretion in trial judges. One evident example is case management. As you read cases in Civil Procedure, notice how frequently appellate courts review the decisions of trial judges under an *abuse of discretion* standard. Despite our penchant in law schools to examine cases from the Supreme Court or the appellate courts, the reality is that discretionary rules vest significant power in American trial courts.

Discretionary rules act more as guidelines than as hard-and-fast requirements. The original purpose of providing discretionary power was to allow judges to tailor procedures to the needs of individual cases, thus helping to ensure that procedural rules never obscured the merits of the controversy. Stated in this way, it is difficult to resist the idea of judicial discretion.

But discretion also opens up a number of troubling prospects. It is expensive to reinvent the procedural wheel for every case. It gives adversaries one more thing to wrangle over in the effort to achieve victory. Discretion provides a judge with the power to achieve objectives other than reaching the merits, should a judge decide that another goal is more worthwhile. For instance, most of the discretion invested in judges under the case management authority of Rule 16 was not intended to help cases achieve accurate decisions, but rather to make litigation faster and cheaper. These two goals are not the same.

Discretion also raises the specter of less uniformity and more variability in substantive outcome. Procedural rules affect the outcomes of cases. If that were not true — in other words, if every set of procedural rules yielded exactly the same outcome — there would be little point in concerning ourselves with procedure. In one case study, however, a group of judges was given a hypothetical scenario involving a complex case, and asked to decide which case management procedures to apply to the case. One judge chose a set of procedures that would likely have resulted in dismissal of the case. Another chose procedures that would likely have resulted in a multi-million-dollar settlement. This example is extreme, but other experimental data also show that different procedural choices result in different outcomes. Substance and procedure are inextricably intertwined.

This fact does not decide the question of how much discretion individual judges should possess, nor is it intended to suggest that we should throw up our hands and view procedure as nothing more than masked substantive policy. But it does suggest the difficulty of designing a system to decide cases accurately. The procedures we choose in part determine what the merits of a dispute are. So, do we prefer a legal system with more discretion (and hence more variability in outcome and more cost) or a system with more rigidity (and hence more risk that cases will be determined on the basis of procedural technicalities or traps)? We cannot have it both ways. There is no perfectly flexible, perfectly uniform, perfectly accurate system of procedure.

THE AMERICAN PRETRIAL PROCESS IN CONTEXT

We have tried to stress the interconnectedness of the components of the pretrial process. On the one hand, the process must accomplish certain goals — giving notice, developing factual and legal issues, and narrowing issues — but it cannot accomplish each goal perfectly. On the other hand, the process has certain mechanisms — pleading, disclosure and discovery devices, and issue-narrowing devices. The trick is to use the available mechanisms to achieve, as nearly as possible, the desired goals. For instance, we have seen that our system gives more weight to the goals of notice and developing the case than to the goal of narrowing issues in advance of trial. Should we wish to give more weight to narrowing issues, we would need to make adjustments elsewhere, perhaps by requiring more specificity in the pleadings or reducing the scope of discovery. As we do so, we also compromise the modern American ideal of accurate decision making.

So should we compromise this ideal? Perhaps you will find an international perspective helpful. When the rest of the world looks at the American system of litigation, discovery rivals jury trial as its most controversial feature. No other country permits discovery on a comparably unfettered scale. Like domestic opponents, many foreigners view discovery as an expensive process that, with virtually no judicial oversight, can expose private information and extort settlements through the threat of a vast discovery campaign. Other legal systems place significant restraints on the methods and scope of discovery, but make up the difference in potentially reduced accuracy by requiring greater specificity in the pleadings, placing a judge in charge of discovery, or interspersing pretrial with trial to keep the issues focused.

If we return to our own shores, most of the reforms in American procedure since the 1970s have been direct or indirect efforts to curtail the perceived excesses of discovery. The mandatory disclosure system, the introduction of a proportionality requirement, the shrinking of the definition of relevance, and Rule 26(g) are all direct attempts to limit the problems of discovery. Rule 11 and the case management apparatus of Rule 16 are two of the principal indirect efforts.

But all of these changes nibble at the corners of discovery. At present, there is less agreement about whether the core of the pretrial system needs to be changed. One oft-discussed reform is more specificity in the pleadings. On a couple of occasions, Congress has enacted heightened pleading requirements for a statutory cause of action, but a general reform of Rule 8 seems unlikely. Radical reforms to discovery (for instance, abolishing depositions) are rarely mentioned. The empirical data suggest that American lawyers, judges, and litigants are satisfied with discovery; except in a small subset of cases (in general, the most complex ones), the perceived problems of discovery do not exceed its perceived benefits. International pressure that might instigate reform has to some extent escaped through the relief valve of arbitration agreements that keep some transnational disputes out of American courts. For now, discovery is likely to remain the centerpiece of the American-style effort to achieve accurate decision making.

⌇ 5 ⌇

Procedural Fairness

An underlying goal of any procedural regime is fair adjudication. Other factors, such as *accuracy* and preferences for an *adversarial system* and *trial by jury*, also influence procedural choices. But ultimately, a procedural regime must make fundamental choices about *process*: defining the minimum procedural protections to which litigants are entitled. If these minimums are not met, then litigants have both a moral and a legal right to complain. Regardless of the outcome on the merits, litigants who do not receive fair procedures are not adequately served by the adjudicatory system.

In the American system, multiple sources provide guidance on these minimum procedural protections. The *Due Process Clauses* of the Fifth and Fourteenth Amendments to the Constitution require all federal and state courts to provide litigants with *due process*. The other sources include statutes, the Federal Rules of Civil Procedure, and common law doctrines such as *preclusion*. It might help to think of the constitutional limitations as a floor and the other sources as furniture: No furniture can fall below the level of the floor, but the actual placement of the furniture—the implementation of the constitutional minimums—is not constitutionally mandated, and many different arrangements might provide adequate procedural protection.

In this chapter, we look first at the constitutional requirement of due process and then at particular implementations of that requirement; in other words, we first construct the floor, and then see where the furniture is placed. Finally, we examine *class actions*, which raise unique questions under both the Constitution and the Federal Rules.

THE FLOOR: CONSTITUTIONAL DUE PROCESS

Both the Fifth and Fourteenth Amendments prohibit the government from depriving individuals of "life, liberty, or property, without due process of law." The phrase *due process of law* comes to us from seventeenth-century English legal commentators. They drew on the Magna Carta, which English nobles forced King John to sign in 1215. The earliest forerunner of our Constitution, the Magna Carta provides (among other things) that the king shall not take various actions against his subjects except in accordance with "the law of the land." In the hands of seventeenth-century English jurists, "law of the land" became "due process of law." The two phrases are still interpreted alike, as are the Fifth and Fourteenth Amendments.*

For purposes of civil procedure, constitutional due process is thought to have three components. It is, first, a limit on the power of the state to exercise *jurisdiction* over those who do not consent to such jurisdiction. Second, a court must provide parties *notice* and *an opportunity to be heard* on all matters that might affect the outcome of the case. Third, the Due Process Clause requires the hearing to be conducted by a

---

* The Fifth Amendment, ratified in 1791, applies to the federal government; the Fourteenth Amendment, ratified in 1868 after the Civil War, applies to the states.

neutral decision maker. * As a matter of both fairness and accuracy, the need for a neutral decision maker is self-evident. In the remainder of this section, we examine the requirements of jurisdiction, notice, and an opportunity to be heard.

Jurisdictional Power

A court cannot be said to provide sufficient procedural protection (due process) if it reaches beyond its legitimate authority. Whatever else we decide about the types of procedures we will allow or require, we must begin by ensuring that the court before which a dispute is brought is legally entitled to resolve the dispute and bases it decision on the appropriate legal authorities. These questions in turn implicate two others: Does the court have the authority to tell the parties what to do, and what sources of law may it consult in deciding? The first is a question of *personal jurisdiction* (or *jurisdiction over the person*) and the second a question of *choice of law*. You will probably study personal jurisdiction in your Civil Procedure course, but you might or might not cover choice of law — and if you do, it will probably be limited to the question of when federal courts must apply state law, rather than the more general question of the constitutional limits on sources of law. Thus, we begin with personal jurisdiction and then deal only briefly with choice of law.

Personal Jurisdiction Personal jurisdiction concerns the scope of a court's power to issue a *judgment* that binds a party and is enforceable against that party anywhere in the country (even in courts other than the one that issued the judgment). Remember that the Constitution sets the floor

---

* You will learn in your Constitutional Law course that a fourth component of due process is *substantive due process*, which places limits on the types of laws that legislatures may enact. That very controversial topic is, fortunately, not relevant to Civil Procedure.

for personal jurisdiction, but statutes and other sources provide the implementation. A court can exercise jurisdiction over a person, then, only when some statute or court rule authorizes it. Begin with state courts. (We discuss federal courts later in the chapter.) As a general matter, a statute or court rule will give a state court the power to exercise jurisdiction over parties physically present within the state's borders. *Long-arm statutes* also allow state courts to reach out across state lines and enter a valid judgment against parties who are not physically present in the state. The Due Process Clause confines the reach of these statutes and court rules. A state statute or court rule cannot reach beneath the constitutional floor and authorize its courts to exercise jurisdiction over everyone all over the country.

The idea that a court does not have unlimited authority over every person predates the adoption of either the Fifth Amendment or the Fourteenth Amendment. In its first significant decision involving the question of personal jurisdiction, the Supreme Court focused on common law doctrines, noting almost as an afterthought that the Due Process Clause of the recently ratified Fourteenth Amendment incorporated "those rules and principles which have been established in our systems of jurisprudence for the protection and enforcement of private rights."[1] Since then, the Court's personal jurisdiction jurisprudence has always been anchored in due process.

Defining the contours of due process in the context of personal jurisdiction, however, is not an easy task. The underlying principle is a relatively simple proposition of political theory: A sovereign nation — including its courts — does not have legal authority over everyone in the world, but may only exercise power over those who have a sufficient connection to that nation. The difficulty lies in specifying how to determine the sufficiency of the connection. And in the United States, that task is complicated by considerations of *federalism*, which is discussed in Chapter 8 and concerns the relationships among the different state and federal courts. (For that reason, we postpone a full treatment of the Court's personal jurisdiction doctrines until later, and present only the basic outlines here.)

It is easy to see that a citizen of a particular state (in the generic sense of a sovereign political entity) should be subject to that state's jurisdiction. But what about citizens of other states? Is it enough if they cause harm to a citizen of that state, or must they have a closer connection? From a political or moral standpoint, there is no right answer to that question. Nor does the language or history of the Constitution give much guidance. But as a matter of legal doctrine, since 1945 the Supreme Court has answered the question by holding that

> due process requires . . . that in order to subject a defendant*
> to a judgment . . . if he be not present within the territory of
> the forum, he have certain minimum contacts with it such
> that the maintenance of the suit does not offend "traditional
> notions of fair play and substantial justice."[2]

The personal jurisdiction cases you will read in your Civil Procedure course are mostly attempts to flesh out the meanings of *"minimum contacts"* and "traditional notions of fair play and substantial justice" and apply them to different factual situations. Because reasonable people can differ on the underlying question of how close a connection is required for a state's exercise of jurisdiction to be politically legitimate, it should not surprise you to find that courts and judges have disagreed on the meaning of these two crucial phrases capturing the core of due process.

---

* By bringing suit in a particular forum, plaintiffs are considered to have consented to jurisdiction. Thus, except in the case of class actions (discussed *infra* at pp. 160-161), personal jurisdiction questions typically arise only in connection with defendants.

Choice of Law The constitutional limitations on choice of law are even more ambiguous. The question whether a particular state has jurisdiction to decide a dispute is not the same as whether that state has a right to impose its own substantive law on the parties. Imagine, for example, that the parties have signed a contract providing that all disputes between them will be litigated in the United States (because they prefer the adversarial system) but governed by French law (because they prefer French substantive law). Unless there is some reason — independent of due process concerns — why the contract should not be enforced, an American court will hear the dispute but resolve it using French law. There is no due process problem, because both parties have agreed to subject themselves to American jurisdiction and French law.

In the abstract, then, there is no reason to assume that the forum exercising personal jurisdiction will always apply its own substantive law. But the underlying political theory suggests that the due process limits should be similar, because in both contexts we are determining whether actions by an individual are enough to subject him or her to the state's authority. Perhaps it should be somewhat easier to exercise personal jurisdiction than to apply the forum's substantive law, as the former is only a question of where the defendant will be sued, while the latter actually determines his or her liability.

In fact, however, the doctrines are the reverse of what we might expect. Due process imposes fewer limitations on the application of a forum's substantive law than it does on the exercise of personal jurisdiction. The exercise of personal jurisdiction requires both minimum contacts and fairness, and, as you can see from many of the leading cases, one or the other is often found to be lacking.[3] But a state is permitted to apply its own law to any dispute as long as doing so is not arbitrary or fundamentally unfair.[4] In practice, moreover, courts have taken a hands-off approach to choice of law: Except in nationwide class actions, application of the forum's law is almost never held to be arbitrary or unfair. Although you are not likely to study choice of law in Civil Procedure (it is generally covered in an upper level course on Conflict of Laws), you should know that it implicates due process concerns and that comparing choice of law and personal jurisdiction doctrines creates a puzzle.

Notice and the Opportunity to Be Heard

In our adversarial system, each party is responsible for presenting his or her own case. No one looks out for the rights of those who are absent, and if a defendant does not respond to the plaintiff's *complaint* the court may enter a *default judgment* in favor of the plaintiff. It is therefore vitally important that every party have both notice that his or her rights might be at stake and an opportunity to present his or her case. The Due Process Clause guarantees both these rights. The opportunity to be heard is more fundamental, but it cannot be exercised without notice of the proceeding. We therefore begin with notice and then turn to the right to be heard.

Notice The Due Process Clause right to be heard necessarily includes the right to adequate notice, although what constitutes adequate notice can vary with the circumstances. State and federal courts are subject to the same constitutional requirements. The basic rule for all cases, state and federal, is that the notice must be "reasonably calculated, under all the circumstances, to apprise interested parties of the pendency of the action and afford them an opportunity to present their objections."[5] This formulation, the Court has said, requires more than "a mere gesture," but must rather use a method that a person "desirous of informing the absentee might reasonably adopt to accomplish it."[6]

Because the reasonableness of the method depends on the circumstances, a method might be adequate in one set of circumstances but not in another. Thus, the Court has approved notice by publication for some parties but not for others; approved notice by certified mail in one case but disapproved it in another; and held that even the posting of a notice of eviction on an apartment door was insufficient when other tenants frequently removed such notices.[7] The standard thus does not require either a particular means of service or the most effective means, but instead sets a floor that must be determined case by case.

Opportunity to Be Heard In most civil cases involving private parties, the opportunity to be heard is automatic and unproblematic. No judge will decide a case — or even a single issue within the case — without giving the opposing party a chance to present his or her side.* But the question of an opportunity to be heard does come up in three circumstances. First, because class actions by definition contemplate parties who will not themselves be heard in court but whose interests will be protected by *class representatives*, the Due Process Clause imposes certain minimum requirements. Those requirements have been codified in Rule 23, however, so we put off the discussion of class actions until later in this chapter.

Second, due process questions have sometimes arisen in the context of government deprivation of various rights and benefits. If the state takes away someone's welfare benefits

---

* There are exceptions, and two of the most important are (1) that a judge may issue a *temporary restraining order* (TRO) without hearing from both sides, and (2) a judge may order the temporary *attachment* (or *sequestration*) of property without hearing from both sides if the judge fears that the possessor of the property will abscond with or destroy the property. Such *ex parte* orders are only issued when stringent requirements are met, and only temporarily prohibit the restrained party from acting. After issuing a TRO or attachment order, the judge must quickly give the restrained party an opportunity to respond. After hearing from both sides, the judge can extend the life of a TRO by issuing a *preliminary injunction* or — then or later — a *permanent injunction*. Similarly, a judge can extend an order attaching property, at least until the possessor posts a bond for the property's value.

or terminates his or her parental rights, for example, what procedural protections must it afford to satisfy the due process requirement of an opportunity to be heard? The two most common questions are whether the government must provide a hearing *before* (rather than after) it terminates the right or benefit, and whether — as is true in criminal cases — it must provide a lawyer for anyone who is too poor to hire one.

Because these types of cases involve a specialized field of law, you might not learn about them in your Civil Procedure class. You might find them helpful in understanding the basic contours of the right to be heard, however, and so we include a brief discussion here. *Goldberg v. Kelly*,[8] decided in 1970, held that New York could not terminate welfare benefits without first holding a hearing to determine whether the recipient's benefits should be stopped. Some of its language also suggested that the Court might ultimately interpret the right to be heard very broadly, imposing on the states the obligation to provide a great deal of process in these sorts of cases. But in 1976, the Court in *Mathews v. Eldridge*[9] allowed the federal government to terminate disability benefits without a pretermination hearing, and announced a test that still governs:

> [I]dentification of the specific dictates of due process generally requires consideration of three distinct factors: First, the private interests that will be affected by the official action; second, the risk of an erroneous deprivation of such interest through the procedures used, and the probable value, if any, of additional or substitute procedural safeguards; and finally, the Government's interest, including the function involved and the fiscal and administrative burdens that the additional or substitute procedural requirement would entail.[10]

This rather amorphous balancing test has since been applied to require only minimal procedural protections. Pretermination hearings are rarely required, and the state usually need not provide a lawyer to indigents unless the proceeding at issue might result in a deprivation of physical liberty.[11] The breadth of protection hinted at in *Goldberg* has never materialized.

The third circumstance in which the right to be heard is implicated is under doctrines of preclusion, sometimes called *res judicata*. Most of preclusion law is *common law* rather than constitutional, but you need to understand the basic common law doctrines to see how the Constitution establishes limits. Preclusion doctrines govern the relationship between an initial lawsuit and subsequent suits that involve some of the same parties, claims, or issues.

Preclusion is an easy concept to comprehend when the second suit involves the same parties as the first suit: *Claim preclusion* (also called *res judicata* or *merger and bar*) prohibits a party from bringing a second suit against the same defendant on the same claim.* Nor can one relitigate previously resolved issues by changing the claim (for example, from tort to contract in a consumer injury case): Under the rules of *issue preclusion* (or *collateral estoppel*), a party who has previously litigated an issue cannot relitigate it, but is instead bound by the previous adjudication's determination of that issue.

But what about new parties? If you are involved in a bus accident, what happens if you first bring, and win, a suit against the bus driver and then bring a second suit against the bus company? Is the bus company bound by the jury's earlier finding that its driver was at fault? If you lose your suit against the driver because the accident was not his or her fault, can you relitigate that question in your suit against the bus company? What if you sue the bus company, and then another passenger who was injured in the accident brings a separate suit against the company? If you win your suit, is the bus company in the second passenger's suit bound by the

---

* It also prevents a party from bringing a new claim, if that claim should have been brought in the first suit. The *transactionalism* principle that determines whether a claim "should have been brought" is explored in Chapter 7.

finding in your case that it was at fault? If you lose your suit, because the bus company was not at fault, is the other passenger bound by *that* finding?

Due process imposes an almost absolute barrier against using a previous judgment against someone who was not a party to that previous litigation, because doing so would deprive the person of the opportunity to be heard on the issue.* So the bus company cannot be bound by your judgment against the driver, and the second passenger cannot be bound by the fact that your jury found the bus company not to be at fault.[12]

Early cases also imposed a common law requirement of *mutuality*: If one party in the second suit could not be bound by the prior judgment, then neither party could. Thus, because the bus company could not be bound by the first suit if you won against the driver, your losing against the driver did not bind you and you could relitigate fault in your suit against the bus company. Similarly, because the bus company could not, in the second passenger's suit, use a prior finding that it was not at fault, the second passenger could not use a prior finding that the bus company was at fault.

Many jurisdictions, including federal courts, have abandoned the doctrine of mutuality. Most jurisdictions allow what is called *defensive non-mutual issue preclusion*, so that a new party can defend itself from a lawsuit brought by a plaintiff who has already lost on the same factual issue against a different adversary. If you lose against the bus driver because it was not his or her fault, you cannot relitigate whether it was the driver's fault when you sue the bus company. (You might be

---

* The barrier is not absolute, because a prior judgment binds both parties to that judgment and those in *privity* with them (their *privies*). Determining whether two parties are in privity with one another is sometimes difficult, but the paradigm case is a successor company. Where a company is involved in litigation and is then sold, the new owners are bound by any judgments previously obtained against the old owners.

able to raise other issues of fault that were not litigated in the first suit: Perhaps the company failed to maintain the bus properly, so that the accident was the company's fault even though it was not the driver's fault.)

You should be able to see the superficial appeal of the mutuality doctrine. It seems unfair, at some basic level, to treat the two opposing parties differently: If A and B are involved in a lawsuit, why should A be bound by a prior result if B is not? And yet if we delve deeper into due process, looking at it primarily as guaranteeing an opportunity to be heard, the two parties are in different positions: If A has already been heard but B has not, it is fair to hold A to the prior judgment even though it is unfair — and indeed violates B's due process right to be heard — to hold B to that judgment.

The second passenger's suit raises somewhat different issues. If you lose your suit against the bus driver and then sue the bus company, the bus company wants to use the earlier judgment against you as a *shield*, to defend itself from your claims. But in the hypothetical involving the second passenger, we are assuming that you won your case against the bus company. Here the second passenger wants to use your earlier judgment as a *sword*, to support his or her own claims against the bus company. This raises the question of whether to permit *offensive non-mutual issue preclusion*. In federal court — and in some state courts, but not as many as allow defensive non-mutual issue preclusion — there is no absolute requirement of mutuality in this circumstance. But there are due-process-based limits: Offensive non-mutual issue preclusion is not permitted where it would be "unfair to a defendant."[13] (It is also not permitted if the plaintiff could easily have joined the first suit.) Examples of unfairness include cases in which the defendant did not have an incentive to defend the first suit vigorously (perhaps it was for very little money), the defendant did not have procedural opportunities to defend the first case that are available in the second case, or there are several prior judgments that are inconsistent with each other (some passengers have won their suits against the bus company and others have lost).

Preclusion doctrines as a whole, then, reflect the courts' attempt to make sure that every party has one—and only one—full and fair opportunity to be heard. At bottom, the limitations on the use of prior judgments are often a matter of constitutional due process.

Understanding Due Process

This brief discussion of the requirements of constitutional due process should suggest some similarities among the various components of due process. The minimum contacts and "fair play and substantial justice" tests for personal jurisdiction, the choice of law rules requiring the avoidance of arbitrariness or fundamental unfairness, the "reasonably calculated" language of the notice requirement, the multipart balancing test for determining the contours of the opportunity to be heard, and the "unfair to the defendant" limit on offensive non-mutual issue preclusion are all flexible rather than mechanical. Each asks a court to consider whether, under all the circumstances, there are enough procedural protections to conclude that minimum standards of fairness have been met. The Due Process Clauses require no more and no less.

If this all-things-considered approach makes you uncomfortable, you are not alone among law students. Many people come to law school expecting to be taught "the law"; that is, to learn the "right" answers to legal questions. But if most legal questions had single right answers, we would not need law schools. Anyone could just look in the right book or on the right Web site and find the answer to his or her legal question. If you want to know the date of the Magna Carta, or the author of *To Kill a Mockingbird*, or the atomic number of oxygen, that is what you do. With sophisticated search engines, you might not even need to know exactly what you are looking for: Knowing that you need the ancient English document that sets out basic rights, or the name of a classic novel about a white southern lawyer defending a black defendant, or information about the air we breathe, might be enough.

Law is not like that (and keeping law schools in business has nothing to do with it!). The *writ* system described in Chapter 1 tried to accomplish that sort of simple certainty, and ended up unjust. A legal system needs flexibility if it is to deal with the endless variation (and ingenuity) of human conduct, the uniqueness of each dispute, and the constantly evolving legal and moral standards. And the broader the scope of the legal provision at issue — the more cases it must govern — the more flexible it needs to be. A rule that determines how legal holidays should be counted for purposes of filing deadlines can be much more specific than a constitutional provision like the Due Process Clause, which was designed to guarantee basic procedural justice in every case.

At the same time, a legal system cannot function if it simply directs courts to do justice. Without some consistency, certainty, and predictability in the legal regime, citizens would neither know what the law requires of them nor be able to rely on the laws to protect them. Would you enter into a business contract if you knew that the terms might be changed at any time if a court thought justice would be better served by doing so? How would you feel about driving a car if a judge might make you pay to repair the car of a driver who rear-ended you simply because you are rich or have insurance and the other driver is poor and uninsured and the judge considers that a just result?

The dilemma of any legal system is figuring out how to navigate between these two extremes, to provide both certainty and flexibility. Although the dilemma can arise anywhere in the legal system, it is most common and most acute in the context of constitutional provisions. The Supreme Court's primary solution — in due process cases and elsewhere in constitutional law — is to try to give some guidance without tying courts' hands. And the only way to judge whether the Court has been successful is to see how it works in practice. As you read the cases on constitutional due process, think about whether you would have reached the same result, and if not, how you would change the doctrinal framework.

THE FURNITURE: THE FEDERAL RULES OF CIVIL PROCEDURE

The Federal Rules of Civil Procedure implement the due process principles of jurisdictional authority, notice, and an opportunity to be heard. They give more specific content to the constitutional requirements, primarily using two basic concepts: *notice* and *prejudice*. The Rules are designed to make sure that every party has sufficient notice of the issues in the case to respond, and that no party is unduly prejudiced by procedural decisions. Both concepts stem from due process concerns and from our basic commitment to deciding cases accurately. The two concepts are also interrelated, because prejudice often arises from insufficient notice, although there are other aspects of prejudice as well. In this section, we focus on a few discrete issues — personal jurisdiction and notice, *pleading, case management*, and *alternative methods of dispute resolution* — to provide a sense of how the concern for due process and the desire for procedural fairness find their way into concrete practices.

Jurisdiction and Notice

We saw that a court cannot exercise jurisdiction over a person unless it has both constitutional authority and authority under a statute or court rule. Courts must also provide persons with adequate notice of the suit. In federal court, Federal Rule of Civil Procedure 4 both provides the authority to exercise jurisdiction and specifies how the requirement of notice is to be satisfied.

Rule 4(k) is the federal equivalent of a state long-arm statute, setting out the reach of the federal courts in various situations. Most cases are covered by Rule 4(k)(1)(A), which authorizes jurisdiction over those persons, and only those persons, who would be subject to jurisdiction in the courts of the state. Rule 4(k)(1)(A) thus incorporates by reference the doctrines we have already discussed regarding state law and its constitutional limits. The rest of the Rule creates some exceptions, authorizing personal jurisdiction in circumstances in which the state courts might or might not have jurisdiction. Under these exceptions, courts often differ as to the constitutional limits on jurisdiction: It is a disputed question, for example, whether a defendant served under a federal statute authorizing nationwide *service of process* (consistent with Rule 4(k)(1)(D)) must have minimum contacts with the state in which the federal court sits, or only minimum contacts with the United States as a whole. Aside from these exceptional issues, however, Rule 4(k) does not raise any questions different from those raised by state courts' exercise of personal jurisdiction.

Rule 4 also specifies the federal court requirements for service of process, which must follow the filing of the complaint. The Rule provides that every defendant must be served with a *summons* and a copy of the complaint, and describes a variety of ways in which service might be accomplished. Importantly, service cannot ordinarily be accomplished by mail, but must be served personally on the defendant or an appropriate substitute.* Rule 4 thus implements the constitutional

---

* The exception is that Rule 4(i) allows service by registered or certified mail on the United States and its agencies, corporations, officers, or employees.

requirement of notice by specifying particular procedures that will satisfy it. In general, the drafters succeeded in placing Rule 4's furniture above the constitutional floor: If process is served in accordance with the basic standards of Rule 4 — in particular, if it satisfies the requirements of Rule 4(d) or 4(e)(2) for service on individuals, or the equivalent part of Rule 4(h)(1) for service on corporations — then the notice should be constitutionally adequate.

Two aspects of Rule 4 can give rise to due process concerns about the adequacy of notice, however. Several parts of the Rule — including 4(e)(1), 4(g), 4(h)(1), and 4(j) — allow service of process in federal court pursuant to *state* law. Similarly, Rule 4(f) provides various means for serving foreign defendants, including as permitted by international treaty, as allowed under the law of the foreign country, or as authorized by the judge in the particular case. Service under one of these provisions does not necessarily satisfy due process requirements. Each method of service must be tested against the constitutional standard to see whether it is "reasonably calculated" to give actual notice. Most such methods will withstand constitutional scrutiny, but occasionally a court will find that one fails to give adequate notice.

Notice Pleading

Due process requires notice of the lawsuit itself, but does not have anything to say about what must be in that notice. One reason for the omission is that pleading rules, old and new, have always required some notice of what the lawsuit is about; in other words, the furniture has always been placed high enough to avoid falling through any possible floor. It might indeed violate due process for a plaintiff to serve notice that said only "I am suing you in such-and-such a federal court," but because we have never had a pleading regime that would allow that bare-bones claim there has never been an opportunity to consider the constitutional floor. So this aspect of notice turns out to be governed entirely by the pleading rules.

The underlying principle of the pleading regime established by the Federal Rules of Civil Procedure is *notice pleading*. The pleadings, in other words, are not designed to narrow the issues, to detect and dismiss claims unlikely to prevail, or to discover or provide evidence — all three of which should ideally be accomplished before trial. Instead, the pleadings are meant only to give enough notice about the party's claims to allow the formulation of an appropriate response. *Discovery, judicial case management* under Rule 16, and *summary judgment* under Rule 56 perform the other necessary *pretrial* functions.

The sufficiency of a pleading turns on a delicate balance between providing enough notice to the opposing party and preventing procedural technicalities from interfering with adjudication on the merits. The Rules themselves provide rough guidelines, but their language is only minimally helpful, and the real meaning is fleshed out in the cases applying them. Think of Rule 8(a)(2), which requires a complaint to contain "a short and plain statement of the claim showing that the pleader is entitled to relief"; Rule 8(b), which asks for a party's defenses to be stated "in short and plain terms"; or Rule 12(e), which allows a party to move for a more definite statement if a pleading "is so vague and ambiguous that a party cannot reasonably be required to frame a responsive pleading." You cannot tell just by looking at one of these Rules — or at most of the other pleading Rules, for that matter — just how much or how little is required. We spent several pages in Chapter 4 trying to pinpoint where the line should be drawn, and you may spend several days, or even weeks, of your Civil Procedure course reading cases (interpreting Rules 8 and 12) in which the main issue is whether a particular pleading satisfies the Federal Rules. In this chapter we focus on how the minimal notice requirements are structured to avoid prejudice to the opposing party.

The primary purpose of our pleading system, as already noted, is to provide notice while avoiding technical or procedural traps. The Supreme Court has frequently reiterated that the Federal Rules "reject the approach that pleading is a game of skill in which one misstep by counsel may be decisive to the outcome."[14] That should be a signal that very little is required in the way of pleading: just enough to give the other party enough notice so that he or she is not prejudiced in preparing his or her own case. Thus, courts — and, consequently, opposing parties — are required to give a party's pleading the benefit of the doubt. They must read the pleading generously, draw reasonable inferences, and interpret the pleading in the light most favorable to the pleader. As Rule 8(f) directs, "[a]ll pleadings shall be construed as to do substantial justice." A party who merely hints at a particular claim or defense is thus likely to survive a *motion to dismiss* under Rule 12(b)(6) or a motion to strike under Rule 12(f) (although good lawyering requires more than the minimum required by the Rules!).

The principles of notice and prejudice are pervasive in the pleading system, going well beyond the determination of whether a particular pleading is sufficient under the Rules. Rule 8(c) allows a court to treat an *affirmative defense* as a counterclaim or a counterclaim as an affirmative defense. Why? Because the procedural misstep of improper designation does not deprive the opposing party of notice or otherwise prejudice him or her. Rule 13(f) permits amending a pleading to add an omitted counterclaim "when justice requires." Similarly, Rule 15 allows liberal *amendment* of the pleadings, limited only by the principle (explicit in some parts of the Rule itself and supplemented by judicial interpretation of other parts) that the amendment should not prejudice the opposing party. Some courts have gone still further: Despite the language of Rule 8(c) that a party responding to a pleading must set forth any affirmative defenses, courts have allowed parties to raise unpleaded affirmative defenses, without even amending the pleading, as long as the opposing party is not prejudiced.[15] Under Rules 12(b) and 12(c), a motion to dismiss for failure to state claim or for judgment on the pleadings will convert to a motion for summary judgment if it includes matters outside the pleadings. Again, mislabeling a motion is not likely to hurt the opposing party—and the Rule makes certain that it does not, by requiring that all parties be given an opportunity to respond to the redesignated motion.

The minimal requirements of notice pleading can be frustrating. Courts—and law students—sometimes feel that our system of notice pleading makes it too easy for plaintiffs to raise weak or even frivolous claims (or, more rarely, that it makes it too easy for defendants to interpose frivolous defenses or counterclaims). Especially in certain contexts such as employment discrimination cases or civil cases brought by prisoners, many lower court judges have concluded based on experience that the ratio of frivolous to meritorious—or even colorable—suits is too high. Indeed, several important Supreme Court cases, which we discussed in Chapter 4, arose as a result of lower courts imposing *heightened pleading* standards on plaintiffs, dismissing cases that the Supreme Court ultimately reinstated. Although the frustration is understandable, heightened pleading requirements are inconsistent with the division of labor set up by the Federal Rules: Pleading only provides notice, and other Rules attempt to deter (think of Rule 11) or weed out (think of Rule 56) claims that are plainly without merit.

One caveat to the minimum pleading requirements: Occasionally the frustration reaches Congress, which then enacts statutes imposing heightened pleading requirements on certain kinds of cases. Such statutes, of course, trump the Federal Rules of Civil Procedure; courts must follow the specific statute rather than the general Rule. Two relatively recent examples are the Private Litigation Securities Reform Act of 1995, and the Y2K Act of 1999, both of which require plaintiffs to plead with more specificity and detail than Rule 8(a) would normally mandate.

You might think about — and may even discuss in class — whether such statutes, or other heightened pleading requirements, are a good idea. Should the pleading requirements remain *trans-substantive*, as originally intended, or should they vary depending on context? The answer might depend on your view of how well the system works in practice: Do heightened pleading requirements keep too many meritorious cases from being adjudicated on the merits, or do minimal pleading requirements allow the filing of too many frivolous claims? And if it is the latter, is the best solution to alter the pleading requirements or to alter other Rules, such as Rule 11 and Rule 56? What problems might follow from either heightened pleading requirements (remember the writ system and *code pleading*) or attempts to strengthen Rule 11 (an experiment already tried and arguably failed, as we discussed in Chapter 2) or Rule 56? As with many of the topics we discuss in this book, notice pleading has both costs and benefits, and the Federal Rules of Civil Procedure as a whole are an attempt to capture as many of the benefits and avoid as many of the costs as possible. And again, we can only judge the success of that attempt by seeing how it works in practice.

Other Fairness Concerns Arising Under the Federal Rules

Notice pleading, however different it may be from earlier pleading regimes, is still consistent with both due process and the adversarial system. The parties bear the responsibility for directing the litigation, and due process requirements set some ground rules. But one relatively recent innovation in the Federal Rules is in tension with the adversarial system and has raised due process concerns among scholars (although not generally among judges). The strengthening and increased use of Rule 16 has meant that judges are taking a more active role in managing litigation. Three aspects of *managerial judging* are of particular concern: management of the pretrial process, judicial pressure toward settlement, and the use of alternative dispute resolution (ADR) mechanisms.

Rule 16 gives the judge a great deal of authority over the pretrial process, from setting deadlines to controlling discovery. The judge often works closely with the lawyers during this process, possibly compromising his or her impartiality. Moreover, many of these managerial decisions are not subject to the procedural safeguards that accompany most judicial decisions: As one scholar has noted, "[m]anagerial judges frequently work beyond the public view, off the record, with no obligation to provide written, reasoned opinions, and out of reach of appellate review."[16] The image of a potentially partisan judge, working in secret and in collusion with one side or the other, is inconsistent with a basic requirement of due process: an impartial decision maker whose actions are open to public scrutiny. Although there is no evidence that managerial judging has actually manifested any departure from impartial decision making, some scholars are concerned about the potential effect on the litigation process.

Other scholars have focused on settlement, especially to the extent that Rule 16 allows judges to encourage — or coerce, depending on your point of view — *settlements*. At their best, settlements are efficient, fair, and Pareto optimal: Everyone goes away happy and less time and money are spent resolving the dispute. Settlement fulfills the ideal that litigation should be the parties' last resort and trials should be rare. Indeed, the original drafters of the Federal Rules believed that the availability of broad discovery would lead to more settlements as parties rationally evaluated their own and their opponents' cases. But that rosy view assumes that the parties are equally situated with regard to settlements. In fact, a difference in party resources can exert a great pressure on the poorer party to settle, and to settle for less. This type of economic coercion might not raise substantial due process concerns; after all, the adversarial system and the *American Rule* that each side pays its own attorneys' fees make it inevitable that such results will sometimes occur. It is the involvement of the *judge* that makes settlement problematic. It is one thing for a party's capitulation to be coerced by economic circumstances, and quite another for a government official to add to the coercion. If the judge believes that settlement — or settlement at a particular price — is in a party's best interest, the behind-the-scenes mechanisms of Rule 16 offer an opportunity for the judge to pressure the party into giving up his or her right to a trial. Does this happen? It's hard to know, but whether the gains in *efficiency* outweigh any actual diminution in due process is a question you might want to consider.

Finally, there is a raging dispute about whether ADR, which is sometimes judicially compelled as part of the pretrial process, does, can, or should satisfy the requirements of due process. ADR differs from formal adjudication in many ways, including the selection (and compensation) of the decision maker, the evidentiary rules, and the opportunity for appellate review. Is that a problem? It depends on one's view of due process, or, more basically, on one's view of justice. One important article on ADR suggests that unlike opponents, "advocates of ADR . . . assume not that justice is something people get from the government but that it is something people give to one another."[17] On this view, imposing due process requirements on people's negotiations with each other is an impediment rather than a safeguard. Or, as Grant Gilmore, one of the most noted scholars of American jurisprudence, observed in a somewhat different context:

> The better the society, the less law there will be. . . . The worse the society, the more law there will be. In Hell there

will be nothing but law, and due process will be meticulously observed.[18]

Your view of ADR as compared to formal adjudication might ultimately depend, then, on how good a society you believe we have.

Due process concerns about judicial case management, settlement, and ADR are on the cutting edge of the law. There are few cases and many open questions. As a practicing lawyer, you will help to shape the answers.

CLASS ACTIONS

The Rule in which due process plays the most significant role is Rule 23, governing class actions. The class action is a device by which the similar claims of many individuals (the *class members*) are consolidated into a single suit, which is prosecuted by a subset of the class members (the class representatives). The due process problem is easy to see: A judgment or settlement in a class action is binding on all class members, although most of them have little or no opportunity to participate in the litigation. Instead, they are — at least in theory — represented by the named class representative. Even more troubling, in practice class actions are often wholly directed by class counsel, with little or no consultation with the class representative (who may in fact have been solicited by the lawyers, rather than the representative seeking out counsel).

Even before Rule 23 saw much use, the Supreme Court recognized constitutional due process limitations on class actions. In *Hansberry v. Lee,*[19] which involved a state court class action and thus was outside the Federal Rules, the Court held that a judgment could not bind absent class members unless they were "adequately represented" in the litigation. Rule 23 incorporates this due process requirement of adequate representation in a number of ways.

First, Rule 23(a) describes four findings a judge must make before he or she certifies a case to proceed as a class action. These four prerequisites work together to ensure adequate representation. Rule 23(a)(4) directly insists on a finding that "the representative parties will fairly and adequately protect the interests of the class." The other prerequisites also contribute to the adequacy of the representation: Rule 23(a)(2) requires that there be "questions of law or fact common to the class," and Rule 23(a)(3) requires that the class representative's claims be "typical" of the claims of class members, thus helping ensure that the litigation interests of the class representative align with the interests of the absent class members. Even the numerosity requirement of Rule 23(a)(1) — that the class be "so numerous that joinder of all members is impracticable" — helps ensure adequate representation by prohibiting class certification when each plaintiff could instead reasonably participate directly in his or her own lawsuit.

Other provisions of Rule 23 also address due process concerns. Rule 23(c)(2) provides for notice to absent class members, including, where appropriate, notice of their right to opt out of the suit. Rule 23(e) requires that the court approve any settlement among the parties (including a voluntary dismissal of the lawsuit), specifically mandating a hearing and a finding that the settlement is "fair, reasonable, and adequate." In most cases, the judge is a neutral arbiter and the parties look after their own interests, but Rule 23(e) requires the judge to protect the interests of absent parties. This prevents the class representatives from colluding with the defendants for their own benefit at the expense of the absent parties (or, more benignly, from inadvertently failing to represent the class well). Even the provisions governing the appointment of class counsel — contained in Rule 23(g), which was added in 2003 — require a court to find that the class counsel will "fairly and adequately represent the interests of the class."

Despite this foundational protection for the due process rights of absent class members, Rule 23 does not resolve all the due process concerns surrounding class actions. Moreover, because the due process concerns about class actions are ultimately constitutional, state class actions, although not subject to Rule 23, also raise due process concerns. The courts have had to step in and fill all these gaps, and there is debate about whether they have always done so correctly. Think first about personal jurisdiction. As noted earlier, plaintiffs are considered to have consented to jurisdiction when they bring suit in a particular forum. But can we really say that absent class members have consented to jurisdiction? In *Phillips Petroleum Co. v. Shutts*,[20] the Supreme Court held that, at least when class members have an opportunity to opt out of the class, there is no constitutional impediment to a court exercising jurisdiction over them even if they have no contacts with the forum.* The Court relied primarily on the fact that a lawsuit does not place on absent class members the same burdens that it does on defendants, and thus does not require them to have contacts with the forum. The only consequence for absent plaintiffs is that they will be bound by the judgment, and as long as they have notice and an opportunity to opt out, they are effectively consenting to be bound. It is still an open question how far a court may exercise jurisdiction over unconsenting absent class members in a mandatory class under Rule 23(b)(1) or (b)(2), which does not allow class members to opt out.

---

* There are two types of class actions: *mandatory* and *opt-out*. Both types must meet the requirements of Rule 23(a), which determine adequacy. But every class action must also meet one of the four requirements listed in Rule 23(b). The first three of these class actions — the class actions described in Rules 23(b)(1)(A), (b)(1)(B), and (b)(2) — are mandatory. Class members cannot remove themselves from the class action, and are bound by the result. The fourth class action — the Rule 23(b)(3) class action — allows class members to excuse themselves from the case. A class member who opts out is not bound by the judgment in the class action, and is free to file a separate lawsuit. All class members in a Rule 23(b)(3) class action must receive notice of their opportunity to opt out.

On the other hand, *Shutts* also held that the forum state was not entitled to apply its own law to the claims of absent class members who lacked any contact with the forum. *Shutts* is thus one of the rare cases in which the Court found more constitutional constraints on choice of law than on the exercise of personal jurisdiction. Nationwide class actions, whether in state or federal court, will always raise difficult choice-of-law questions. Because these questions are rarely addressed in a first-year Civil Procedure course, and are instead usually left for an advanced course in Complex Litigation, we do not consider them further here.

Another constitutional due process issue left unanswered by Rule 23 is the preclusive effect of a finding of adequacy of representation. You should recall that it is a violation of due process to be bound by a judgment in which one has not had an opportunity to participate. In the class action setting, the right to be heard is fulfilled by a finding that the class representative adequately represents the interests of the absent class members. But the absent class members, especially those whose injuries are manifested only after the class action is completed, usually have no opportunity to participate in the proceeding that determines the adequacy of representation. Can they be bound by the finding of adequacy? If so, they are bound by a determination in which they were never heard, and by an eventual judgment as to which they may not have been adequately represented. But if not, then a class action judgment (including a settlement) can never be final, because an absent class member can always collaterally attack the finding of adequacy, and, if he or she persuades a court that he or she was *not* adequately represented, will not be bound by the judgment. Because one benefit of a class action is that it "buys peace" for the defendant by settling all related claims, the lack of finality is a serious detriment. Courts have split on how this question should be answered, although the recent trend seems to be toward holding the finding of adequacy binding on class members.[21]

The class action fits awkwardly within our litigation paradigm, so it is not surprising that it challenges our notion of due process. Whether or not you study class actions in your Civil Procedure course, understanding how they put pressure on our conception of due process will help you attain a deeper comprehension of the meaning of due process in other contexts. It may also lead you to question the design of our procedural system, the interpretation of due process, or both. And it is those sorts of questions that will engage scholars, judges, law reformers, and litigators for the foreseeable future.

~ 6 ~

Efficiency

Rule 1 of the Federal Rules of Civil Procedure states that all of the Federal Rules should be "construed and administered to secure the just, speedy, and inexpensive determination of every action." This famous phrase encapsulates the aspirations of the federal procedural system — or, indeed, just about any modern procedural system. In this chapter, we examine in greater detail the latter two goals: speed and inexpensiveness. Delay and cost are two of the most telling criticisms that can be leveled against any procedural system; indeed, when you study procedural systems around the world and across the years, complaints about delay and cost are universal. Delay and cost are especially associated with procedural regimes, like the ancient *equity* system, that employ a great deal of judicial *discretion* to tailor procedural justice to the individual case as a way to reach the most accurate decisions. Because this equitable orientation is essentially the approach of the Federal Rules of Civil Procedure, it is not surprising that delay and cost are common criticisms of the modern American procedural system.

Delay and cost are part of the same concern: inefficiency in the operation of a procedural system. As a general matter, every system seeks to be as efficient as possible. But the rub lies in the words "as possible." One of the most important questions in designing a procedural system is the role that *efficiency* should play. Should it be a cardinal consideration, of the same stature as the *adversarial system, jury trial,* or *due process,* so that these other principles must bend to the demands of efficiency? Or should efficiency be a second-order consideration that comes into play only after the primary principles have already blocked in the procedural system — in effect, a tie-breaker to choose between specific procedural rules that are equally consistent with the cardinal principles? Traditionally, in Anglo-American procedure, efficiency has tended at most to occupy the latter role. In more recent years, as the law-and-economics movement has gained strength, efficiency has tried to break into the first rank of procedural principles. In this chapter, we begin with an overview of the law-and-economics account of procedure, then explore the ways in which the concern for efficiency has helped to shape procedural doctrines and practices.

A FORMAL THEORY OF PROCEDURAL EFFICIENCY

The economic account of law asserts either that, over time, the law has selected rules of behavior that are economically efficient (the descriptive argument) or that, to the extent that the law has not done so, it should select rules that induce efficient behavior (the normative argument). Both approaches try to determine the incentives that possible legal arrangements create for individuals or entities to engage in desirable (in other words, economically efficient) behavior.

One of the fundamental insights of economic theory is the Coase Theorem, which asserts that, in the absence of transaction costs, any legal rule is allocatively efficient. This theorem seems counterintuitive: *Every* legal rule is efficient? The answer is "Yes". Suppose that a plaintiff expects to suffer a $100 injury from the defendant's conduct, but the defendant can avoid the injury at a cost of $50. From the viewpoint of efficiency, the defendant should spend the $50, because it avoids a greater loss of $100. What legal rule will induce the defendant to do so? According to the Coase Theorem, any rule will. Here is a quick proof. First, suppose that the legal rule is strict liability (thus, the defendant is liable for any injury he or she causes, regardless of fault). An economically rational defendant will spend $50 to avoid the liability of $100. Thus a rule of strict liability leads to the efficient result. Now consider the opposite legal rule: The law does nothing to hold the defendant liable. In this case, the plaintiff will have an incentive to pay the defendant $50 to bribe the defendant to take care. This result is also efficient. The plaintiff will be better off because he or she will avoid a $100 loss with a $50 payment, and the defendant is no worse off after being reimbursed by the plaintiff to take care. Now suppose that the law selects a rule somewhere between strict liability and no liability—for instance, liability when the defendant is negligent. The same result obtains. If we define negligence to require a defendant to take cost-effective accident-prevention measures, a defendant again will spend $50 to avoid a liability of $100. Of course, different rules can have important distributional differences. Under a rule of strict liability or negligence, the defendant must pay the $50 to avoid the injury; under a rule of no liability, the plaintiff must pay the $50. But neoclassical economic theory principally concerns itself with allocative efficiency, and leaves questions of distribution to political or other processes.

Note the important caveat in the Coase Theorem: *in the absence of transaction costs.* In the real world, positive transaction costs always exist. For instance, in the preceding hypothetical, if we choose the no-liability rule, the negotiations between the plaintiff and the defendant will be costly, and they might break down without the defendant's agreement to spend $50. The existence of positive transaction costs can lead us to prefer some legal rules over others. If negotiations are costly and if no other transaction costs exist, it makes sense to choose either a rule of strict liability or a rule of negligence rather than a rule of no liability, because either of these rules induces the defendant to take care without incurring the costs of negotiation. A general summary of the economic approach to law is this: In a world of positive transaction costs, the legal rule that best advances overall social welfare is the rule that minimizes the *sum* of the costs of injuries, the costs of avoiding injuries, and the transaction costs.

One of the principal types of transaction costs is the cost of litigation. To return to the hypothetical, assume that we choose a rule of strict liability. Under this rule we have a new transaction cost with which to contend: the cost of the lawsuit. Like the cost of negotiation, the cost of litigation can affect our choice of legal rule. In the preceding hypothetical, assume that the plaintiff will need to spend $80 and the defendant $40 to litigate a strict liability case. With these numbers, it is socially efficient to use a no-liability rule, because it is cheaper to let the $100 injury happen than to give the plaintiff a legal entitlement that costs society $120 in litigation expenses.

Because litigation is a significant source of transaction costs, the law-and-economics approach is naturally interested in questions of procedure and jurisdiction. Economic theory has identified two different types of cost that procedural and jurisdictional rules impose. One is the direct cost of litigation, including attorneys' fees, filing fees, witness and travel expenses, and so on. The other is the indirect cost of errors. As we said in Chapter 1, we can design a litigation system with very low direct cost: We can decide lawsuits by flipping coins. One obvious reason that we do not flip coins is that we want lawsuits to determine the truth of what really happened. But there is also an economic explanation. Erroneous decisions impose economic costs on society. Bill Gates has little incentive to accumulate wealth if it can be taken away from him with a coin flip.

In general, direct litigation costs and error costs are inversely proportional to each other. The more we spend on litigation, the less likely it is that we will make errors; the less we spend on litigation, the more likely it is that we will make errors. That fact might lead you to think that, if we are trying to be efficient, our goal should be to incur the least overall expense from litigation — in other words, to minimize the sum of direct litigation costs and indirect error costs for each case. In fact, it is not quite that simple. First, in the United States, not every plaintiff who *can* bring a lawsuit actually *does* so. One thing that deters some plaintiffs from litigating is the expense. Therefore, if we reduce the litigation costs for each case, we are likely to induce more plaintiffs to file lawsuits. The costs of more lawsuits could more than offset the savings realized in each case. Second, recall that the ultimate goal is maximizing overall social welfare by minimizing the sum of the cost of accidents, accident-prevention expenses, and transaction costs. The costs of litigation are only one component of transaction costs. It is a logical fallacy to think that what is true of the whole is true of each part; in other words, it is not necessarily true that if we are trying to reduce overall costs we must reduce a component of those costs to its minimum. Lower costs in one area might actually create higher costs in another.*

---

* It can be shown that, under certain conditions, higher rather than lower litigation expenses can create a socially efficient incentive to take care. To take a very crude example, suppose that the plaintiff's $100 injury can be avoided by the defendant's expenditure of $50. It is efficient for *someone* to spend the $50 to avoid the $100 cost. But assume that the law does not require the defendant to take care and the cost to the plaintiff of negotiating with the defendant is so high that the plaintiff will not pay the defendant $50 to take care. If it costs the defendant $60 to litigate and prove his or her lack of liability, the defendant will take care. But if it only costs the defendant $40 to litigate, he or she will not take care — an inefficient result.

THE MEANING OF EFFICIENCY IN AMERICAN PROCEDURE

Efficiency gets far less precise and rigorous treatment in the rough and tumble environment of American civil procedure. In the previous chapters, we examined many of the doctrinal components of the American procedural system through the lens of the constitutional and historical principles that shaped them. With each doctrine, a concern for efficiency lurks just beneath the surface. For instance, although our pretrial system is designed principally to assure that cases are decided accurately (in other words, without error costs), concerns for the costliness of this system (in other words, direct litigation costs) have led to the creation of *mandatory disclosure* and cutbacks in *discovery*.* Likewise, the primary argument for the incursion of *case management* into classic adversarial process is the need for greater efficiency in litigation. Efficiency emerges again in *summary judgment*, which seeks to render a judgment on the merits as quickly as possible and without the error costs that an unreasonable jury can impose. Efficiency also emerges in the principle of procedural fairness. *Mathews v. Eldridge*[1] gives due process a decidedly economic cast: We can depart from adversarial process when the gains in less costly process (direct litigation costs) exceed expected losses in accurate decision making (error costs). Efficiency has time and again proven itself to be a principle that checked the complete realization of other procedural principles.

In some areas of procedural law, however, concerns for efficiency have done more than lurk beneath the surface: They have driven certain doctrines and practices. In the rest

---

* Perhaps the most evident manifestation of this economic concern is the *proportionality* limitation, contained in Rule 26(b)(2), which explicitly balances the costs of providing information against the expected benefits of the information.

of this section, we briefly examine three of these areas: *venue*, *appeal* and finality, and *alternative dispute resolution* (ADR).

Venue

Most court systems contain various divisions or districts. For instance, in most states, the state trial court system is broken down by county: The state courts located in Smith County have separate courthouses and trial judges from the state courts located in Jones County (and if Smith County is large enough, it might even have more than more than one courthouse and set of judges). Similarly, at the federal level, the federal trial courts are divided into districts. There are 94 districts in all; every state contains at least one federal district court, and some contain as many as four.[2]

The plaintiff must choose one of these courts. To some extent, that choice is dictated by the rules of *subject matter jurisdiction*, which we discuss in Chapters 7 and 8: Certain courts might lack the authority to decide certain types of cases. To some extent, the choice of court is dictated by the rules of *personal jurisdiction*, which we discuss in Chapters 5 and 8: Certain courts might lack the authority to enter a judgment against defendants who have insufficient contact with the state in which the court sits. But the choice is also dictated by a third set of rules: the rules of venue.

To understand how venue works, consider a hypothetical car accident that occurs in Los Angeles between the plaintiff, who lives in and is a citizen of Oregon, and the defendant, who lives in and is a citizen of New York. The plaintiff's damages are severe, in this case $1 million. The plaintiff decides to sue in federal court (which is appropriate, under a type of subject matter jurisdiction called *diversity jurisdiction*). Assuming that the defendant has sufficient contacts with New York and California (and only New York and California), the rules of personal jurisdiction would allow the plaintiff to bring suit in a federal court located in either New York or California. But here's the problem: There are four federal districts within the state of California (the Central, Eastern, Northern, and Southern Districts), and four more within the state of New York (the Eastern, Northern, Southern, and Western Districts). So can the plaintiff pick any of these eight courts to sue in?

No, and the reason is the requirement of venue. Every court system has venue rules that decide which courts within that court system can hear a particular dispute. In the federal system, the basic venue rule is 28 U.S.C. §1391, which allows the case to be filed only in those districts that meet one of the three following criteria: a district in which "any defendant resides, if all defendants reside in the same state"; a district in which "a substantial part of the events or omissions giving rise to the claim occurred"; and if (but only if) neither of these first two criteria yield a district court, then a district in which "any defendant is subject to personal jurisdiction."[3] Let's assume that the defendant resides in Manhattan, which is within the Southern District of New York. Los Angeles is within the Central District of California. Therefore, the only two federal courts that have venue over the plaintiff's case are the Southern District of New York (where the defendant resides) and the Central District of California (where the accident occurred). The other courts in New York and California lack venue, and cannot hear the case.

If you are thinking that the rules of venue and personal jurisdiction seem to overlap, you are somewhat correct. Both limit which courts can hear a particular case; both keep courts that have no connection to a case from hearing it. Indeed, our doctrine of personal jurisdiction grew out of older doctrines of venue that applied under the laws of nations. But the two doctrines are distinct, and each one must be satisfied for a court to hear a case.

Perhaps the best way to keep them distinct is to understand what each one is trying to achieve. As we discuss in Chapters 5 and 8, the motivating forces behind personal jurisdiction are procedural fairness and federalism. With venue, however, the motivating force is convenience to the parties, the witnesses, and the court. In a sense, venue rules try to make sure that the costs of litigation stay down. By locating the case near the events that caused it (where much of the evidence and many witnesses will probably be) or near the defendant, the parties generally will spend less money and time than if the case could be filed in the District of Hawaii.

Of course, the word "generally" in the last sentence is important. We can hypothesize a situation in which some other forum is even more convenient than the ones the statute authorizes. In our example, if the plaintiff chooses the Central District of California, both sides will suffer inconvenience, possibly more than would be suffered if the case were filed in the Southern District of New York. The venue statutes are a fairly crude tool for reducing litigation costs.

Traditionally, the one doctrine that addressed this problem was *forum non conveniens*. A party (usually the defendant) could claim that, although the case was technically filed in a proper venue, the venue was, under the circumstances, very inconvenient. A court had the power under this doctrine to dismiss the case, thus leaving to the plaintiff the responsibility of finding a more convenient court that also had venue. *Forum non conveniens* is still a doctrine of some importance in international litigation and in litigation in state court, but for the most part, it has been abandoned in federal court. Rather than subjecting the plaintiff to the hassle of dismissal and refiling, 28 U.S.C. §1404(a) allows a federal court to transfer the case directly to another federal court that is also a proper venue whenever the transfer is "[f]or the convenience of parties and witnesses, in the interests of justice." This *transfer of venue* mechanism is smoother and more efficient, and thus consistent with the basic goal of venue to avoid the inefficiencies of inconvenient litigation.

Appeal and Finality

Although most of your Civil Procedure course concerns the procedures used in the trial courts, you will probably spend at least a bit of time on the appellate system. As you know, a typical American court system — whether state or federal — has three tiers: the localized trial courts, the intermediate court or courts of appeals, and a court of last resort (usually called a supreme court) at the top.* For the most part, courts of appeals and supreme courts are appellate courts; the bulk of their work is to hear appeals from the immediately lower court. So the courts of appeals hear appeals from the trial courts, and the supreme court hears appeals from the courts of appeals. There are plenty of exceptions and qualifications to this structure, of course, but it describes the usual system.

One question is why we have an appellate process at all. After all, we have poured an awful lot of resources into the case at the trial level. We have afforded the parties many procedural opportunities, and we have undertaken a conscientious effort to decide the case accurately. Having another court or two reexamine the same decision seems wasteful and inefficient, doesn't it? Not necessarily. Recall that there are two counter-balancing components in the efficiency calculus: direct litigation costs *and* error costs. Undoubtedly, the availability of appeal increases the direct litigation costs in each case. But the appellate process is designed to reduce the number of errors, and thus helps to eliminate the costs associated with erroneous decisions. Moreover, because courts of appeals cover a larger geographical area than lower courts, an appellate decision about the proper scope of the law has a larger influence, thus making the law more uniform and reducing the need to litigate the same issues in other trial courts in

---

* Some states do not have an intermediate court of appeals.

the same region. Thus, an appellate process can also eliminate direct litigation expenses in future cases.

This last insight explains a couple of the common issues in appellate practice. First, as a general matter, a trial court needs to resolve factual issues and legal issues to enter a *judgment*. In most cases, many more resources go into determining the facts than determining the law (as we have said, the disclosure-and-discovery process is the single most expensive part of American litigation). In determining whether the judgment was correct, an appellate court might need to examine both the factual and the legal merits of the case. Should courts of appeals rehear all the evidence that the trial court heard to decide whether the *factual findings* at trial were correct? In the American system, the answer has always been "No." Appellate courts defer a great deal to the factual findings from the trial level. A jury's verdict can be overturned only if it can be shown that the verdict was unreasonable or against the weight of the evidence.* According to Rule 52(a), the trial judge's findings of fact can be overturned only if they contain *clear error*. Likewise, on matters left to the trial judge's discretion, an appellate court can overturn the trial judge's decision only if there was an *abuse of discretion*. But in reviewing the legal determinations made in the trial court, the court of appeals exercises *de novo review*; in other words, the court of appeals does not defer at all to the legal views of the lower court.

Thus, courts of appeals tend to exercise one of three *standards of review* — clear error for factual findings, abuse of discretion for discretionary rulings, and *de novo* for legal conclusions — depending on the nature of the issue they are

---

* In Chapter 3, we examined in more detail motions for *judgment as a matter of law* (claiming that the jury acted unreasonably) and motions for *new trial* (claiming that the verdict was against the weight of the evidence). Assuming that a party made these motions in the trial court, the only issue on appeal is whether these motions should have been granted or not. Thus, a court of appeals has no more power to review the factual findings of a jury than a trial judge has.

deciding. Two of these standards are highly deferential to the lower court; the third does not defer at all. This division makes sense economically. Limiting the scope of review on appeal for the most expensive aspects of litigation (factual development and discretionary litigation structure) represents an effort to balance our desire to get it right against our need to keep litigation inexpensive. Because uniformity in legal standards can reduce future litigation costs, allowing courts of appeals to reexamine legal issues without limiting the scope of review also makes economic sense.

A second important issue in appellate practice is the timing of an appeal. Suppose that a judge denies a Rule 12(b)(6) *motion to dismiss*, or orders a party to answer a discovery request. The party who lost the motion believes that the judge is wrong. Can the party immediately file an appeal and get the views of the court of appeals on the question, or must the party wait until the entire case has wrapped up and file one appeal on everything? You can see the arguments on both sides of these questions. On the one hand, if we allow an appeal every time a judge enters an order that a party dislikes, a single case might bounce back and forth between the trial and appellate courts for a generation. On the other hand, if we do not allow an appeal, a lot of wasted time and effort might go into trying a case that the court of appeals would have tossed out at the stage of the motion to dismiss, or retrying a case because of an error a judge made in a discovery ruling. The problem is a classic economic one: Which set of risks is greater?

In the federal courts and in most state courts, the balance has been struck in favor of making the parties wait to appeal until the final judgment has been entered. This *final judgment rule* is codified at the federal level in 28 U.S.C. §1291, which authorizes appeals from "final decisions of the district courts." But in particular circumstances, a party can appeal before final judgment is entered. Congress and the Supreme Court have created a number of exceptions or qualifications to the final judgment rule. As you might expect, these exceptions and qualifications for the most part describe situations in which delaying an appeal either promises no gains in efficiency (because the contested issue is distinct from the rest of the case) or might cause more litigation or error costs than an immediate appeal. For instance, the most noteworthy exception, 28 U.S.C. §1292, permits an *interlocutory appeal* either when a trial judge has entered a *preliminary injunction* or when the judge certifies (and the court of appeals agrees) that an immediate decision on a debatable and "controlling question of law" will "materially advance the ultimate termination of the litigation."

Efficiency can also provide a useful tool for understanding another aspect of litigation: the problem of finality. Suppose that the plaintiff loses a case at trial, and the court of appeals affirms the judgment. The very next day, the plaintiff stumbles across a piece of evidence that proves that he or she should, in fact, have won. Can the plaintiff go back into court and reopen the case? Or file a brand new case? If we look at the problem solely from the viewpoint of accuracy (or, in economic terms, error cost), we want the case to be decided correctly. But error cost is not the only issue that matters. We also have to think about the direct litigation costs of the reopened case, as well as the cost and delay that will arise in all the other cases on the judge's docket because scarce judicial resources are still being devoted to a case already decided.

Quite sensibly, therefore, our system gives parties one very full bite at the apple, and then generally invokes the principle of finality to prevent relitigation of decided matters. Once again, the word "generally" is important; some exceptions exist. In limited circumstances a party can reopen a case by moving to vacate the judgment.[4] In limited circumstances a party can escape the effects of *claim preclusion* and *issue preclusion* (doctrines we discuss in Chapters 5 and 7), and relitigate a claim or issue in another case. But generally, a judgment is the final word. Litigation is costly, and we have made the policy judgment that the cost of continual litigation over decided matters outweighs any marginal benefits from more accurate decision making.

Alternative Dispute Resolution

So far, we have talked about the role of efficiency in adjudicated cases — whether efficiency should be a consideration in the design and selection of procedural rules. More generally, this book has treated civil procedure from the perspective of adjudication. In recent years, however, a number of lawyers, judges, and scholars have argued that this focus on civil procedure is myopic. Viewed not through the lens of adjudication but rather through the lens of dispute resolution, litigation is merely one of numerous ways in which people resolve disputes, and frankly, not even the most important way. These other processes are collectively referred to as alternative dispute resolution (ADR) processes.

Dispute resolution processes lie on a continuum from settlement to adjudication. The four classic models are *settlement, mediation, arbitration,* and *adjudication.* Settlement, in the pure sense, involves an agreement — a contract — mutually agreed on by the parties; no one else is involved. Mediation also results in an agreed-on settlement, but it differs from a settlement in that a third party (the mediator) assists the parties in arriving at their agreement. Arbitration also involves a third party (the arbitrator); unlike mediation, the arbitrator has the authority to resolve the dispute even if one or both of the parties refuses to agree to the resolution. In this regard, arbitration is like adjudication, but it differs from adjudication because the arbitrator is usually a private person who does not necessarily resolve the case according to legal principles, nor are the arbitrator or the parties necessarily bound by the rules of procedure that the judges and litigants in court must respect. Some hybrid ADR processes combine aspects of these dispute resolution models. According to ADR proponents, an exclusive focus on adjudication presents a false picture of the dispute resolution world, which is fuller, richer, more creative, and sometimes more efficient than the limited (albeit important) world of the lawsuit.

Indeed, disputes that are resolved by trial are rare. Despite Americans' perceived penchant for suing at the drop of a hat, studies suggest that only 8 to 12 percent of all disputes with possible legal merit ever reach litigation. (Think back in your own experience. Were you ever in a car accident? Was the matter handled by negotiations among insurance companies without the dispute ending up in court?) Of the civil cases that reach the courthouse, very few reach the courtroom. According to the most recent data, only 1.4 percent of the civil cases filed in federal court are resolved through a trial.* What happens to the remaining 98.6 percent? Roughly 18 percent are resolved through motions to dismiss or for summary judgment. The vast majority — around 81 percent — either settle or are withdrawn by the plaintiff. Therefore, even among the small percentage of cases that find the courthouse to begin with, the overwhelming majority end through an ADR process.

ADR proponents argue that our procedural system should focus on the needs of this majority. For instance, in the real world, parties often conduct discovery with an eye toward developing the information they need to settle the case, not the information they need to try it; and they file motions for summary judgment not with the hope of victory but with the

---

* This figure represents the percentage of civil cases reaching trial in 2005, which is the most recent year for which data existed at the time of the writing of this book. Numbers for state courts are comparable. The 2005 figure is not an aberration. The 2003 number was 1.8 percent, and the 2004 number was 1.6 percent. Trial rates have been dropping for years; in the 1990s, the rate hovered at 3 to 5 percent.

desire to achieve more favorable settlement terms. Perhaps, therefore, it makes sense to focus discovery on the information that the parties need to negotiate a proper settlement rather than the information that they need to go to trial. In other words, maybe our procedural system should be geared more toward resolving disputes, and less toward formal adjudication.

Economic analysis enters into this argument in two ways. At one level, it can model the circumstances under which parties choose to litigate, arbitrate, mediate, or settle. The plaintiff wants the highest expected recovery at the lowest cost. A rational plaintiff therefore compares adjudication and the various ADR alternatives by analyzing what each method is likely to bring by way of recovery, subtracting the costs of that method, and choosing the one that yields the greatest net expected recovery.* Faced with the plaintiff's choice of method (whether adjudication, arbitration, mediation, or settlement), the defendant now wants to minimize any exposure to liability. This requires the defendant to consider how likely it is that he or she will be required to pay something to the plaintiff, how much that payment will be, and how much the costs of the defense will be. The calculus of both parties is subject to change as events unfold. For instance, a plaintiff might choose adjudication because the defendant is unwilling to settle, mediate, or arbitrate the case willingly. But once the lawsuit commences, both parties might develop an incentive to settle. Assume that the plaintiff believes that he or she has a 50 percent chance of winning $100,000, but it will cost $20,000 to try the case. The plaintiff's expected recovery in litigation is therefore $30,000 ([.50 × $100,000]−$20,000). The defendant agrees with the plaintiff's assessment that there is a 50 percent chance of losing $100,000; in addition, the

_____

* This model is somewhat simplistic. Sometimes, when the parties have a preexisting relationship, they select a dispute resolution method before the dispute arises; the party with superior bargaining power often forces the choice of a method that favors that party.

defendant faces trial expenses of $15,000. As a result, the defendant is looking at an expected loss at trial of $65,000 ([.50 × $100,000] + $15,000). Under these facts, both the plaintiff and the defendant are better off if they settle the case for anything between $30,000 and $65,000. This is a very simple model, but economic analysis can add necessary refinements and analyze the parties' behavior under different, more realistic assumptions. Economic efficiency has proven a very useful concept in thinking about the role of ADR in relation to adjudication, and in thinking about why so few cases go to trial.

Second, efficiency has been a primary argument behind the rise of something called *court-annexed ADR* — in other words, ADR methods that courts themselves sponsor and either require or suggest that litigants consider using in lieu of trial. Today many courts are spurring the parties toward ADR and away from trial. The Alternative Dispute Resolution Act of 1998[5] requires every federal district court in the country to "devise and implement its own alternative dispute resolution program." Many state courts sponsor comparable ADR programs. The range and sophistication of such programs vary widely among courts, but the common thread is the goal of bringing cases to an amicable conclusion as efficiently as possible.

Considered in this light, the law school focus on Civil Procedure seems misplaced. Instead, perhaps you should be learning about, and then comparing and contrasting, the procedures used in litigation, settlement, meditation, and arbitration. Rather than considering how to design a litigation system intended to end with trial and judgment, perhaps we should be thinking about how to design a procedural system that most effectively and efficiently induces the parties to settle.

To a degree, the value of ADR depends on its basic premise: that its methods resolve disputes more efficiently than adjudication. In some cases, that premise is assuredly true. But most of those cases never enter the litigation system. Among the cases that are litigated, the data are less promising. In one comprehensive study conducted in the 1990s, before the passage of the ADR Act, courts that aggressively used ADR methods did not achieve lower costs or less delay than courts that sponsored no ADR methods. On the other hand, these courts had no greater cost or delay either. It seems that the extra cost and delay occasioned by the use of ADR in the cases in which it was unsuccessful counterbalanced the savings in terms of cost and delay in the cases in which ADR was successful.[6] So efficiency turns out not to be a compelling argument for the use of ADR in lawsuits. At the same time, it is not a compelling argument against the use of ADR, either.

Critics of ADR point out that adjudication has an intrinsic value that ADR cannot supply. Adjudication establishes the legal principles that form the basis for many ADR processes. Moreover, ADR methods necessarily operate in the shadow of the law; a principal reason to settle or mediate any dispute is the threat that the law might give one of the parties a legal entitlement. Private agreements forged through ADR are also more likely than adjudication to replicate and reinforce already existing inequalities among parties. The vaunted procedural flexibility of many ADR processes can be seen instead as a disturbing lack of procedural regularity. Indeed, adjudicatory procedure acts as a principal check on the overbearing tendencies of the powerful. As Justice Frankfurter once observed, "The history of liberty has largely been the history of observance of procedural safeguards."[7] On this view, courts should respond to competition from ADR by making adjudication more accessible, rather than by sloughing off their responsibility onto court-annexed ADR processes.

EFFICIENCY IN CONTEXT

Economic analysis can help us to understand the incentives that various procedural rules create. Sometimes using sophisticated econometric modeling, the economic literature has explored the economics of such diverse procedural issues as pleading, discovery, summary judgment, *joinder*, attorneys' fees, and incentives for settlement or the use of other ADR methods. To take a couple of examples, economic analysis has shown that the existence of summary judgment tends to depress the settlement amounts that plaintiffs might expect to receive. Similarly, in allowing parties to seek discovery while requiring their opponents to pay for the costs of producing it, our system generally encourages more discovery than a system in which the requesting party must also pay for the costs of production. (These are general claims; there are, of course, some exceptions.)

Economic considerations also underlie or help to inform many of our procedural rules. But even when concerns for efficiency spur policymakers to rein in or change procedural practices, the policymakers rarely engage in the kind of sophisticated analysis of direct litigation costs, error costs, and maximization of overall social welfare that a serious commitment to economic analysis requires. Generally, when policymakers argue that a change in a procedural or jurisdictional rule will be more "efficient," they mean that the change will reduce direct litigation costs. As we have seen, however, that claim is far from economically adequate. Even if a change in a rule successfully reduces direct litigation costs, it will nonetheless be inefficient if (1) the reduction in direct litigation costs is offset by a larger increase in error costs, (2) the new rule induces the filing of enough additional suits that the savings in direct litigation costs are eaten up by the costs of more lawsuits, or (3) the new rule increases the combined costs of accidents and accident-prevention measures more than the savings in direct litigation costs. In choosing whether to adopt a rule that reduces direct litigation costs, policymakers have not historically balanced the reductions against these potential costs.

Therefore, although efficiency is one of the central thematic elements in modern American litigation, it is not yet a principal force in the design of the procedural system. Efficiency reins in other principles, and it tinkers at the margins of procedural rules. But a legal system that began with efficiency as its first and most foundational principle would look very different from the one that we have designed. For instance, take proportionality. A hard-bitten economic approach would ask whether the marginal gain in accuracy from each piece of discovery outweighed the marginal cost of discovery. But proportionality is construed far more loosely than that. Proportionality bars discovery only when the balance against discovery is overwhelming. American procedure uses the efficiency principle more as a brake on grossly inefficient practices (and not even always then; you will see very little consideration of efficiency in the jurisdictional principles you will study in Chapter 8) than as a design principle of the first order.

That said, we do not mean to downplay the importance of efficiency in American litigation. Words like "economy," "expedition," "speed," "convenience," and "expense" appear throughout the Federal Rules of Civil Procedure,[8] as well as in some statutory provisions.[9] These words are even more common in the Advisory Committee Notes, which explain the reasoning behind the Federal Rules. Economy and efficiency are also a common theme in judicial opinions that interpret jurisdictional statutes and procedural rules,[10] and in various manuals that judges rely on to select the case management techniques used in specific cases.[11]

Efficiency probably exercises its greatest influence at the level of the particular. In individual cases, a party might suggest a more efficient way to handle an aspect of the case or suggest how, on the facts of the case, the party's interpretation of an ambiguous procedural rule will lead to greater efficiency than the opponent's reading. Indeed, when a particular procedure allows a case to be handled with less expense but just as well, this procedure probably should be employed. As we have seen, judges have great discretion to tailor procedural rules to individual cases. Achieving greater efficiency within the case is almost always a powerful argument to motivate a judge to exercise his or her discretion in one way rather than another. In exercising discretion to achieve efficiency, however, judges usually fail to consider efficiency in the broader context of maximizing overall social welfare. We have few tools with which to compare the true costs and benefits of case-specific procedural choices. In light of such imponderables, judges often ask only the most readily answerable question: Which rule best reduces direct litigation costs in this case?

Economic analysis also reminds us about two facts of which it is easy to lose sight: First, procedural rules affect parties' behavior; second (and relatedly), they affect the outcome of cases. Every rule creates certain behavioral incentives; thus, every rule affects the expected outcome in litigation. Some procedural rules (for example, whether to file a pleading on $8\frac{1}{2}'' \times 11''$ or $8\frac{1}{2}'' \times 14''$ paper) are fairly neutral in their substantive effect. But the major design choices in a procedural system invariably have significant effects on the outcomes of cases. It is vital to keep that fact in mind as we evaluate how we should distill our sometimes conflicting procedural principles into specific procedural rules.

～ 7 ～

Transactionalism

How big should a lawsuit be? Answering that question implicates all of the principles we have already discussed. If it is too big or too small, we might run into inefficiencies: too big, and resolving it will take too long and be too complicated; too small, and we might end up with multiple lawsuits resolving the same question(s) over and over. Overly large cases might also place too great a burden on jurors, who cannot give up months or years of their lives to hear thousands of claims; a large number of claims also taxes a jury's capacity to keep the claims straight and reach an accurate decision on the individual merits of each one. A judge could resolve a case in fits and starts, fitting it in much the way a computer locates empty space to store the bits and bytes of a file, but a case with thousands of individual claims strains a judge's resources and comprehension as well. *Procedural fairness* also plays a role in shaping the case: Not only must the case be small and manageable enough that the parties can get a fair trial, but it must also be large enough to ensure that the disputes between opposing parties do not end up being resolved in conflicting ways by different juries. Even the *adversarial system* affects the size of a case. First, there is the basic party-autonomy principle of the adversarial system, the *master of the complaint* rule, which holds that the shape of the lawsuit is determined principally by the plaintiff. Second, the need to afford each party an *opportunity to be heard* imposes practical limits on the scope of a lawsuit.

Thus, the question of the size of the litigation presents an excellent study of how we might balance the procedural principles that we have already studied. If we choose any one of these principles to define the minimum or maximum size of a lawsuit, we might run afoul of one of the others. A principle of pure *efficiency* might bring in claims and parties that the existing parties do not wish to include, or it might divide claims that all the parties do wish to litigate. Letting the parties decide could produce great inefficiencies and potential unfairness. What if a plaintiff decided to litigate each of multiple related claims against the defendant one case at a time? What if a car accident victim brought separate suits for a broken arm, cracked ribs, and a damaged car? Or if he or she wanted to litigate a tort claim against a negligent driver, a contract claim against his or her employer, and a property claim against his or her neighbor all in one suit?

Our judicial system uses the principle of *transactionalism* to mediate among these various pressures in determining the structure of the lawsuit. In many places in the Federal Rules of Civil Procedure, as well in other procedural doctrines such as *preclusion*, different consequences follow depending on whether a claim is transactionally related to other claims in the lawsuit. In other words, our procedural system contemplates an ideal lawsuit as one that involves all of the claims, and only those claims, that arise out of a single transaction. But no lawsuit is ideal, and exactly how transactionalism works in each context often depends on how much pressure comes from one of the other principles. Efficiency, party autonomy, and fairness can all influence how transactionalism functions within each doctrine.

It is confusing enough that the same principle — transactionalism — might vary in application depending on context. You must also understand that the principle of transactionalism is sometimes described in different language. And just as the same language does not necessarily get applied identically, sometimes two different formulations *are* applied identically. This chapter sorts out all these permutations.

JOINDER AND PRECLUSION RULES

One basic question you will study in your Civil Procedure course is the circumstances under which additional claims and parties may be included in the lawsuit (beyond one plaintiff suing one defendant for a single wrongful action). Various Federal Rules of Civil Procedure govern when such claims or parties *may* be added, and together the Federal Rules and doctrines of preclusion determine when such claims or parties *must* be added. There is the also the question of when a federal court has *subject matter jurisdiction* over the additional claims or parties; we discuss that in the next section of this chapter. Keep in mind, however, that as long as there is subject matter jurisdiction, various Rules give the judge a great deal of control over the actual shape of the litigation: Rules 20(b), 21, and 42(b) allow the judge to divide claims, parties, or both into separately tried cases (and Rule 42(a) allows the judge to consolidate cases).

At the outset, it is important to understand the two categories of *joinder* and how they work in tandem with preclusion rules. A simple lawsuit involves one plaintiff suing one defendant on one claim. Rules of *claim joinder* determine the circumstances under which additional claims can be added, and rules of *party joinder* determine the circumstances under which additional parties can join the original plaintiff and defendant in the case. Preclusion doctrines work in tandem with claim joinder by determining when someone is barred from litigating a claim because it was (or should have been) litigated in a prior suit. Thus, claim joinder rules set the outer boundary on the parties' opportunity to expand the claims in the first case, and preclusion rules provide a use-it-or-lose-it hammer that effectively requires the parties to accept that opportunity in certain situations. Because of this interrelationship, the rules of claim joinder must be at least large enough to permit the joinder of claims that would be barred by the preclusion doctrines (although claim joinder may also be even larger). Preclusion has less effect on the shape of party joinder, however, because of a basic tenet of *due process*: A person can in most situations be precluded from litigating a claim or issue in a later case only if he or she was joined as a party in the prior case.* Party joinder doctrines are thus independent of preclusion doctrines (except to the extent that broader rules of party joinder permit the joinder of more parties, and broader joinder extends the preclusive effect of a single judgment to more people).

The unifying principle of the joinder and preclusion rules is transactionalism, but the principle works differently depending on whether we are talking about new claims against parties already involved in the lawsuit or new claims against new parties. In general (although there are exceptions, which we talk about later), transactionally related claims against existing parties *must* be brought, or they will be precluded forever; unrelated claims against those parties *may* be brought, but will not be precluded if they are not; transactionally related claims against new parties *may* be brought, but again will not be precluded if they are not; and unrelated claims against new parties *may not* be brought. It might help to think of a staircase, from required to permitted to prohibited:

Required	Permitted	Prohibited
Related claims against **existing** parties		
	Unrelated claims against **existing** parties	
	Related claims against **new** parties	
		Unrelated claims against **new** parties

---

* Prior judgments are preclusive for the parties and those *in privity* with them. So sometimes an individual — or, more likely, a corporation — may be bound by a lawsuit in which he or she was not a party.

These general principles are the way that our procedural system accommodates efficiency, fairness, and party autonomy.

Claims

Begin with *permissive* claim joinder. If two parties are already involved in a lawsuit, it is fair and efficient to allow them to litigate all of their disputes — whether related or not — in that single lawsuit. (Remember, if it might confuse the jury to hear two completely unrelated claims, the judge always has the option to sever them.) Rule 18(a) therefore allows unlimited claim joinder against a single opposing party, and Rules 13(a) and (b) together allow unlimited *counterclaims*. Thus a plaintiff *may* join related and unrelated claims in a single complaint, and a defendant *may* raise any and all counterclaims regardless of whether they are related to the plaintiff's claims or to each other.

Forcing the parties to bring all their claims together, however, impinges on their freedom to structure the lawsuit. So deciding whether to *require* claim joinder, even for claimants who are already parties to the lawsuit, creates some tension between efficiency and the adversarial system's preference for party-driven structure. The federal legal regime resolves this tension by making claim joinder mandatory only where the claims are transactionally related. This principle is most clear with regard to counterclaims. Rule 13(a) says that a counterclaim that "arises out of the transaction or occurrence" that gives rise to the plaintiff's claim must be brought,* and Rule 13(b) provides that a counterclaim that does not arise out of the same transaction or occurrence as the plaintiff's claim may (but need not) be brought. The Federal Rules never say what the consequence of failing to assert a Rule 13(a) counterclaim is, but courts have developed the *compulsory counterclaim* rule, which states that a defendant cannot

---

* There are a few narrow exceptions, all listed in Rule 13(a).

assert in later litigation a claim that should have been asserted under Rule 13(a) in an earlier case. Thus, transactionally related counterclaims (under Rule 13(a)) are compulsory, and transactionally unrelated counterclaims (under Rule 13(b)) are permissive.

The same principle applies to claims by the plaintiff, but the source is preclusion doctrine rather than the Federal Rules of Civil Procedure. All jurisdictions prohibit *claim-splitting*, applying the doctrine of *claim preclusion* or *res judicata* or *merger and bar* (all different names for the same thing) to prevent a party from bringing a claim that should have been litigated in a prior suit against the same opponent. How does a court decide whether a claim should have been brought in an earlier lawsuit? In federal court and in most state courts, claim preclusion embodies the principle of transactionalism: A subsequent claim is barred by claim preclusion if, in the words of the *Restatement (Second) of Judgments*, it arises out of the same "transaction, or series of connected transactions" as the original lawsuit.[1] A later claim is not barred, however, if it is unrelated to the claim in the original suit.

Exactly what constitutes the same transaction or series of transactions for claim preclusion purposes, of course, is no more pellucid than what constitutes the same transaction or occurrence for purposes of Rule 13(a). The *Restatement* explicitly recognizes this uncertainty, providing that:

> What factual grouping constitutes a "transaction," and what groupings constitute a "series," are to be determined pragmatically, giving weight to such considerations as whether the facts are related in time, space, origin, or motivation, whether they form a convenient trial unit, and whether their treatment as a unit conforms to the parties' expectations or business understandings or usage.[2]

This inherent lack of definitional clarity allows courts to accommodate the various pressures on transactionalism. For example, preclusion (whether for claims or counterclaims) is a draconian consequence for a procedural misstep: If a party mistakenly omits a transactionally related claim or counterclaim, that claim is lost forever, never to be determined "on the merits." In cases that might plausibly be characterized either way (as related or unrelated), we might therefore want to define "transactionally related" more narrowly in the context of claim preclusion than in some other contexts. It should nevertheless be defined broadly enough to prevent strategic omissions or gross inefficiencies. And, in fact, that is what we find in many court decisions: The definition of a transactional relationship is at its narrowest in cases involving preclusion. So despite the similarity of language, the interpretation will vary depending on the context.

The rules governing *cross-claims* present a variation on the principles of pure transactionalism for existing parties. Cross-claims are claims asserted against a co-party — a co-plaintiff or co-defendant who has been joined in the case. Typically, they are claims asserted by one defendant against a co-defendant. Rule 13(g) provides that a party "may" bring a cross-claim against a co-party, but only if the claim arises out of the same "transaction or occurrence" as either the original suit or a counterclaim. But Rule 13(g) is not compulsory: A defendant who fails to bring a related claim against a co-defendant is not barred from raising the claim in a subsequent lawsuit. In light of the fact that both defendants are already parties, why does Rule 13(g) depart from the general rule that would make related claims between them compulsory? And why doesn't it allow permissive, unrelated claims, the way that Rule 13(b) does for counterclaims?

Here efficiency and respect for the plaintiff's principal role in establishing the litigation structure work together to push the system away from the choices made in Rules 18(a) and 13(b). It would almost always be inefficient for the defendants to be fighting among themselves about issues unrelated to the underlying dispute between the plaintiff and the defendants, and it would distort the structure the plaintiff had created for the case. So rather than make unlimited joinder the default rule, with a judicial option to sever, Rule 13(g) simply bars unrelated claims. But, carrying the interplay among the principles one step further, if a party does have a transactionally related claim against a co-party, Rule 18(a) allows him or her to join to it any other claims, related or not. Once the defendants are fighting among themselves about one transaction, they might as well be allowed to resolve all their disputes.

Similar considerations shed light on the permissive nature of Rule 13(g). Although we are willing to force the plaintiff to join all of his or her related claims in one complaint, and to force defendants to respond by raising all related counter-claims, the efficiency of forcing the defendants to litigate their claims against each other is uncertain. If the plaintiff fails to prevail against the defendants, the cross-claims usually collapse as well, so time might have been wasted on them. Moreover, the idea of compulsory cross-claims impinges significantly on the principle that the plaintiff is the primary architect of the lawsuit.

These considerations are not dispositive as an abstract matter. Perhaps unrelated cross-claims should be allowed at the option of the judge. In other words, you may or may not agree with how Rule 13(g) has accommodated the tension among the various principles. But you should recognize that it *is* an accommodation, and that the differences in the application of transactionalism among the various parts of Rule 13 (as well as Rule 18 and the preclusion doctrines) stem from these competing considerations.

Parties

Now let us turn to party joinder. Here efficiency concerns are more likely to cut against joinder, and all the principles become more complicated. If two parties are already involved in a lawsuit, it is easy to make an argument that it is generally efficient to allow them — and often fair to require them — to litigate claims other than those that first motivated the plaintiff to sue. But dragging more parties into the suit is a different matter: More parties increases the likelihood of jury confusion, inaccuracy, and ultimately inefficiency; it implicates the due process rights of the additional parties; and it trespasses ever more deeply on the original parties' (especially the original plaintiff's) decisions about how to structure the lawsuit.

Permissive Party Joinder: Rule 20   The Federal Rules recognize these distinctions by imposing different transactional requirements where multiple parties are involved. In general, the scope of both permissive and mandatory party joinder is narrower than the scope of claim joinder.

Compare permissive claim joinder under Rule 18 with permissive party joinder under Rule 20. The former is unlimited, but the latter requires a transactional relationship: Rule 20(a) allows plaintiffs to join together, or plaintiffs to join multiple defendants, in a single suit only if the claims "aris[e] out of the same transaction, occurrence, or series of transactions or occurrences" and have at least one common question of law or fact. Notice, however, that although Rule 20(a) requires some transactional relationship among claims, this formulation of the transactionalism principle is broader than that of Rule 13(a) or 13(g) because it includes a "series" of transactions or occurrences. Rule 20 thus requires more connection among the claims of multiple plaintiffs (or against multiple defendants) than among the multiple claims of a single plaintiff, yet it does not require as much connection as cross-claims or compulsory counterclaims. Why? Because this is how the Rules' drafters chose to make the trade-offs between efficiency, party autonomy, and the overarching idea that a lawsuit should generally involve claims that are transactionally related. Just as with

193

Rule 13(g), this is not the only plausible resolution, and you may disagree with it.

The commitment to party autonomy, as well as due process considerations, exerts an even stronger influence against efficiency when it comes to preclusion doctrines. Recall that parties are required to litigate all of their transactionally related *claims* in a single lawsuit, or forfeit the right to bring them later. But preclusion doctrines do not require the joinder of all transactionally related *parties*. Failure to join a party has no consequences for subsequent lawsuits: A plaintiff may always bring a subsequent suit against a different defendant; although *issue preclusion* may sometimes prevent the plaintiff from relitigating issues he or she has already lost, claim preclusion will not bar the suit. Similarly, preclusion doctrines rarely bind plaintiffs who could have, but did not, join a prior lawsuit, and the Supreme Court has suggested that it is generally unconstitutional to do so.[3]

Impleader: Rule 14 Rule 14 takes a narrower approach to permissive party joinder than Rules 18(a) and 13(b) take with regard to permissive claim joinder, Rule 13(a) takes with regard to compulsory counterclaims, or Rule 20(a) takes with regard to initial party joinder. Rule 14 allows a defendant (or a plaintiff against whom a claim has been filed) to *implead* additional parties. But Rule 14 imposes a stricter requirement of transactionalism: A party may only implead a *third-party defendant* who "is or may be liable" to him or her for "all or part of [an opposing party's] claim" against him or her. In other words, only parties whose liability to the defendant stems from some claim of *contribution* or *indemnification* — parties whose indebtedness to the defendant *rests on* or *derives from* the defendant's indebtedness to the plaintiff — may be impleaded. As an example, consider a simple suit about a car accident. The plaintiff alleges that the defendant's car ran into her car, causing her injury. If the defendant claims that a third driver caused him to swerve and hit the plaintiff's car, he may implead the third driver. But if the defendant claims instead that his car did not hit the plaintiff's car at all (perhaps it is a hit and run, and the defendant's car happens to look like and share some license plate numbers with another car, but he was not there) and that the real culprit was the third driver, he cannot implead the third driver. He must simply deny the facts alleged in the plaintiff's complaint. Assuming that the defendant prevails, it will then be up to the plaintiff to sue the third driver.

Under Rule 14, then, the kind of "same transaction or occurrence" relationship that obligates a defendant to bring a compulsory counterclaim and permits the defendant to bring a cross-claim against a co-defendant is not sufficient to allow the defendant to implead a third party. (All of these same limitations also apply to a plaintiff seeking to implead a third party in response to a counterclaim.) Like Rule 20, however, impleader under Rule 14 is permissive rather than mandatory: If a plaintiff or defendant fails to implead a third party, he or she is nevertheless permitted to bring a subsequent suit for contribution or indemnification against that third party.

Again, we can explain these differences among related joinder rules by looking at the competing considerations. The plaintiff has chosen not to bring the impleaded parties into the original suit, so we should have an especially good reason before we allow the defendant to alter that choice. The heightened transactional relationship between the plaintiff's claim against the defendant and the defendant's claim against the third party supplies that reason. (Similarly, the defendant bringing a counterclaim has chosen not to invoke Rule 13(h) to join additional parties, and the plaintiff should not be able to do so without good reason.) We might also believe that bringing more parties into the suit is likely to create rather than reduce inefficiency unless the claims against the additional parties are very closely related to the original claims. Finally, consider whether it would be fair to the hapless third parties to have their liability determined in a proceeding that is not really supposed to be about them or their wrongdoing, but rather about their accuser's wrongdoing. Unless the accuser (the impleading defendant) can explain why the suit *is* about a third party's wrongdoing as well as his or her own, we might want to make the accuser wait and sue the third party separately, which is just what Rule 14 does. Remember, you do not have to agree with these choices, but only recognize that some choice must be made and understand why the drafters might have chosen as they did.

Mandatory Party Joinder: Rule 19   Mandatory party joinder is even more problematic, and thus is almost never required. If a person does not want to join a particular lawsuit, it seems to violate every principle of due process and the adversarial system to require him or her to do so. And forcing a plaintiff who wants to sue some defendants but not others to join the additional defendants would be a very large step away from the basic notion that the plaintiff is the master of the complaint. In both situations, mandating joinder is also likely to be counterproductive as long as the parties — especially the plaintiff — retain control over the course of the lawsuit.

One Rule does provide for mandatory party joinder. Rule 19(a) directs that a person must be joined as a party in three circumstances: if complete relief cannot be accorded to the existing parties in the absence of the third party, if the third party's own interests will be impaired or impeded in his or her absence, or if the absence of the third party might subject one of the existing parties to the risk of inconsistent or multiple obligations. How should we explain the existence and contours of Rule 19? Transactionalism principles do not help much, because Rule 19 does not require the joinder of all persons involved in the transaction. The same can be said of efficiency principles. The considerations of due process and party autonomy that we have already discussed might explain why Rule 19 *does not* require joinder of everyone involved in the transaction, but those same considerations cut against mandatory joinder at all.

To give one example of how Rule 19 might work, assume that a trust pays out $1 million a year to four beneficiaries. The trustee, who lives in New York, distributes the proceeds equally among all four. One of the beneficiaries, A, believes that she deserves 50 percent of the annual distribution, so she sues the trustee in New York. Assume as well that the other three beneficiaries all live in Hawaii, and have no contact with New York. As a result, the New York court has no jurisdiction over B, C, and D, so A does not join them as parties. This scenario presents a classic case for the use of Rule 19(a). A wants a larger slice of the pie, which will inevitably reduce the shares of one or more of the other beneficiaries. If B, C, and D are not joined, the interests of B, C, and D run the risk of being impaired; the trustee also runs the risk of having inconsistent obligations to A and separately to B, C, and D. Therefore, Rule 19(a) demands that B, C, and D be joined if feasible. But, on these facts, it is not feasible because a New York court has no personal jurisdiction over B, C, and D. So now Rule 19(b) comes into play. Applying the factors listed in Rule 19(b), the New York court needs to decide whether to *dismiss* A's case or to limp along without B, C, and D. (On these facts, the one factor that is likely to weigh most heavily is whether A can refile the case in an Hawaiian court, joining B, C, D, and the trustee. If so, the New York case is likely to be dismissed. If not, the New York court has a very hard decision to make.)

Ultimately, what seems to unify the three circumstances where Rule 19 makes party joinder mandatory is an overall balance of fairness, to both the original parties and the putative third party, which strongly tips in favor of joinder. The litigation process is steaming toward a train wreck: Either the plaintiff cannot get effective relief, the defendant will face excessive liability, or the third party will be shut out of his or her legal rights. The concern for fairness is reaffirmed in Rule 19(b), which specifies the factors that should be considered in deciding whether the case should be dismissed if it proves impossible to join a party identified as necessary under Rule 19(a). In general terms, these factors try to measure the degree to which the plaintiff, defendant, absent party, and court will be harmed by non-joinder, and requires dismissal when the harm is so great that it is better for a possibly meritorious case to be dismissed than for it to proceed. This dismissal due to the *indispensability* of an absent party is one of the most remarkable limits on the principles of deciding cases accurately and affording the plaintiff the adversarial right to be master of the complaint.

Intervention: Rule 24   So far, we have seen two approaches to joinder. One is permissive joinder, in which plaintiffs (and to a limited extent defendants) determine the party structure, subject to the constraints of transactionalism. The other is mandatory joinder, in which certain parties must be present in the case even if the plaintiff and the defendant have not otherwise joined them. *Intervention* presents yet another model: Under certain circumstances, the absent third party has the opportunity to join the case if he or she wishes. If the absent party does not wish to join the case, he or she can sit happily on the sidelines, secure in the knowledge that, as a nonparty, he or she cannot be bound by the judgment in the case. But if the absent party wants, he or she can also join the case, become a party, and become bound by the outcome.

On the one hand, intervention promises a more fair and efficient process; rather than two lawsuits, there will be only one, and the dispute will be resolved with additional perspectives and a fuller context. On the other hand, intervention threatens to undo the plaintiff's primary right to establish the party structure, and could veer the case off in new directions only tangentially related to the initial dispute. Rule 24 tries to mediate between these concerns. It allows two types of intervention: *permissive intervention* and *intervention of right.** Permissive intervention has minimal criteria specified in Rule 24(b), principally, that the underlying case and the intervenor's case share "a question of law or fact in common." This standard is even broader than the transactional principle, but its breadth is tempered by the court's ability to impose significant restrictions on the ability of the permissive intervenor to participate in the case. Intervention of right gives the intervenor full rights of participation as a party. As a result, you might expect that the standard for intervention of right is higher, and seeks to adjust the various interests of the plaintiff, the defendant, the putative intervenor, and the court.

You find that expectation vindicated in the requirements of Rule 24(a). An intervenor of right must show "an interest relating to the property or transaction" in the lawsuit, must demonstrate that the lawsuit "may as a practical matter impair or impede the . . . ability [of the person seeking intervention] to protect that interest," and must prove that none of the present parties "adequately represent[s]" that interest. None of these requirements is crystal clear. One common formulation states that Rule 24(a)'s "impairment of interest" requirement should be interpreted to permit as much joinder "as is compatible with efficiency and due process."[4] A number of cases hold that the only impairment of interest that an intervenor needs to show to obtain party status is a possible *stare decisis* effect of the case on some future litigation in which the putative intervenor might be a party. Other cases reflect a higher standard,

---

* Be careful about one piece of vocabulary. "Permissive" intervention is different from other types of "permissive" party joinder in an important way. When we generally speak of permissive party joinder (especially Rule 20 joinder), we mean that joinder to the transactional maximum is permissible as long as the plaintiff allows the joinder. With permissive intervention, we mean that the intervention is permissible because the court allows it, even if the plaintiff would prefer not to allow it.

insisting on a "significantly protectable interest"[5] and denying intervention that will significantly alter the present focus of the case. As a practical matter, the cases show that intervention of right becomes much harder to achieve when all the parties object to the intervention.*

Throughout this chapter, we have been showing how the words "transaction or occurrence" have different meanings depending on the context in which they are used and the procedural principles that are in play in that context. A microcosm of that argument also exists in the language of Rules 19(a) and 24(a). Rule 19(a) mandates the joinder of persons who claim an "interest" in a case that "may . . . as a practical matter impair or impede the person's ability to protect" this interest. Rule 24(a) authorizes intervention of right when potential intervenors claim an "interest" in a case that "may as a practical matter impair or impede the . . . ability [of the person seeking intervention] to protect" this interest. The language of these two rules is almost identical. But that does not seem to make sense. Rule 19 mandates the joinder of such people. Rule 24 permits them to enter the case if they wish. It cannot be both, so which is it? Must they be forced to join, or may they choose to join if they wish?

The key to the answer is to understand that, although the words are the same, the context for their use is not. Mandatory joinder invokes concerns for the autonomy of the plaintiff, the defendant, and the absent party; it also raises the specter that a meritorious lawsuit will be dismissed under Rule 19(b). In that context, we would expect the quoted language to be construed very narrowly, and it is. With intervention of right, however, no threat of a dismissal for non-joinder looms, and the potential intervenor is exercising his or her autonomy to join the case.

---

* One doctrine that has not proven much of a barrier is the requirement of adequate representation. The Supreme Court has been clear that even minor differences in litigation incentive between a party and a putative intervenor satisfy this requirement.

Intervention also helps to expand the case in the direction of a single, efficient resolution of all transactionally related claims. Hence, you would expect to see the language in Rule 24(a) interpreted more generously, and it is.

Class Actions: Rule 23   The most controversial of the party joinder devices is the *class action*. We already described the rough outline of class actions in Chapter 5, where we examined the unique due process challenges that they pose. Here we can look at the device through the lens of transactionalism and the multitude of procedural principles that feed into the transactional balance.

At its most basic level, a class action allows one person (the *class representative*) to bring a claim on his or her own behalf and on behalf of those who are similarly situated (the *class members*). The judgment that the class representative receives then binds the class members; put differently, class members are precluded from asserting in future litigation the claims that the representative prosecuted or defended. Thus, class actions can be seen either as a party joinder device, in which class members join the class representative's case, or as a preclusion device, in which the class members never join the case but are nonetheless barred. It does not matter which view you take; the result — that the claims of class members are precluded — is the same either way. Because any joinder of class members is really a legal fiction, perhaps it is better to see class actions as a rule of preclusion.

Class actions pose a dilemma at numerous levels. At the level of theory, binding class members to a judgment in which they had no individual opportunity to be heard seems inconsistent with both due process and the individual autonomy that underlies the adversarial system. At the level of practice, class actions can sometimes hold out the promise of enormous financial reward for one side, and the threat of financial ruin for the other; with so much at stake, it is inevitable that class actions raise concerns — whether well founded or not — about the risk of collusion among the class representative, the class counsel, and the opponent to sell out the interests of the class. The judge must inevitably become more active in managing such class actions to protect the rights of all.

In light of these concerns, we need strong affirmative reasons for using class actions. As a general matter, the affirmative arguments for the class action are fairness and efficiency. For instance, assume that a credit-card company has illegally over-billed each of 100,000 customers $10. Very few individual claims will be filed; it is not worth most people's time or trouble to sue for $10. We could use Rule 20 to join together similarly situated plaintiffs, but the cost of identifying who they are and getting each plaintiff's consent would eat up most of the $10. The class action is much more efficient. It also has an important advantage in terms of fairness. Because individual lawsuits are unlikely, the credit-card company stands to pocket $1 million in illegal gains. The class action is the only effective way to deter this unlawful behavior.

Our system has decided that, in some situations, these concerns for fairness and efficiency outweigh the adversarial preference that makes each plaintiff the master of his or her own complaint (and the due process concern about the opportunity to be heard, which we discussed more extensively in Chapter 5). The Rule encapsulates this balance. The elements of Rules 23(a) and 23(b) together ensure that the class action is the fairest and most efficient way of proceeding. The requirement in Rule 23(a)(1) that "the class is so numerous that joinder of all members is impracticable," as well as the (a)(2), (a)(3), and (a)(4) requirements of commonality, typicality, and adequacy of representation, limit class treatment to large-scale litigation in which the greatest efficiencies from consolidated treatment can be realized while still ensuring vigorous advocacy of individual claims. A class action must also meet at least one of the Rule 23(b) requirements. Rule 23(b) states four circumstances in which it is appropriate to require individuals to relinquish control of their own legal claims. Some familiar patterns emerge. For instance, in Rule 23(b)(1)(A), class treatment is appropriate when the person opposing the class is subject to a risk of "inconsistent or varying adjudications" from individual lawsuits; here, as in Rule 19, we worry about unfair treatment to the defendant from multiple lawsuits brought by plaintiffs, none of whom could be bound by a prior judgment obtained by another similarly situated plaintiff. Rule 23(b)(1)(B) sounds a note we have heard in both Rule 19(a) and Rule 24(a): Joinder should be authorized when lawsuits by individual class members would "as a practical matter . . . substantially impair or impede their ability to protect their interests."* Rule 23(b)(2) is a riff on Rule 23(b)(1)(A), permitting class treatment when injunctive relief in favor of class members is appropriate. Rule 23(b)(3), however, is a new concept; it allows class treatment when the common questions of law or fact "predominate" over individual issues and class treatment is "superior" to other available methods for fairly and efficiently adjudicating the controversy. Rule 23(b)(3) was first created in 1966; it reflected a policy judgment that, when the transactional commonalities exceed the individual differences, fairness and efficiency should overpower our adversarial preference.

A considerable body of law has arisen around each of these four types of class action. Let us focus on several thematic issues. First, an important distinction separates the first three types of class action from the (b)(3) class action. Each of the first three class actions is *mandatory*. In other words, class members are stuck in the class; they cannot remove themselves and

---

* As we saw when we examined Rules 19 and 24, the same language does not mean the same interpretation. Context matters. With a different mix of concerns over efficiency, due process, and the adversarial system, it is not surprising that the language in Rule 23(b)(1)(B) has been given a meaning different from its meaning in either Rule 19(a) or Rule 24(a).

bring individual actions. If class members could leave the class, the very unfairness that the class action is seeking to avoid will occur. On the other hand, Rule 23(b)(3) is an *opt-out* class action. Individual class members can remove themselves from the class action if they wish. Even though the class action is thought by the judge to be the best way of tackling the dispute, our respect for the adversarial right of litigants to control their own lawsuit requires a compromise in the form of an opt-out right.

Second, like Rule 19, Rule 23 is a form of mandatory joinder; people who might not wish to be parties in a case nonetheless find themselves embroiled in a lawsuit whose judgment will bind them. Like Rule 19, our respect for the adversarial rights of individuals to control their cases keeps us from extending this mandatory joinder to the full scope of the transaction; the four Rule 23(b) categories, combined with the fairly stingy interpretation most courts have given them, still leave many transactionally related cases ineligible for class treatment. The strongest claims for class treatment are those found in Rules 23(b)(1) and (b)(2); here, the demands of fair treatment to the person opposing the class or to absent class members do not allow an opt-out right. Rule 23(b)(3) is closer to the line; the strongest claims of unfairness are not present, but the possibility of realizing great efficiency is tantalizing. Unsurprisingly, the Rule 23(b)(3) class action is the most controversial aspect of this most controversial device. The way in which Rule 23(b)(3) funnels the concerns for fairness, efficiency, due process, and adversarial process into the opt-out compromise is a wonderful example of the interaction between principles and practical procedural solutions.

Parties and Claims Together

The drafters of the Rules did not provide for every eventuality, and occasionally a situation might arise in which the lenient rules of claim joinder meet the more tailored rules governing party joinder. For example, Rule 14 permits impleader for claims of indemnification or contribution. But under Rule 18(a), a defendant can join other, unrelated claims against the third party to his or her claim for indemnification or contribution. Or think about the provision of Rule 14(a) that allows an impleaded party to assert claims against the original plaintiff as long as the claims are transactionally related to the plaintiff's claims against the defendant. This language reflects the spirit of Rule 14. Because it is primarily a rule about party joinder rather than claim joinder, Rule 14 imposes a transactionalism requirement even on a claim that arises between two persons who are already parties to the litigation. But Rule 18 allows a party to join any claims, whether they are related or not. So although Rule 14(a) prohibits the impleaded third party from asserting just an unrelated claim against the plaintiff, Rule 18(a) allows him or her to assert a related claim and an unrelated claim together.[6] There are also other circumstances that create this same conflict between the unlimited claim joinder under Rule 18 and the more transactionally oriented Rules, such as Rule 13(g) and other parts of Rule 14(a). One way to think about these problems is to recognize that party joinder necessarily has claim joinder "baggage": We try to limit who gets invited into the house, but once we invite them we do not exercise any control over what they bring.[7] These interstices between Rules are an opportunity for creative argument on behalf of your client—whether your client is the party who wishes to bring the unrelated claim or the party who wishes to have it dismissed—if you understand how the claim joinder and party joinder Rules are different and the role that transactionalism plays.

The basic joinder and preclusion rules thus might seem bizarre and overly complex at first glance, as each type of joinder seems to follow different rules. But we have tried to make sense out of the jumble of rules and doctrines. We started with the principle that an ideal lawsuit should involve all of the parties and claims — and only those parties and claims — that arise out of the same transaction or occurrence. Sometimes the Rules mandate exactly that result, for example the compulsory counterclaim requirements of Rule 13(a). But sometimes other principles are in tension with this ideal, and the Rules try to reach an appropriate compromise among competing principles. The end result is a multilayered scheme, the rationality of which becomes apparent only with careful study.

SUBJECT MATTER JURISDICTION

A federal court must have *subject matter jurisdiction* over each and every claim in a lawsuit. If it does not, it must dismiss the claims over which jurisdiction is lacking. The Federal Rules of Civil Procedure do not provide subject matter jurisdiction, and thus just because a claim may be joined under the Federal Rules does not necessarily mean that the federal court will have jurisdiction to hear it. So the joinder rules discussed in the previous section only tell us half the story, and indeed complicate the other half. (A court must also have *personal jurisdiction* over each and every party, but those doctrines are governed by principles other than transactionalism and are therefore considered elsewhere in this book.)

Your Civil Procedure course will probably cover the two most important types of federal subject matter jurisdiction, *federal question* jurisdiction and *diversity* jurisdiction. A court has federal question jurisdiction over claims brought under federal law. It has diversity jurisdiction over state law claims brought by citizens of one state against citizens of another state, as long as the amount in controversy exceeds the *jurisdictional amount* of $75,000. (This sum has slowly risen over time, so you may read older cases with a lower jurisdictional minimum.) We discuss these two types of jurisdiction at length

in Chapter 8, when we consider why these types of cases —
and only these types of cases — may be brought in federal
court. As we will see, the basic principle involved is *federalism*,
in particular, a respect for the role of state courts in our system
of divided government. Here we are concerned only with how
transactionalism interacts with federalism to affect jurisdiction
over multiple claims.

What if claims that do not satisfy either diversity or federal
question jurisdiction are joined with claims that do? If the
Tennessee plaintiff in a diversity case asks for $100,000 and
the Indiana defendant wants to counterclaim for $50,000,
there is jurisdiction over the plaintiff's claim (the parties are
diverse, and the amount in controversy is higher than
$75,000), but is there jurisdiction over the counterclaim? If
the defendant wants to implead a third party under Rule 14,
but either the third party is from the same state as the defendant
or the defendant's indemnification claim is less than $75,000,
does the federal court have jurisdiction? Every joinder rule
we have discussed can potentially raise the same question.

These questions are governed by the doctrine of *supplemental jurisdiction*, which, prior to 1990, was called *pendent*,
pendent party, and *ancillary* jurisdiction. And the basic
principle of supplemental jurisdiction is transactionalism: As
a general rule, if a federal court has *independent* or *original*
jurisdiction (diversity or federal question) over one claim, it
has supplemental jurisdiction over all transactionally related
claims. As with joinder and preclusion, however, other principles put pressure on — and sometimes result in the modifica-
tion of — a regime of pure transactionalism.

Supplemental jurisdiction began as a judicially created doctrine, which was codified by Congress in 1990 in 28 U.S.C.
§1367. The modern view of supplemental jurisdiction is
derived primarily from two sources: old-fashioned ancillary
jurisdiction (which encompassed compulsory counterclaims,
cross-claims, impleader, and intervention of right) and the

more modern pendent jurisdiction. A federal court had jurisdiction over ancillary claims when they had a "logical dependence" on claims within federal jurisdiction.[8] Modern pendent
jurisdiction developed in a 1966 Supreme Court case, *United
Mine Workers of America v. Gibbs*.[9] *Gibbs* held that a federal
court has jurisdiction over state claims (between nondiverse
parties) that are joined with federal claims, whenever the state
and federal claims "derive from a common nucleus of operative
fact." Section 1367(a) rephrases this transactionalism requirement, allowing jurisdiction over all claims that "are so related"
to claims over which the court has independent subject matter
jurisdiction "that they form part of the same case or controversy." It is widely accepted that in adopting this language,
Congress meant to codify the *Gibbs* "common nucleus of
operative fact" standard and also to define the transactional
relationship necessary for supplemental jurisdiction as broadly
as the Constitution permits. (Under the Constitution, Congress may not confer on the federal courts jurisdiction to
hear cases beyond those listed in the nine *heads of jurisdiction*
of Article III. Thus, supplemental jurisdiction is constitutionally permissible only when the claims outside of the heads of
jurisdiction are part of the same constitutionally defined case
or controversy as claims within the court's jurisdiction.)

Under both the pre-1990 doctrines and §1367, then, the
key question is the same as in joinder and preclusion: whether
claims are transactionally related. Although the language differs ("same transaction or occurrence" for joinder and preclusion, "logical dependence" for ancillary jurisdiction, "common
nucleus of operative fact" for pendent jurisdiction, and "part of
the same case or controversy" for §1367), the inquiry is the
same: Balance the relevant competing interests to achieve a
pragmatic solution.

As you might expect, the jurisdictional doctrine therefore
mirrors the joinder rules, but only to the extent that the joinder
is premised on a transactional relationship. For example,

compulsory counterclaims are within supplemental jurisdiction but permissive counterclaims are not. So if our hypothetical defendant's $50,000 counterclaim arises out of the same transaction or occurrence as the plaintiff's original claim, the defendant must raise it *and* the federal court has subject matter jurisdiction over it. If the counterclaim does not arise out of the same transaction or occurrence, the defendant may technically raise it under the Rules, but the court has no jurisdiction to entertain it because it does not meet the requirements for independent diversity jurisdiction. In the latter circumstance, the counterclaim will usually be dismissed for lack of jurisdiction (although we note an exception a little later in this section). Similarly, because Rule 18 allows a plaintiff to join multiple claims whether they are transactionally related or not, the jurisdictional inquiry will be separate. Assuming that there is independent federal jurisdiction over one claim in the complaint, there will be supplemental jurisdiction over any claims that are transactionally related to that claim, but not over those that are unrelated.* Again, the Federal Rules of Civil Procedure allow the unrelated claims to be joined but the jurisdictional rules might nevertheless prohibit the court from hearing the claim.

Jurisdiction under Rule 14 works the same way. Because a defendant can only implead parties who are liable to him or her under a theory of contribution, indemnification, or other derivative liability, impleader claims are always sufficiently

---

* It is actually slightly more complicated. The rule in the text works for federal question jurisdiction. But in diversity cases, the only question (assuming that the plaintiff and the defendant are diverse) is whether the total amount the plaintiff seeks to recover from the defendant is more than $75,000. Assume that the plaintiff brings several claims in one lawsuit and none of the claims is worth $75,000, but the claims total more than $75,000. Then there is jurisdiction over the case, even if the claims are unrelated to each other. A single plaintiff's ability to cobble together unrelated claims to create jurisdiction violates the transactional principle we have described. But the rule is an old and venerable one, unlikely to be changed by the Supreme Court. Some jurisdictional rules have a "because I said so" quality that defies logical explanation.

transactionally related to the plaintiff's original claim to satisfy supplemental jurisdiction. Thus, even if the impleaded party is from the same state as the defendant (or, for that matter, the same state as the plaintiff), or the claim is below $75,000, the federal court will still have jurisdiction.

Beyond the impleader itself the jurisdictional rules governing impleader get more complicated. Rule 14(a) allows the impleaded party (or third-party defendant) to assert counterclaims against the original defendant, and those counterclaims are subject to the same jurisdictional rules as any other counterclaim: Counterclaims that are transactionally related to the defendant's claim against the third party are compulsory and within supplemental jurisdiction, but unrelated counterclaims are permissive and are only within the court's jurisdiction if they satisfy the requirements for independent subject matter jurisdiction under diversity or federal question (or some other statutory grant of jurisdiction). Rule 14(a) also permits the third-party defendant to assert against the plaintiff any claims that arise out of the "transaction or occurrence" that is the subject of the plaintiff's claims against the defendant. As with compulsory counterclaims and impleader itself, because Rule 14(a) limits the impleaded party to transactionally related claims against the plaintiff, there will always be supplemental jurisdiction over those claims.

When we bring Rule 18 into the game, however, the picture changes. As we noted earlier, Rule 18 allows a party to join a related claim and an unrelated claim, even where Rule 14 apparently limits the party to related claims. The two examples we discussed are a defendant impleading a third-party defendant on a claim of indemnification and joining an unrelated claim, and an impleaded party bringing both a related and an unrelated claim against the plaintiff. Because Rule 18 does not depend on a transactional relationship among claims, and supplemental jurisdiction does, what is allowed under the Rules is not necessarily allowed under the statutes governing the federal courts' jurisdiction. Unless the additional, unrelated claim (by the defendant against the third-party defendant or by the third-party defendant against the plaintiff) independently meets the requirements for federal court jurisdiction, it will be dismissed. The principle of federalism curbs Rule 18's impulse to expand the litigation beyond the transactional boundary.

There is one final wrinkle for impleader. Imagine that a plaintiff has a dispute — arising out of the same transaction — with two potential defendants, one of whom is from the same state as the plaintiff and one of whom is not. The requirement of *complete diversity* prohibits the plaintiff from bringing suit against both defendants, because no plaintiff may be from the same state as any defendant. So, thinking creatively about the joinder and jurisdictional rules, what might such a plaintiff try to do? He or she might sue the diverse defendant, wait for the diverse defendant to implead the nondiverse party (because the nondiverse third-party defendant "is or may be liable" to the defendant for any liability owed to the plaintiff), and then use Rule 14(a) to make the claim against the nondiverse party that he or she could not bring originally. Because the plaintiff's claim against the nondiverse impleaded party arises from the same transaction as his or her claim against the original defendant, there should be a sufficient transactional relationship to allow both the joinder and the exercise of jurisdiction. But think about that: We have just permitted the plaintiff to use the joinder rules to evade the jurisdictional barrier to a suit against the nondiverse party! The Supreme Court, prior to the enactment of §1367, disallowed this move, finding no jurisdiction in *Owen Equipment & Erection Corp. v. Kroger.*[10] Section 1367(b) codifies *Kroger* by providing that there is no supplemental jurisdiction over claims by a plaintiff against a person made a party under Rule 14. In this circumstance, then, the transactional principle is modified to prevent the evasion of core jurisdictional rules.

So far, we have been assuming that the transactional requirements for supplemental jurisdiction and for joinder are the same. But they might not be. Recall that the tightness of the transactional relationship required might vary depending on context, even if the requirement is linguistically identical. So "same transaction or occurrence" might mean something different if the question is whether preclusion doctrines prevent a party from bringing a claim at all than if the question is whether a claim or party can be joined under the Federal Rules. Jurisdictional transactionalism is at the opposite end of the spectrum from preclusion. Even a fairly loose transactional relationship should suffice to confer supplemental jurisdiction, because allowing a party to include additional claims will generally foster efficiency and party autonomy and will rarely be unfair. (Remember, the question of whether a particular *party* can be added depends on the joinder rules and the doctrines of personal jurisdiction. Once the party is in the lawsuit, the joinder rules and the doctrines of subject matter jurisdiction determine whether a particular *claim* may be brought by or against that party.) As noted earlier, Congress also intended a broad interpretation of the supplemental jurisdiction statute.

What difference might it make if transactionalism is broader and looser in the jurisdictional context than in the preclusion context or even the joinder context? First, the interpretation of Rule 13(a) might vary depending on why the court is looking at the Rule. A court that is asking whether a particular counterclaim is transactionally related to the original claim, and therefore compulsory, to figure out whether it is within supplemental jurisdiction might be inclined to find even a marginally related claim compulsory, because doing so has many advantages and few disadvantages. But if the question is whether a party who failed to raise a counterclaim in an earlier lawsuit should be precluded from bringing it now because it was compulsory in the first suit, the specter of unfairness might incline the court to define Rule 13(a)'s "same transaction or occurrence" more narrowly and hold that a marginally related claim is not sufficiently related to be compulsory.

A second circumstance arises in the gap between joinder and jurisdiction. We know that Congress intended to make supplemental jurisdiction broad and generous. We do not know much about where the drafters of the Federal Rules intended to place the line between compulsory and permissive counterclaims, and we leave it to judicial interpretation. When the rules governing supplemental jurisdiction depended on judge-made doctrines, it made sense to conclude that the "same transaction or occurrence" language of Rule 13(a) should be interpreted the same way as the "common nucleus of operative fact" language of *Gibbs*. Permissive counterclaims were therefore automatically outside of supplemental jurisdiction. But suppose that we read §1367 as broader than Rule 13(a): We might find that some marginally related counterclaims that we would designate as permissive are nevertheless within supplemental jurisdiction. And in fact, at least one court of appeals has done just that. *Channell v. Citicorp National Services*[11] involved a suit brought by consumers under the federal Truth in Lending Act, and the defendant (Citicorp) raised a state law counterclaim that sought to collect the loan balance from the consumers. A pre-§1367 Seventh Circuit case, binding on the *Channell* court, had already held that such a counterclaim was permissive. In *Channell*, the court nevertheless concluded that the counterclaim fell within the supplemental jurisdiction of §1367. The holding only makes sense if we understand that the strength of the transactional relationship that is required to satisfy the principles of transactionalism varies with the context.

Just as with joinder and preclusion, then, the jurisdictional rules depend on transactionalism, but the exact contours are sometimes determined by other factors. What might have seemed like a crazy quilt—joinder under some Federal Rules falls within supplemental jurisdiction, but joinder under others, or even under other parts of the same Rule, does not — should begin to make sense once you start thinking about why we might vary the scope of the transactional requirements.

AMENDED PLEADINGS AND RELATION BACK

You are likely to encounter transactionalism in one other context in your Civil Procedure course. Rule 15(c) allows a claim or defense that is added to a *pleading* by *amendment* to relate back to the date of the original, unamended pleading, if it "arose out of the conduct, transaction, or occurrence" described in the original pleading. To figure out whether to give this language a broad or narrow reading, we need to look at why there is a transactional requirement here and what other principles might be in tension with it.

Rule 15(c) incorporates transactionalism primarily to protect the defendant from prejudice or unfair surprise while still adhering to the principle that cases should be decided on the merits rather than on procedural technicalities. To see this, begin by imagining a typical breach of contract situation, in which both parties might believe that the other has breached. The plaintiff has provided a good or service for which the defendant has failed to pay the full amount, but the defendant believes that the plaintiff did not provide the contractually agreed-on good or service. If the plaintiff sues, the defendant is likely to counterclaim. If the plaintiff does not sue, however, the defendant might not do so either: The defendant might reason that he or she did not get the full value of the contract, but also did not pay the full amount — and the parties are now even.

If we extend this insight to multiple contracts between the same parties, you can see that the defendant's expectations and litigation decisions might be affected by the plaintiff's complaint. So what if the plaintiff sues on one contract, but later wishes to amend the complaint to include a different contract as well? If the statute of limitations has not expired, there is not much problem. Although the defendant might have breathed a small sigh of relief and begun to structure his or her litigation strategy, the defendant knew that he or she was still subject to suit (whether in this lawsuit or in a subsequent one) on the second contract. Allowing the plaintiff to amend the complaint to include a claim on the second contract does not seem unfair.

But what if, between the time the plaintiff files the original complaint and the time he or she seeks to amend it to include the second contract, the statute of limitations for breach of contract has expired on the second contract? Now the defendant can claim unfair treatment: The defendant's interest in *repose* (in knowing that the plaintiff could no longer sue on the second contract) has been disrupted, and his or her litigation strategy might have become fixed at the time the statute of limitations expired. On the other hand, if the statute of limitations bars what might well be a meritorious claim, we have allowed a procedural misstep to trump the merits. Rule 15(c) uses transactionalism to mediate between these two competing interests. The amended complaint will relate back to the original filing — that is, it will be deemed to have been filed *before* the statute of limitations expired — only if it is transactionally related to a claim in the original complaint.

Rule 15(c) thus uses transactionalism to balance two interests that are very important in our legal system: finality and deciding cases accurately. For this reason, Rule 15(c) is likely to fall somewhere in the middle of the spectrum in terms of how broadly or narrowly its requirement of a transactional relationship will be interpreted. Notice also that in the joinder, preclusion, and jurisdiction contexts, transactionalism is a value in itself (we think it is a good idea for lawsuits to involve transactionally related claims). When we modify the principle of transactionalism in those contexts, we do so largely because other values are in tension with the results that would be produced by a purely transactionalist regime. In the context of relation back, however, transactionalism itself is of secondary importance; we require a transactional relationship primarily as a way to mediate between two *other* values. We are therefore likely to find quite a bit of variation in the interpretation of the transactional language of Rule 15(c) at the margins, as different judges balance the competing values of finality (or avoiding prejudice) and deciding cases on the merits.

CONCLUDING THOUGHTS

Knowing how transactionalism works in different contexts — and, more importantly, understanding why it varies — should help you see how the Rules are designed to accomplish numerous and sometimes conflicting goals. There is often no easy or right answer to the question of how the tensions among these goals should be resolved. But that is true not just for transactionalism and not just for the Federal Rules of Civil Procedure. If you take what you have learned about transactionalism and apply it to other interpretive ambiguities in the law, you will be well on your way to becoming a good lawyer.

∽ 8 ∾

Federalism

The architects of any procedural regime will have to grapple with many of the issues we have discussed so far. If the system is *adversarial*, they will face all of them. But the federalist structure of the United States presents a further challenge to a procedural system.

Imagine a country — France, for example — with a single unified government: one executive, one legislature, and a single judicial system. The legislature enacts both the substantive and procedural law, and the courts apply it. Learning civil procedure in such a country might be challenging, as students struggle with changes over time, textual or interpretive ambiguities, linked or cross-referenced rules, the interplay between substance and procedure, and accommodating different goals such as *procedural fairness* or *efficiency*. But some things will be clear. A citizen of France may generally sue another French citizen in any French court that the legislature authorizes, and the suit will be governed by French law, both as to substance and procedure.

In the United States, learning civil procedure is more difficult because of the complications of *federalism*. We do *not* have a single legislature or a single judicial system (or a single executive, either, but that does not matter much for civil procedure). We have more than 50 different systems: one for the federal government, one for each of the 50 states, one for Washington, D.C., and one for each territory and commonwealth. So in addition to the inherent uncertainty and complexity of a procedural regime and its relationship to substantive law, American lawyers and law students are necessarily confronted with the interactions *among* multiple procedural and substantive regimes.

So if a citizen of Tennessee and a citizen of Minnesota get into a car accident in Indiana, the plaintiff has, in the abstract, a choice of at least nine different courts: the state courts of Tennessee, Minnesota, and Indiana, and the federal district courts in each of the three states — one in Minnesota, two in Indiana, and three in Tennessee. Once the suit is brought, there are at least four potential sources of both substantive and procedural law: the laws of each of the three states plus federal law — which might, at least in theory, be legislation enacted by Congress or *common law* created by the federal courts. There is also no particular reason to assume that the same jurisdiction will provide both the substantive law and the procedural rules; a federal court in Minnesota might choose federal procedural law and Tennessee substantive law. Or maybe the plaintiff decides that he or she would like a vacation in Hawaii or that the law of New Hampshire favors his or her case. Are the courts of those states available? Can Hawaii or New Hampshire law govern the lawsuit? It does not end with the choice of forum and governing law. Once the suit is completed, what happens if the plaintiff or the defendant tries to sue again in a different jurisdiction? What if the plaintiff wins in Indiana, but the only way to collect the *judgment* is to seize the defendant's Minnesota bank account?

This chapter is meant to help you understand the complexities of civil procedure that arise from our federal system. We begin with a brief historical overview of the aspects of federalism — often called judicial federalism — that affect courts and lawsuits.

A BRIEF HISTORY OF JUDICIAL FEDERALISM

All of the complications arise from the fact that some two centuries ago, 13 independent colonies decided to unite into a single nation but did not want to give up their separate identities or their sovereignty. It was the genius of the founding generation, led mostly by James Madison, to "split the atom of sovereignty" between the federal government and the states. The Constitution, drafted by a Convention in 1787 and ratified by the state legislatures during 1787 and 1788, tried to separate governmental powers into a federal sphere and a state sphere. But rather than creating a clear and unwavering line between them, the drafters of the Constitution left a fair amount of overlap and a great deal of ambiguity.

The first question the drafters had to confront regarding the judiciary was whether to create a system of federal courts at all. Each state had its own courts, and they were functioning very well, thank you. The drafters agreed without much difficulty that there should be a federal Supreme Court, if for no other reason than to settle disputes among the states.* But what about the ordinary disputes of citizens? One problem was that at least some of the founding generation mistrusted state courts when it came to applying or enforcing federal law. As two members of the Constitutional Convention put it, "[i]nferior tribunals are essential to render the authority of the National Legislature effectual," because "the Courts of the States can not be trusted with the administration of the National laws."[1] Another problem was that few people trusted

---

* In case you were wondering, between 1776 and 1787, under the Articles of Confederation, disputes among the states were settled—but not very successfully—by a complicated procedure that was derogatorily described as "knocking out the brains of the committee" because each side sequentially eliminated potential "commissioners" until only the least controversial remained to decide the case.

the impartiality of state courts when it came to suits between their own citizens and citizens of other states. A third issue was that many of the founders mistrusted state judges and juries — who were seen as likely to interfere with the national economy and national power — and thought that federal judges and juries would be more national in focus.

Nevertheless, some members of the Convention were afraid that federal courts might take power from, or interfere with, state courts. A proposal that the Constitution itself mandate the existence of lower federal courts, the way it does for the Supreme Court, was defeated. Madison immediately proposed the compromise that found its way into Article III and survives to this day: The "judicial power" of the United States is vested in the Supreme Court "and in such inferior Courts as the Congress may from time to time ordain and establish."

Thus, the Constitution gives Congress the power to establish — or not — federal courts below the Supreme Court. Congress did so as one of its very first acts, in the Judiciary Act of 1789.[2] Compared to today, however, the original federal courts had very little *subject matter jurisdiction*. They heard mainly *diversity* cases (cases in which the parties came from different states) and *admiralty* cases (cases that dealt with incidents occurring on the high seas or the nation's navigable waters). Congress did not confer jurisdiction to hear federal statutory or constitutional questions, and indeed did not do so effectively until 1875 — but that is getting ahead of our story.

The basic scheme established by Article III and the Judiciary Act, then, seems to be one in which federal courts are courts of very *limited jurisdiction*, exercising only the power affirmatively granted to them and serving primarily as interstitial supplements to the state judiciaries. But lurking behind this limited view of federal courts is the same dispute that simmered around the federal government generally — especially Congress — for the first 80 years after the adoption of the Constitution. Exactly what was the United States? Was it a nation or a mere confederation of states? The answers to these questions, not resolved until the Civil War, affect the power of the federal judiciary as much as they do the power of Congress. And although the Civil War settled the basic question of national unity, it did not eliminate all disputes between those who view states as quasi-independent sovereigns and those who see them as merely governmental subdivisions. Some of the doctrinal tensions in civil procedure, therefore, stem from attempts to resolve this underlying federalism dispute. For that reason, some of the cases you are likely to read will seem to be more about constitutional law than about procedure.

The men of the Constitutional Convention and the first Congress also foresaw and tried to resolve some of the other complications that might arise in a nation with multiple court systems. One example derives as much from the size of the new United States as from the multiplicity of courts. How far can a plaintiff drag a defendant to answer a suit? In federal court, at least, the initial answer was "not very." The Judiciary Act of 1789 required a federal court plaintiff to *serve* process on the defendant in his home district (which, at the time, was coterminous with his home state) or in any district "in which he shall be found at the time of serving."[3] The question of state court power over noncitizens — which depends in part on how one views the sovereignty of states — was not federally resolved, but was limited by state statutes. Later in this chapter, we will see that courts have had a difficult time with these questions of *personal jurisdiction.*

Another early attempt to deal with potential interjurisdictional problems involved the multiple-suit situation. In a single judicial system, *preclusion* doctrines govern the effect that a court must give to prior judgments.* But what if the first

---

* We have already discussed the general issues of preclusion in Chapter 5 and Chapter 7.

judgment is issued by one jurisdiction and the second suit is brought in a different jurisdiction? Article IV of the Constitution includes the Full Faith and Credit Clause, which tells states that they must respect and enforce the judgments of other states. The first Congress followed up with a statute, the Full Faith and Credit Act,[4] which requires *federal* courts to respect the judgments of state courts. Neither the Constitution nor Congress, however, provided any clear guidance on the preclusive effect of federal court judgments, either in state courts or in other federal courts. That question was left to the Supreme Court to resolve, and the basic answer is that federal common law governs in these situations.

The first Congress also enacted the Rules of Decision Act[5] as part of the Judiciary Act of 1789. That Act — which, like the Full Faith and Credit Act, has remained largely unchanged — provided that "[t]he laws of the several states" should be "regarded as the rules of decision" in federal courts "except where the Constitution or treaties . . . or Acts of Congress otherwise require or provide." The conventional interpretation of this provision is that it was meant to apply state substantive law in federal courts unless there is a federal constitutional, statutory, or treaty provision to the contrary.* (Exactly what types of state law fall within this mandate has been a subject of some controversy, as we shall see.)

As for the procedures to be applied in federal courts, Congress was less perspicacious. The issue is complicated by the separation between common law and *equity*, as discussed in Chapter 1 of this book. The Process Act of 1789[6] and a more detailed substitute enacted in 1792[7] attempted to conform federal procedure for both law and equity to existing procedures, but did so differently for law and for equity. The equity

---

* We return to other possible meanings of the Rules of Decision Act in the last section of this chapter. Modern controversy about the meaning of the Act suggests how much uncertainty still exists as to the founding generation's view of federalism.

solution was both simpler and more long-lasting (surviving until the Federal Rules of Civil Procedure merged law and equity in 1938): Federal courts sitting in equity were to follow traditional rules of equity except as otherwise provided by either the district courts or the Supreme Court. In 1822, the Supreme Court promulgated the first of several sets of equity rules, and federal court equity practice continued to develop independent of state law.

The early history of federal procedure in cases at law was not so smooth. Congress first specified that the procedural rules in federal courts were to be "the same in each state . . . as are *now* used or allowed in the supreme courts" of the state. In other words, the federal courts were apparently supposed to follow the state procedural rules as they existed in 1789, when the law was enacted. (The 1792 act merely said that federal courts should use the same procedures that they had been using under the 1789 act.) What if state courts changed their procedural rules — should federal courts continue to use old state rules or change to the new ones? In 1825, the Supreme Court answered the question: Procedures in federal court must "conform to the law of the state, as it existed in September 1789 . . . not as it might afterwards be made."[8] Congress tinkered with the system in 1828 and again in 1842, but did not change the basic rule that prevented federal courts from following changes in state procedural rules.* Federal court procedure thus grew more and more anachronistic.

In 1872 Congress finally passed the Conformity Act,[9] which told federal courts to apply *current* state rules of procedure in common law cases. Even then, however, the Conformity Act and judicial interpretations of it allowed individual federal courts a great deal of leeway to depart from state rules.

---

* The 1792 act also authorized federal courts, including the Supreme Court, to adopt their own procedural rules in cases at law (as they did in equity), but the Supreme Court never promulgated any such rules and lower courts were reluctant to strike out on their own.

This often meant that any particular federal court followed neither the state rule nor a uniform federal rule. It was not until the adoption of the Federal Rules of Civil Procedure in 1938 that federal courts were required to follow uniform, and distinctly federal, procedural law. Again, however, the long history of the relationship between state and federal procedure helps to explain some of the modern disputes about the Federal Rules.

Thus on questions of jurisdiction, the force of judgments, and substantive and procedural law, Congress took different routes — some more successful than others — in accommodating the difficulties created by the coexistence of multiple court systems. All these choices had repercussions that persist into our own era, as courts try to adapt for the modern United States statutes and doctrines from a time very different from our own.

One further development is worth noting. After the Civil War, Congress proposed and the states ratified the Thirteenth, Fourteenth, and Fifteenth Amendments to the Constitution, collectively known as the Reconstruction Amendments. Two aspects of the Reconstruction Amendments are important for understanding modern civil procedure. First, the Fourteenth Amendment provides that no state may "deprive any person of life, liberty, or property, without due process of law." As we discussed in Chapter 5, the *Due Process Clause* (together with its federal counterpart in the Fifth Amendment) imposes limits on the exercise of jurisdiction by both state and federal courts.

But the Reconstruction Amendments also represented a major reversal of American attitudes about the relationship between federal and state governments. To the extent that some members of the founding generation viewed the states as the primary sources of positive legislation and the state courts as primary guarantors of individual rights and liberty, the experience of secession and the Civil War undermined the legitimacy of that view. The Reconstruction Amendments are widely seen by historians as transferring to the federal government, at least symbolically, both the primary power and the primary responsibility for governing the lives of American citizens. Federal courts, although still courts of limited jurisdiction, took on enhanced authority. Congress's establishment of general *federal question jurisdiction* (in 1875, at the height of Reconstruction) is one illustration of the change in attitudes.

Keep in mind, however, that just as there were dissenters from the views that prevailed in the late eighteenth century, some Americans remained opposed to an expansion of federal power and loyal to the sovereignty of states. Federalism complicates procedural doctrines not only because of the interactions among courts, but because of the continuing diversity of views about the appropriate shape of those interactions.

JUDICIAL FEDERALISM AND CIVIL PROCEDURE: HOW IT MATTERS

Subject Matter Jurisdiction of the Federal Courts

The subject matter of the federal courts is controlled by both Article III of the Constitution and federal statutes. Article III sets the outer limits of jurisdiction: Congress cannot confer on federal courts any jurisdiction beyond the nine *heads of jurisdiction* listed in Article III. But within those broad boundaries, Congress is largely free to shape the jurisdiction as it sees fit. At first, Congress conferred very little jurisdiction on federal courts, and even today the statutes do not give federal courts all of the jurisdiction that is permitted under Article III. The statutory grants of jurisdiction are interpreted and applied by the courts themselves. In addition, in most cases the federal courts and the state courts have *concurrent jurisdiction* (unless Congress chooses to make federal jurisdiction *exclusive*), so litigants have a choice of whether to file in state or federal court.

225

The two most important sources of federal court jurisdiction are federal question (or "arising under") jurisdiction, which depends on the nature of the claim and is authorized by 28 U.S.C. §1331, and diversity jurisdiction, which depends on the citizenship of the parties and is authorized by 28 U.S.C. §1332. Different aspects of judicial federalism are relevant to these two different types of federal jurisdiction. In addition, 28 U.S.C. §1367 permits federal courts to exercise *supplemental jurisdiction* over claims that are related to those properly before it, and 28 U.S.C. §1441 gives defendants who are sued in state court the right to *remove* the case to federal court if it could have been brought there in the first place.

Jurisdiction over claims brought under supplemental jurisdiction, and over cases removed to federal court, both depend on the existence of some claim over which the federal court has *original* or *independent* jurisdiction. (Supplemental jurisdiction also depends on the transactional relationship among the claims, and for that reason is discussed in Chapter 7.) The independent jurisdiction must come from diversity of citizenship, a federal question, or satisfaction of the requirements of one of the other (less important) statutes conferring original jurisdiction on the federal courts. Ultimately, then, jurisdiction over almost every claim brought in federal court hinges on the meaning of diversity jurisdiction or federal question jurisdiction. We turn now to those doctrines.

Diversity Jurisdiction Diversity jurisdiction allows federal courts to hear disputes between citizens of different states (or between citizens of a state and citizens of a foreign nation). It is, as you have just learned, as old as the nation itself. It is based at least in part on a fear that state courts will treat their own citizens better than citizens of other states (or countries). In 1789, this was probably a legitimate fear. The states had been separate colonies and then separate and independent states, each with its own constitution and full-scale government.

Most Americans considered themselves citizens of a state rather than citizens of the United States. During the period between 1776 and 1789, the states bickered with one another over tariffs, land, and trade. In that atmosphere, citizens of one state might justifiably fear that business dealings with citizens of another state might ultimately put them at a disadvantage if anything went wrong and the matter landed in state court, especially because, as noted earlier, there was mistrust of state juries as well as judges.

A second concern was whether state courts might interfere with the growing national economy. Many of the framers were worried specifically that state courts exhibited a bias against creditors, especially (but not solely) out-of-state creditors. This problem was especially acute because some of these creditors were British, and Britain continued to maintain some troops on American soil during the 1780s for the ostensible reason that the United States was not complying with its treaty obligations to honor British debts. Interposing federal courts — and federal juries — between creditors and pro-debtor popular sentiment was a solution to these problems.

The more relevant question, however, is whether any of these fears are justifiable in the modern United States. Are today's state courts likely to mete out impartial justice regardless of the citizenship of the parties? Or are they likely to favor local interests at the expense of outsiders? Do state courts protect debtors and consumers at the expense of creditors and corporations? No systematic study has been able to answer these questions one way or the other. Many lawyers certainly believe that there is reason to fear — or to take advantage of — state court biases. Anecdotal evidence suggests that at least in some parts of some states, outsiders are not likely to fare well in suits against state citizens, and large corporations are at a particular disadvantage.

Two sources are suggested for the possible bias of state courts. Some argue that state judges, who are usually elected, are too likely to be influenced by the need to please state citizens so that they can be reelected. Federal judges, once appointed, serve for life unless they choose to retire. State court judges, on the other hand, usually have to stand for reelection every few years. Justice O'Connor recently noted that "the very practice of electing judges undermines" the actual and perceived impartiality of the state judiciary.[10] Others contend that it is state court juries who are the more likely source of bias.

A few well-publicized examples have fueled a belief that only federal courts can offer a neutral forum. For example, when Cincinnati Reds manager (and former star player) Pete Rose was accused of betting on baseball, he brought suit against Major League Baseball Commissioner Bart Giamatti in state court and got a temporary injunction prohibiting Giamatti from holding any hearing on the charges. The judge who issued the injunction was up for reelection the following year. Giamatti removed the suit to federal court, and his lawyer explained to the federal judge why diversity jurisdiction was necessary:

> In the State Court in Cincinnati, I need not describe Mr. Rose's standing. He is a local hero, perhaps the first citizen of Cincinnati. And Commissioner Giamatti is viewed suspiciously as a foreigner from New York, trapped in an ivory tower, accused of bias by Mr. Rose. Your Honor, this is a textbook example of why diversity jurisdiction was created in the Federal Courts and why it exists to this very day.[11]

When Rose could not get the case moved back to state court, he gave up the fight and accepted a lifetime ban from baseball. Both parties and their lawyers apparently believed that the federal court would be a more neutral arbiter than the state court.

Similarly, in the hearings before Congress on the bill that became the Class Action Fairness Act of 2005, some evidence concerned the tendency of state courts in a few jurisdictions to impose large damage awards in consumer actions against corporations, especially out-of-state corporations. Other anecdotes lament the alleged bias of rural state court juries as contrasted to the more sophisticated urbanites who tend to populate federal court juries because those courts are often located in urban areas.

Without systematic evidence of either bias or neutrality, however, it is hard to know what to make of these accounts. It is therefore no surprise that the need for — and appropriate contours of — diversity jurisdiction is a matter of controversy. The American Law Institute (an influential law reform group) has long urged the abolition of diversity jurisdiction. Congress has responded by periodically raising the *jurisdictional amount* required for diversity jurisdiction, which is currently any amount greater than $75,000. Federal question jurisdiction, on the other hand, has not required a minimum jurisdictional amount since 1980.

Despite the continued existence of diversity jurisdiction, the minimum jurisdictional amount and other statutory limits on diversity seem to reflect its questionable modern foundations. In diversity cases (but not federal question cases), a defendant may not remove to federal court if the plaintiff sues in state court in the defendant's home state, yet a plaintiff is permitted to file the suit originally in federal court in the plaintiff's home state. A defendant also may not remove a diversity case from state to federal court more than a year after it has been filed, even if the plaintiff originally asks for less than $75,000 and only asks for more *after* a year. For federal question cases, by contrast, the only time limit on removal is that the defendant must remove within 30 days of discovering that it is within the federal court's jurisdiction (even if that happens more than a year after the suit is filed). Similarly, the limits on the exercise of supplemental jurisdiction contained in 28 U.S.C. §1367(b) apply only to diversity cases and not to federal question cases.

Judicial interpretation and application of §1332 also seems to indicate some ambivalence about diversity jurisdiction. Since 1806, diversity jurisdiction has required *complete diversity*; that is, no plaintiff may be from the same state as any defendant. Complete diversity is not constitutionally required; Congress may provide for jurisdiction whenever there is *minimal diversity* (any two opposing parties are from different states). Nor is complete diversity explicitly mentioned in §1332. Nevertheless, the Supreme Court has held that complete diversity is required under §1332. The Court has also suggested that in the absence of complete diversity the federal courts have no jurisdiction over the case at all, even as to the claims of parties who are diverse from each other.[12] In theory, then, a court faced with incomplete diversity should *dismiss* the whole case. Both the minimum jurisdictional amount for diversity, and the existence of federal question jurisdiction, on the other hand, are decided claim by claim or party by party, so that if jurisdiction exists for some claims or parties, the court may dismiss the claims or parties over which it lacks jurisdiction and decide the claims over which it has jurisdiction.* Moreover, a court can exercise supplemental jurisdiction over a plaintiff who lacks the minimum amount (but not over a nondiverse party) if his or her claim is transactionally related to that of a co-plaintiff who does meet the jurisdictional minimum. Again, then, the

---

* There is some confusion about whether courts *must* dismiss a whole case in the absence of complete diversity, or whether it may simply dismiss the nondiverse parties. Before *Exxon Mobil Corp. v. Allapattah Servs., Inc.*, 545 U.S. 546 (2005), Supreme Court precedent allowed dismissal of the nondiverse parties. *See Newman-Green, Inc. v. Alfonzo-Larrain*, 490 U.S. 826 (1989). In holding that courts have no jurisdiction at all over cases that lack complete diversity, however, *Allapattah*, without mentioning *Newman-Green*, necessarily implied that the whole case must be dismissed. Many lower courts nevertheless continue to dismiss nondiverse parties and exercise jurisdiction over the claims of the remaining parties. In other words, they view themselves as having jurisdiction over the case, but not over all of the claims.

requirement of complete diversity places significant limits on federal court jurisdiction.

Finally, consider the basic rule that the party invoking federal jurisdiction bears the burden of showing that the case is within the court's jurisdiction. In most cases, this allocation will not matter much, because it will be clear whether the parties are diverse or whether the case arises under federal law. But in some cases it is difficult to tell the citizenship of a party. Many courts seem to put a thumb on the scale against diversity jurisdiction, leaning toward whichever finding of citizenship will defeat rather than confer federal court jurisdiction.

Whether these complicated and sometimes subtle limits strike the right balance depends on one's view of judicial federalism. Those who see the states as "little laboratories" or as bulwarks against overfederalization of our jurisprudence might view diversity jurisdiction as an anachronistic anomaly and seek to curtail it as much as possible. Some strong nationalists, worried that diversity cases distract federal courts from their principal role in enforcing federal rights, agree. Other nationalists, however, distrust state courts and prefer to see diversity jurisdiction expanded. Thus as you read cases and statutes related to diversity jurisdiction, you should not be surprised to find some tensions and inconsistencies.

Federal Question Jurisdiction   Federal question jurisdiction raises a different sort of federalism concern. Instead of concern that state courts might favor their own citizens over citizens of other states, federal question jurisdiction rests on a fear that state courts might favor state law or disfavor federal law.

Some of the fear of state court bias in federal question cases stems from the same sources as the fear in diversity cases: biased jurors or popularly elected judges. The concern is especially acute in cases involving protection of unpopular minorities or the exercise of controversial individual rights. Consider

again the Pete Rose case: If a state judge is unable to stand up
to a local baseball hero, how likely is he or she to stand up for
the rights of unpopular speakers, political activists, or racial or
religious minorities? As one scholar put it, continuing the
sports motif, "Imagine, for a moment, that the Chicago Cubs
announced that from this point forward, they would hire
umpires, unilaterally determine their salaries, and retain unre-
viewable discretion to fire them at any time. Can anyone imagine that we could trust a call at second base?"[13]

But jurisdiction in federal question cases has implications
beyond the generalized concern that elected state judges (or
state juries) might be unwilling or unable to protect federal
rights. Federal question cases by definition require the application of federal law. Presumably, we want the most accurate
and uniform interpretation and implementation of federal law.
Federal judges are in a better position to provide that accurate
and uniform interpretation for several reasons.

First, there are many fewer federal judges than there are
state judges. This means that there are both a smaller number
of likely interpretations and a lower likelihood of a single judge
taking a unique position. Together with the requirement that
the president and the Senate concur on their appointment, it
also means that they are more likely to be the cream of the crop.
Indeed, federal judges are often appointed from the state
judiciary, and one hopes that it is the best of the state judges
who are chosen. And although the vast majority of state court
judges are competent and hard working, it is much easier (and
more likely, simply given the huge numbers of state court
judges) for an incompetent, lazy, or corrupt judge to sneak
onto a state bench than onto the federal bench. As one scholar
put it, "[a]s in any bureaucracy, it is far easier to maintain a high
level of quality when appointing a relatively small number of
officials than when staffing a huge department."[14]

Federal judges are also more experienced in deciding questions of federal law, at least after a few years on the federal

bench. They have lower caseloads and larger staffs, which also helps the quality of their decision making. Finally, their institutional loyalties lie with the Supreme Court and the federal government, perhaps influencing them to try harder to divine the true meaning of federal statutes and Supreme Court cases.

Of course, there are reasons to distrust the federal courts as well. Federal judges may be too insensitive to state interests, and thus may overenforce federal law. The same federal appointment process and life tenure that insulates them from majoritarian pressures may leave them too free of constraints on their decision making. And the relatively recent politicization of the appointment process may yield a federal bench that is systematically biased in one direction or another, but state courts may still vary from location to location.

As with diversity jurisdiction, then, there are fundamental disagreements about the importance of the availability of a federal forum to decide federal questions. One context in which there is some disagreement among scholars (although not among courts) is whether federal courts should have jurisdiction over federal questions that are raised only in the defendant's answer, whether as a defense or as a counterclaim. The *well-pleaded complaint* rule of *Louisville & Nashville Railroad Co. v. Mottley*[15] definitively denies jurisdiction in such cases. Unless the federal question is a necessary element of the plaintiff's claim, there is no federal jurisdiction over the case, even if it turns out that because of a federal defense or counterclaim, the most significant dispute — or even the only dispute — between the parties will turn on federal law.

The rule of *Mottley* is clear but the rationale is not. The rule is not constitutionally required: *Mottley* is an interpretation of §1331, and the Supreme Court has long held that the Constitution permits Congress to authorize jurisdiction over any federal question, including those raised by way of counterclaims or defenses.[16] If it is important that federal law be interpreted and applied by federal courts, the need for such interpretation does not disappear simply because it is the defendant rather than the plaintiff who raises the federal question. One answer is that plaintiffs cannot know at the time they file suit whether there will be a federal defense or counterclaim, and if we allow them to anticipate one, many of the cases filed in federal court will end up involving no federal law at all. But that response does not explain why cases cannot be removed to federal court once it becomes clear that federal law will be an important part of the case, and a number of scholars — as well as the American Law Institute — have occasionally proposed amending the removal statutes to allow removal of these types of cases. However, Congress has never done so, and cases based on state law, but with a federal defense or counterclaim, must stay in state court.

Another area of disagreement involves federal questions that are embedded in a state cause of action. If the plaintiff pleads a claim under state law, but resolution of that claim requires the court to decide a federal question, is there federal jurisdiction? The Supreme Court has adopted different approaches to this question over time, creating a patchwork of inconsistent cases.

The Court first held in *American Well Works Co. v. Layne & Bowler Co.*[17] that "[a] suit arises under the law that creates the cause of action," suggesting that *no* claim under state law gives rise to federal jurisdiction. But a few years later in *Smith v. Kansas City Title and Trust Co.*,[18] the Court approved jurisdiction over a federal question embedded in a state cause of action. In *Smith*, the plaintiff claimed that a corporation had violated state law by making "unauthorized" investments; the plaintiff argued that the investments were unauthorized because they were federal government bonds that were alleged to be federally unconstitutional. Thus, a court could not rule on the plaintiff's claim without interpreting the Constitution. Jurisdiction existed, according to the Court, because the plaintiff's "right to relief depend[ed] upon the construction or application of the Constitution or laws of the United States." Justice Holmes, who had written the Court's opinion in *American Well Works,* dissented because the plaintiff's cause of action was created by state law rather than federal law. Federal courts reconciled the two cases by suggesting that the *American Well Works* formulation was "more useful for inclusion" than for exclusion:[19] A federal cause of action creates federal jurisdiction, but the lack of federal cause of action does not necessarily defeat federal jurisdiction. To complicate matters further, however, the Court denied jurisdiction in *Moore v. Chesapeake & Ohio Railway Co.,*[20] which, like *Smith,* was a case in which the plaintiff's state law claim could not be resolved without examining and deciding a question of federal law (in *Moore,* it was a question of federal statutory law under the Federal Safety Appliance Act).

Two modern cases complete the picture but do not make it any clearer. In *Merrell Dow Pharmaceuticals Inc. v. Thompson,*[21] the Court rejected jurisdiction. The plaintiff's state law tort claim alleged that the defendant had been negligent by failing to label its product in conformity with the federal Food, Drug, and Cosmetic Act (FDCA). The Court held that the complaint did not raise a "substantial" question of federal law, resting the holding primarily — some might say solely — on the fact that Congress had not created any private cause of action directly under the FDCA. But then in *Grable & Sons Metal Products, Inc. v. Darue Engineering & Manufacturing,*[22] the Court found jurisdiction over a federal question embedded in a state cause of action even though there was no private cause of action directly under the federal statute. Grable's property had been sold to Darue by the Internal Revenue Service (IRS), which had seized it from Grable for failure to pay taxes. Grable sued Darue under state law to recover the property, but ownership turned on whether the IRS had given Grable adequate notice of the sale under federal law. The

Court in *Grable* interpreted *Merrell Dow* as applying a balancing test that permits a federal court to exercise jurisdiction over a state law claim if it "necessarily raise[s] a stated federal issue, actually disputed and substantial, which a federal forum may entertain without disturbing the congressionally approved balance of federal and state judicial responsibilities."

If this sequence of cases does not make sense to you, you are not alone. The Court has been inconsistent, but the question is also inherently difficult because it implicates complicated and intersecting questions of federalism. Consider first the approach of *American Well Works*: If no embedded federal question gives rise to federal jurisdiction, then we have lost some of the advantages of federal court expertise and uniformity. On the other had, if *every* embedded federal question creates federal jurisdiction, state courts and state legislatures will often have the power to control whether there is federal jurisdiction over state law claims, because they can choose whether or not to make the violation of federal law an element of the state cause of action. (Think about the *Merrell Dow* case: State law controlled whether violation of a federal statute did or did not amount to negligence.) Neither of these alternatives is appealing. Ultimately, therefore, we are stuck with some kind of more or less strict balancing test. The contours of the test, in turn, depend on both the value that is placed on having a federal forum decide federal questions and the willingness to displace state court jurisdiction over state law claims.

Luckily for Civil Procedure students, however, other disagreements over the scope of federal question jurisdiction tend to manifest themselves only in more sophisticated doctrinal contexts not usually covered in a first-year course. The basic level of agreement is higher for federal question jurisdiction than for diversity jurisdiction, and so the statutes and judicial interpretations impose relatively few limits on the exercise of federal jurisdiction over most federal claims.

Personal Jurisdiction

To decide a case, a court must have both jurisdiction over the particular claims (that is, subject matter jurisdiction) and jurisdiction over the parties (that is, personal jurisdiction, or, as it is sometimes called, *in personam jurisdiction*). As a matter of political theory, no government institution, including the judiciary, can justify its actions as to particular individuals without explaining why it has the right to exercise authority over those individuals. As a matter of practical reality, in most circumstances a court's decision is useful only insofar as there exists the threat of governmental coercion to enforce it, and a government cannot enforce a judgment over someone who is not subject to its authority. Thus personal jurisdiction is really just an aspect of a much broader notion of government power. Because our Constitution divides governmental power, federalism complicates personal jurisdiction doctrines at least as much as it complicates subject matter jurisdiction.

The abstract question of personal jurisdiction arises even in countries with a unified judiciary. First, of course, there is always the problem of citizens of other countries. When should a plaintiff be entitled to force a citizen of one nation to appear before another nation's courts? The possible answers range from "always" to "never," but the ones closest to "always" run counter to our strong intuitions that neither a nation nor its courts should be able to exercise sovereignty over everyone in the world. Moreover, even with regard to citizens of a single country with a unified judiciary, we might expect that considerations such as distance and convenience could lead to limits on the geographic reach of each court; it seems wrong to require someone who lives at one end of the country to come before a court at the other end unless we can point to some reason to litigate the dispute there.

In the United States, the exacerbating effect of federalism arises primarily from controversy and uncertainty about whether a suit in one state against a resident of another state is more like the suit against a citizen of another nation or more like the suit forcing a citizen to travel to the far corner of his or her own nation. The former raises fundamental questions of governmental sovereignty and power and the latter is more focused on fairness to individuals. And the range of views on federalism — on the question of whether states should be treated more like independent sovereigns or more like governmental subdivisions — ensures that there will be wide disagreement about how far personal jurisdiction should reach. Cases on personal jurisdiction (especially the Supreme Court decisions you are likely to read for your Civil Procedure course) are confused and confusing because even the Supreme Court cannot seem to make up its mind on this issue.

The Supreme Court originally considered personal jurisdiction a matter of state sovereignty, holding in 1877 in *Pennoyer v. Neff*[23] that "every State possesses exclusive jurisdiction and sovereignty over persons and property within its territory." Thus, no state could exercise jurisdiction over noncitizens unless they were served with process while inside the state. (States could, however, exercise *in rem jurisdiction* over property located within the state.) But with the growth of a national economy and national corporations, and the advent of the automobile, the *Pennoyer* formulation became more and more impractical. Citizens of one state, both people and corporations, often caused harm in other states.

In 1945, after chipping away at *Pennoyer* for decades, the Court finally abandoned the formalist line drawn by *Pennoyer* in favor of a functionalist analysis. In *International Shoe Co. v. Washington*[24] the Court laid down the basic test that still governs personal jurisdiction. Although courts still have jurisdiction over citizens of their own state (and over noncitizens who are served with process in the state), state legislatures can also create jurisdiction over noncitizens by enacting *long-arm statutes*. If authorized by a state long-arm statute, state courts may exercise jurisdiction over noncitizens who have sufficient contacts with the state to make the exercise of jurisdiction consistent with "traditional notions of fair play and substantial justice." For specific jurisdiction — that is, for claims arising out of the defendant's* contacts with the state — this test has evolved into a two-part requirement: The defendant must have *minimum contacts* with the state, and the exercise of jurisdiction must be fair, taking into consideration the interests of the plaintiff, the defendant, and the state, as well as the shared interests of all the states. Both parts of the test must be met for the court to exercise personal jurisdiction. The test for general jurisdiction — that is, for claims that do not arise out of the defendant's contacts — is somewhat stricter, requiring a showing of "continuous and systematic" contacts (as well as fairness).

These tests are easy to state but very difficult to apply in all but the simplest cases, and the Court's jurisprudence exhibits a great deal of internal inconsistency. Part of the reason is that none of the tests are self-defining, and must be filled out on a case-by-case basis. But a deeper problem lies in the conflicting notions of federalism that underlie personal jurisdiction doctrines. If states are independent sovereigns, then we might expect strict limits on the exercise of jurisdiction over noncitizens: Only if a party has by his or her actions subjected himself or herself to the sovereignty of the state (perhaps through contacts with the state) may the state's courts exercise jurisdiction over him or her. If, on the other hand, states are governmental subdivisions and the United States is more like a unified nation, we would expect that the only limits on the exercise of jurisdiction would relate to fairness and convenience. Moreover, limits in the latter case would more likely be statutory than constitutional, similar to the *venue*

---

* Because plaintiffs are considered to have consented to jurisdiction by filing suit in a particular state, it is only personal jurisdiction over defendants that usually causes any difficulties. In Chapter 5, we described one situation in which personal jurisdiction over plaintiffs is an issue: class actions.

statutes that currently place additional limits on where a suit can be brought even if personal jurisdiction exists in more than one forum. The two prongs of specific jurisdiction, in other words, seem to be based on two different views of federalism. Because the two views are inconsistent, it is unsurprising that the cases applying the test sometimes seem incoherent.

The Court has wavered on its views of federalism and thus on the underlying basis for limits on personal jurisdiction. Even after it abandoned *Pennoyer*, the Court as late as 1980 (in *World-Wide Volkswagen Corp. v. Woodson*[25]) held that doctrines of limited personal jurisdiction serve "two related, but distinguishable functions:" They both "protect[] the defendant against the burdens of litigation in a distant or inconvenient forum," and ensure that states "do not reach out beyond the limits imposed on them by their status as co-equal sovereigns in a federal system." But only two years later, the Court backed away from the latter basis, stating in *Insurance Corp. of Ireland v. Compagnie des Bauxites de Guinée*[26] that limited personal jurisdiction "represents a restriction on judicial power not as a matter of sovereignty but as a matter of individual liberty."

The puzzle, then, is why a doctrine based in personal liberty — grounded in the Due Process Clause of the Fourteenth Amendment — cares about artificial boundaries between states. Why should a defendant who lives in New York City automatically be subject to jurisdiction in Buffalo, New York (some 400 miles from New York City), while remaining immune from jurisdiction in Newark, New Jersey (a 15-minute subway ride across the Hudson River from New York City) unless he or she has minimum contacts with the *state* of New Jersey? Substitute any similar locales, and the result will be the same: A defendant's inconvenience is constitutionally irrelevant* when it comes to suits in the far corner of his or

---

* The choice of forums *within* a state is governed by state and federal venue statutes, and is not ordinarily a matter of constitutional concern.

her own state, and the *lack* of inconvenience is constitutionally irrelevant when the suit crosses a state border. Such results suggest that limits on personal jurisdiction must sound more in state sovereignty than in personal liberty, but the Supreme Court has held just the opposite. No wonder the cases seem confusing!

From a doctrinal perspective, the problem seems to be with the minimum contacts strand of the test for personal jurisdiction. An all-things-considered test of fairness is consistent with the notion that personal jurisdiction limits stem from the liberty interest of the defendant (and is also consistent with most notions of state sovereignty, except the very strongest form represented in *Pennoyer*). But the idea that a defendant must also have minimum contacts with a state is difficult to explain as a matter of personal liberty and convenience. Remember, personal jurisdiction is not about *whether* a defendant can be sued, but about *where*. Why should a defendant care that some artificial line has been crossed on his or her way to the courthouse?

One reason a defendant might care about the location of the courthouse is if it affects the substantive law that will be applied to the case. A New York City defendant might be happier in Buffalo than in Newark if he or she thinks that New York law is more favorable and will be applied in the former court but not the latter. Unfortunately, that explanation will not work. First, limiting the *jurisdiction* of a court seems like an inefficient and roundabout method of constraining which state's *substantive law* will apply. (Think about the fact that federal question jurisdiction is concurrent, and that raising a federal defense does not create federal jurisdiction. Both these doctrines mean that sometimes state courts will apply federal law. We do not have a problem with that, so why should we have a problem allowing New Jersey to apply New York law?) Why not use a notion of minimum contacts to decide which state's law will apply instead of to determine the courthouse in which the trial will be held?

A more fundamental problem with explaining limits on personal jurisdiction by reference to substantive law is that the Supreme Court has, in fact, imposed almost no limits on which state's law can apply. As we saw in Chapter 5, a state may choose to apply its own law in almost any situation, regardless of the parties' connection to the state. If jurisdiction is obtained despite the absence of minimum contacts (as it can be if the defendant consents to jurisdiction or is served within the state, for example), the state is nevertheless permitted to apply its own law to the dispute. As one commentator has noted, this seems exactly backward: "To believe that a defendant's contacts with the forum state should be stronger under the Due Process Clause for jurisdictional purposes than for choice of law is to believe that the accused is more concerned with where he will be hanged than with whether."[27] Such a regime makes little sense, but until the Supreme Court settles on a single consistent view of federalism, we are likely to be stuck with it.

Before we leave personal jurisdiction, we must deal with one last wrinkle. To the extent that limits are based on state sovereignty at all, those limits should not apply in federal courts. Indeed, as a constitutional matter, federal courts do have nationwide personal jurisdiction, limited only by concerns of due process — the exercise of jurisdiction must always be fair. But Federal Rule of Civil Procedure 4(k) dictates that, with rare specified exceptions, a federal court has personal jurisdiction only when a state court in the same state would have personal jurisdiction. Thus, all of the nuances of minimum contacts and fairness apply in federal courts as well as state courts, although they do so as a matter of procedural choice rather than by constitutional command.

In the context of doctrines of personal jurisdiction, underlying disputes about federalism have led not only to complexity but also to incoherence. Lower courts do the best they can to reconcile the Court's conflicting cases and rationales, and to accommodate the interests of the states and the parties. But in the end, if we reject both the extreme limits of *Pennoyer* and the converse of allowing personal jurisdiction anywhere in the United States,* doctrines of personal jurisdiction in a federal system will always be complex and uncertain.

Choice of Law

Federalism complicates one final aspect of modern civil procedure. The existence of multiple jurisdictions means courts may often find themselves hearing disputes that arise under or implicate the law of a different jurisdiction. Begin by considering substantive law. State courts have concurrent jurisdiction to decide questions of federal law. They also hear cases in which it might make sense to apply the law of a sister state: for example, if the dispute arose in another state, or one or both of the parties resides there, or a contract specifies that the law of a particular state will govern. And federal courts in diversity cases hear ordinary disputes about property, torts, contracts, and the like, for which Congress has enacted no governing legislation; therefore, state law governs. Each of these three different situations — state courts hearing federal questions, state courts choosing which state law to apply, and federal courts hearing diversity cases — involves principles of *choice of law*, but each is governed by a somewhat different set of rules.

The first situation is the easiest. When a state court hears federal claims (for example, claims that an employer discriminated in violation of federal law, or that a state statute violates

---

* Nationwide personal jurisdiction has never been the rule in the United States, but it is in Australia, another federal system. *See* Austl. Act. P., Jurisdiction of Courts (Cross-Vesting) Act 1987 (No. 24).

the federal Constitution), it *must* apply federal substantive law. The federal law of employment discrimination does not differ depending on whether it occurs in Utah or in Florida, nor on whether the dispute is litigated in state or federal court. Recall that the Constitution leaves open the possibility of having no lower federal courts at all. The expectation was that if no federal courts existed, state courts would necessarily have to enforce federal law. The Supremacy Clause of the Constitution requires state courts to do so: It makes the Constitution and federal statutes and treaties "the supreme Law of the Land" and requires that "the Judges in every State shall be bound" by federal law.

Second, a state court's decision about which state's law to apply — *horizontal choice of law* — is generally not covered in an introductory Civil Procedure course. Instead, it is usually the subject of an upper level course on Conflict of Laws. But it is helpful to know a few things about this aspect of choice of law. As we have already mentioned, there are few constitutional or other federal constraints on a state court's choice of governing law. A state can apply its own substantive law as long as it has a connection with the case such that the application of forum law is neither arbitrary nor fundamentally unfair. Each state has adopted one (or more) of six different theories or methodologies that judges and scholars have created to handle horizontal choice-of-law decisions. These range from a strong preference for the law of the state in which the court sits to a decision based on which state's law is best or produces the most just results. Needless to say, most of the methodologies contain a great deal of wiggle room, which is one reason that this subject can fill an entire course.

The third question — what law to apply in diversity cases, sometimes called *vertical choice of law* — has most bedeviled the federal courts. By definition, a court hearing a case that is in federal court solely because of the diversity of the parties has no statutory federal law to invoke (if it did, it would be within federal question jurisdiction). So where should it find the governing law to decide the case? The Supreme Court gave one answer to this question in the mid-nineteenth century and changed its mind a hundred years later. Although the second answer still prevails, both scholarly disputes and questions of application still remain. The rest of this section describes this most difficult problem in judicial federalism, known as the *Erie* doctrine.

As you already know, the first Congress anticipated the question of choice of law in the federal courts. The Rules of Decision Act of 1789 provided that "[t]he laws of the several states" should provide the rules of decision (the substantive law), and the Process Act did the same for the rules of procedure. Let us leave aside procedure for the moment, and focus on the Rules of Decision Act.

In 1842, the Supreme Court made a momentous ruling in *Swift v. Tyson*.[28] It held that "the laws of the several states" included only state statutory law, not state common law. Where no state statute specifically governed the dispute, a federal court was free to use "general reasoning and legal analogies" to reach its own decision, even if a state court following state common law would apply a different rule. For almost 100 years thereafter, federal courts developed federal common law case by case, often deviating substantially from the law that would be followed if the dispute had landed in state court. Courts even found ways to ignore state statutory law in some cases. The inherent advantages and disadvantages of a federal forum (discussed in this chapter in the context of subject matter jurisdiction) were magnified by the differences in the substantive law that would apply depending on whether the suit ended up in state or federal court. Not surprisingly, parties aggressively sought to litigate their disputes in the most favorable forum, with corporations sometimes even changing their citizenship by reincorporating in a different state to obtain (or, more rarely, to avoid) federal jurisdiction.

The Supreme Court finally overruled *Swift* in *Erie Railroad v. Tompkins*,[29] interpreting "laws of the several states" to include both statutory law and state common law as declared by its courts. The basis for this holding is a matter of some dispute. Justice Brandeis's majority opinion made three arguments, all of which have given rise to later controversies. First, *Swift* was incorrect as a matter of statutory interpretation. Second, the regime of *Swift* had "introduced grave discrimination by noncitizens against citizens," especially to the extent that it encouraged unfair or abusive forum-shopping tactics (most often by corporations).

Finally, in the most famous and most controversial part of the opinion, Justice Brandeis wrote that the *Swift v. Tyson* approach was unconstitutional: "There is no federal general common law" because "Congress has no power to declare substantive rules of common law applicable in a state." Justice Reed's concurrence specifically disagreed with this last rationale, and later Justices — including, most notably, Justice Frankfurter — sought to distance the Court from it. The Court has never again suggested that the rule of *Erie* is constitutionally required, but Justice Brandeis's reasoning has influenced both individual Justices and particular cases.

Between *Swift* and *Erie* lies the core question of federalism: Exactly where should the line be drawn between state and federal power? We might begin with the Rules of Decision Act itself. Recall the historical background from the first section of this chapter. The founding generation, which first enacted the Rules of Decision Act, mistrusted the neutrality of state courts when it came to noncitizens. But there is a great deal of evidence that many of the strongest proponents of the Constitution (including James Madison, James Wilson, and other prominent Federalists) also mistrusted state legislators, especially when it came to the treatment of out-of-state creditors. Wilson, trying to persuade his fellow Pennsylvanians to ratify the Constitution, asked his listeners how they would feel to have their "property lie at the mercy of the laws of Rhode Island."[30] Based on this mistrust and other historical evidence (including the use of the phrase "laws of the *several* states" instead of "laws of the *respective* states") one scholar has argued that the Rules of Decision Act was not meant as a directive for federal courts to apply state law at all, whether statutory or common law. Instead, he argues, it told federal courts to apply *American* law rather than *English* law, which presumably required federal courts to develop an American, or federal, common law.[31] As a matter of statutory interpretation, then, *Swift* might be closer than *Erie* to the original meaning of the Rules of Decision Act. In any case, Congress did not significantly amend the Act between 1842 and 1938, which makes the Court's statutory about-face in *Erie* harder to justify. Nevertheless, the Court has not wavered from its interpretation in *Erie*.

Leaving aside the historical evidence (which is controversial, to say the least), we are still left with the question of the best interpretation of the Rules of Decision Act. What about Brandeis's concern — later characterized as the "the twin aims of the *Erie* rule"[32] — that the *Swift* interpretation had led to forum shopping and inequities? Forum shopping and the resultant disparate treatment of similarly situated litigants are always possibilities in a multijurisdictional system, and thus arise because of federalism. But unlike many of the other topics we have discussed in this chapter, condemnation of forum shopping and discrimination does not depend much on one's views of the appropriate division of authority between state and federal courts nor on whether states are sovereigns or governmental subdivisions.* Instead, our desire to avoid forum

---

* It is possible to argue, as Brandeis did in other cases, that the value of states as "little laboratories" should encourage us to apply state law whenever possible, but that argument has not played a significant role in the development of the *Erie* doctrine.

shopping is part of our general preference for deciding cases accurately.

But *Erie* does not successfully guard against forum shopping, even if it is strictly applied. The *Erie* doctrine prevents only what is sometimes called *vertical forum shopping*, that is, between state and federal courts. The fact that different states have different laws means that *horizontal forum shopping* is also a troubling possibility: A litigant might choose to sue in one state rather than another to get the benefit of particular laws. A federal court must apply the same state law that would be applied by a court of the state in which the federal court sits.[33] This means that state choice-of-law rules, mentioned earlier, govern in federal court as well. Although this does nothing to reduce the possibility of horizontal forum shopping among federal courts, interaction between this rule and another increases it. Under 28 U.S.C. §1404, a district court is permitted to *transfer* a case to any other district in which it might have been brought, if it is convenient for parties and witnesses and "in the interest of justice." If a plaintiff brings a suit in federal court in State A, whose choice-of-law rules would apply the law of State A, what should happen if the case is transferred to a federal court in State B (if State B's choice-of-law rules would not apply the law of State A)? The Court's answer is that "[a] change of venue under §1404(a) generally should be, with respect to state law, but a change of court-rooms."[34] In other words, the choice-of-law rules of State A still apply. You should be able to see that this leaves plaintiffs with a great opportunity for forum shopping: Even if the litigation should, and eventually does, take place in a federal court in State B, a plaintiff can file in a different state with more favorable laws and then seek a transfer. The opposite rule, of course, would encourage *defendants* to forum shop by seeking transfers to states with more favorable rules. And reverting to *Swift* increases the incentives to shop between state and federal forums, but, by allowing the development of a nationwide federal common law, reduces the probability that litigants will choose among different federal courts based on the substantive law to be applied. In short, in a multi-jurisdictional system, it is not possible to eliminate forum shopping (or even to reduce it very much), only to decide which kind(s) of forum shopping we will allow.

So where does this leave *Erie?* Its persuasiveness may ultimately depend on notions of federalism after all. Two cross-cutting issues can help us. First, we can ask whether a general federal common law is too intrusive on state sovereignty, or too great an exercise of federal power. If so, then *Erie* is preferable to *Swift* regardless of the effects on forum shopping. Alternatively, we can focus on what might be seen in economic terms as a "market for law." Different jurisdictions compete with one another to provide the best or most effective law for some purpose, whether that purpose is attracting corporations or other citizens, providing the most justice, or becoming a magnet for lawsuits. We can ask whether we are more comfortable allowing the states to compete solely with one another in the market for (common) law than we are with allowing the federal government to enter the competition. If states compete with one another, we may end up with a "race to the bottom" as each state tries to attract corporate and other interstate business. On the other hand, if federal common law were to compete, it might end up monopolizing the market and driving out state innovation. The choice between these two potential dangers influences the view of whether the forum-shopping effects of *Swift* are worse than the forum-shopping effects of *Erie* and its progeny. Needless to say, there are no right answers to these questions.

Up to now, we have been considering only whether *Erie* itself was correctly decided. In one sense, that question is irrelevant, because there is no chance that the Supreme Court will overrule it or return to *Swift*. But application of *Erie* is complicated by its intersection with procedural rules, and thus one's view of *Erie* might influence how it is applied. We turn now to that issue.

Like the choice of substantive law, the choice of procedural law arises in three situations: whether a state court should apply the procedural law of a sister state whose substantive law governs, whether a federal court should apply state procedural law when deciding a claim based on state law, and whether a state court should apply federal procedural law when deciding a claim based on federal law. In the first situation, a state court is almost always entitled to apply its own procedural rules to a case, even when it chooses to apply another state's substantive law; and state courts will usually do so. The second situation — which procedural rules federal courts should apply in diversity cases — is one of the most vexing questions you encounter in civil procedure. Federal courts cannot simply apply their own procedural rules, because doing so might in some circumstances re-create the world of *Swift*, in which cases come out differently depending on whether they are in state or federal court.

The year 1938 saw not only the decision in *Erie* but the advent of the Federal Rules of Civil Procedure. Before 1938, *Swift* and the Conformity Act meant that federal courts applied federal substantive law and state procedural rules. After *Erie* and the Federal Rules, federal courts applied state substantive law and federal procedural rules. (The fact that the whole world of federal litigation turned upside down in a single year suggests the complexity and intractability of judicial federalism questions.) The line between substance and procedure, however, is anything but clear. The history of the *Erie* doctrine since 1938 has been a series of cases in which the Court gradually settled on an approach to drawing that line.

The first step of the *Erie* analysis in the procedural area is to determine whether state law and federal law conflict; if there is no conflict, then pragmatically it does not matter whose law applies. If a conflict exists, and the conflict is not clearly about substantive law, the Court eventually settled on a two-track analysis for determining which should govern in diversity cases in federal court. Which track to use depends on the source of the federal law:

- If a statute or a Federal Rule of Civil Procedure creates the conflict, then federal law prevails unless the statute or Federal Rule is beyond the power of the federal government to prescribe.
- If, however, state law conflicts with a federal doctrine not directly derived from a statute or Federal Rule, then the court must decide whether applying the federal doctrine undermines the purposes of *Erie*, either by encouraging forum shopping or by creating inequities. If it does, state law probably* applies.

This multiprong analysis is relatively easy to state (although difficult to extract from the cases) but devilishly difficult to apply. The reason is that most of the tests provide little guidance at crucial junctures, leaving a great deal of room for answers to vary depending on how one allocates authority between the state and federal governments.

Because the analysis differs for the two situations, it is vital to determine whether the conflict derives from a Federal Rule (or statute) or from another federal source. Often, the answer

---

* The caveat is necessary because some lower federal courts still employ an analysis used by the Supreme Court just once, in *Byrd v. Blue Ridge Rural Elec. Coop., Inc.*, 356 U.S. 525 (1958), and seemingly discredited by disuse since then. In *Byrd*, the Court suggested that "affirmative countervailing considerations" — in that case, a preference for the jury rather than the judge to decide disputed issues — might warrant the application of federal law even though that choice might substantially affect the outcome of the litigation. *Byrd* is a difficult precedent on which to rely, both because the Court has never again suggested that countervailing considerations should play a role in the *Erie* analysis and because the Court in *Byrd* rested its decision on multiple grounds and not simply on its "countervailing considerations" analysis. The question is further complicated by a more recent case, *Gasperini v. Center for Humanities, Inc.*, 518 U.S. 415 (1996), in which the Court seemed to apply a *Byrd*-like balancing test without acknowledging that it was doing so.

to this inquiry depends on how broadly or narrowly one reads the Rule at issue. For example, Federal Rule of Civil Procedure 3 provides that "[a] civil action is commenced by filing a complaint with the court." If state law provides that an action is not "commenced" for purposes of the statute of limitations until the defendant is served, which rule should govern a diversity case in which the statute of limitations expires between the time the complaint is filed and the time it is served? The Supreme Court has held in a federal question case (as to which *Erie* does not apply) that Rule 3 means that the statute of limitations is tolled when the complaint is filed.[35] One might therefore think that Rule 3 creates a direct conflict with a contrary state rule in a diversity case. But no. Faced with exactly this situation, the Court held that Rule 3 is not "sufficiently broad to control the issue," essentially interpreting Rule 3 in diversity cases as saying nothing about tolling the statute of limitations.[36] Especially because the Court cautioned that the Federal Rules should not be "narrowly construed in order to avoid" a collision with state law, but should rather be "given their plain meaning," it is hard to justify the differing interpretations of Rule 3 except as a matter of federalism. In other words, reading Rule 3 narrowly in this context allows the *Erie* doctrine more play, limiting the intrusion of federal law on state policies in diversity cases. Other cases seem inconsistent because they interpret Federal Rules more broadly, although the trend as of this writing seems to point toward narrow interpretation. Either way, deciding whether to read the Rules broadly or narrowly is inevitably linked to an underlying vision of the shape of federalism.

The Court's answers to the second question we identified earlier — whether a Rule or statute is beyond the power of the federal government to prescribe — seem to manifest exactly the opposite approach to federalism issues. In *Hanna v. Plumer*[37] the Court concluded that even if a Federal Rule of Civil Procedure has "incidental effects" on the substantive rights of the parties, it is within federal authority as long as it is even arguably procedural. Such a toothless test gives not only Congress, but the Supreme Court as the promulgator of the Federal Rules, almost unlimited power to override state procedural law. In contrast, Justice Harlan, labeling *Erie* "one of the modern cornerstones of our federalism," argued that the majority's standard was too lenient. And as one leading commentator pointed out, the Rules Enabling Act (which authorizes the promulgation of the Federal Rules) provides that Federal Rules must not only be procedural, they also must not "abridge, enlarge or modify any substantive right."[38] The Court's *Hanna* test does not account for the possibility that a rule might be procedural but nevertheless affect substantive rights. Again, the Court's broad reading of federal authority must ultimately rest on a particular, and contestable, view of federalism.

Even determining whether applying federal law (rather than state law) encourages forum shopping or creates inequities is not a mechanical decision, but allows room for the play of federalism. After all, even the most mundane and clearly procedural rule might influence some lawyer to prefer state or federal court and has the potential to create inequities. Courts have generally looked at whether there is a significant potential for forum shopping or substantial inequities, but close cases can go either way.

The third choice-of-law issue in the procedural context is the converse of *Erie*: What law should govern procedure when a state court decides a claim that arises under federal law? It should not surprise you to learn that state procedural rules and federal substantive law apply. But it might surprise you that the Court has never formulated or applied a detailed test, as it did in the post-*Erie* cases, to distinguish between substance and procedure. Instead, the Court has said simply that a state court is not permitted to apply any state rule that overly burdens a federal right, largely leaving the question up to state courts (with only occasional oversight by the Supreme

Court).[39] It seems that the Court is less concerned about state courts treading on federal prerogatives than it is about the opposite, an approach that also rests on views about judicial federalism.

Ultimately, then, federalism matters in *Erie* cases not only because it is the underlying justification for the doctrine itself but also because it influences, at least at the margins, whether state or federal law will govern issues that can be characterized as either procedural or substantive.

CONCLUDING THOUGHTS

The design of a procedural regime is complex enough in a unified judicial system, as the other chapters of this book have shown. Add to this not only multiple jurisdictions but a multiplicity of views on the appropriate relationships among those jurisdictions as well, and you are bound to encounter even greater uncertainty, ambiguities, and inconsistencies. Some students (and lawyers) might find this controlled chaos disconcerting. But as long as litigation depends to any degree on the skill of the lawyer, mastering the intricacies of judicial federalism will give you the opportunity to use your knowledge to your clients' advantage. Whether you are arguing a novel point to a judge, seeking the best forum for a lawsuit, or lobbying a legislature or an administrative agency for a particular legal rule, understanding the theoretical foundations of our federal judicial system will serve you and your clients well.

~ 9 ~

Epilogue: Beyond Civil Procedure

Throughout this book, we have treated civil procedure from a particular perspective: the perspective of how we have, and how we might, design the rules for the American litigation system. Litigation is often viewed as the quintessential work of lawyers. Litigation and trials capture the headlines and the popular imagination. The federal procedural regime, in particular, is both nationwide in scope and imitated by many states. For all these reasons, it is natural for law schools to concentrate on teaching, and for law students to focus on learning, American — and especially federal — civil procedure.

As you complete your introductory Civil Procedure course, however, you should take forward three last insights. First, an introductory Civil Procedure course is just that: an introduction. Your course, and this book, have explored only the tip of the iceberg. If you hope to be a litigator, or even if you are simply interested in the subject, there is still much to learn.

The federal courts confront an increasing number of class actions and other complex cases. These cases can involve hundreds (or even thousands) of parties, hundreds of millions of dollars, and years of discovery. Although we have touched on some basic issues in this book, such cases implicate values and principles well beyond the traditional issues of adjudication. The judgments in these sorts of cases often resemble legislative or administrative problem solving more than they do adjudicative dispute resolution. Courses in class actions or complex litigation explore these important questions.

Each of the steps in the litigation process, moreover, requires a body of knowledge unto itself. Discovery, pretrial motion practice, settlement negotiations, and the like are often taught as separate courses so that law students can build on the knowledge and the skills they have learned in their basic Civil Procedure course.

Similarly, your Civil Procedure course and our discussion of federalism in Chapter 8 consider only the very simplest of questions arising from our federal system. As long as we have multiple court systems, the changing legal landscape and the ingenuity of lawyers and litigants ensure that new questions will keep arising about the relationship among the different courts. A course in conflict of laws (or choice of law) addresses the relationship from the perspective of substantive law: Which jurisdiction's law should apply to the particular dispute? Procedural questions also arise, as when opposing litigants race each other to not just one, but multiple courthouses, asking one court to prohibit or undo what another court is doing, has done, or is about to do. These sorts of questions are generally covered in a course on federal courts or federal jurisdiction. Moreover, both types of federalism questions recur on a global scale, as different countries offer options for both the forum and the substantive law.

This last point brings us to the second idea that you should keep in mind as you move forward in your legal education: The American litigation system is not the only game in town. The globalizing trends of the past half-century complicate dispute resolution in myriad ways. For example, the parties may be from different countries, the evidence needed to prove the case may be located outside the forum's jurisdiction, or a court's judgment may need to be enforced in a foreign country. American litigation can only go so far in resolving disputes with these sorts of international obligations, but more and more, these are the sorts of cases in which many American lawyers are involved. A variety of courses in international law will help you sort through some of these issues.

Additionally, whether domestic or international in scope, litigation is not the only way to resolve disputes. People also resolve disputes through settlement, mediation, arbitration, and a host of hybrid processes that collectively are referred to as alternative dispute resolution (ADR) processes. In all your classes, you read cases that were litigated all the way to a reported decision, typically on appeal. It is easy to forget that such cases are the exception and not the rule. The vast majority of potential legal disputes never reach the courthouse. Of the civil cases that are litigated, only 1.4 percent reach trial. The rest are dismissed, dropped, settled, mediated, or arbitrated. Because ADR takes place against the background of both the substantive law (which gives the parties rights enforceable in adjudication) and the procedural regime (which provides the default enforcement process to which ADR methods are the alternative), it is appropriate to focus on the formal adjudicatory system first. But later courses in ADR and related topics can round out a litigator's education.

Finally, the third and most far-reaching idea to consider as you continue your legal education and career is this: Viewing litigation solely or primarily as a mechanism for resolving private disagreements overlooks its other potential functions. Litigation also establishes the boundaries between the government, which creates legal rules, and its citizens. Lawsuits provide unique opportunities for courts to declare the social expectations under which we should all live. One possible purpose of litigation, then, is to require a public institution, the court, to specify the limits of appropriate social behavior. Procedure is the language of this institution, the way in which we as a society routinize the conduct of courts and hold them accountable to their task. How we structure a procedural system that accomplishes this purpose might differ from the procedural rules we would establish if we limit litigation's purposes to the resolution of private disputes.

We cannot pretend to resolve for each of you the correct way of viewing the purposes of litigation or the role of procedure in it. Our goal has been to expose the fundamental principles of civil procedure, as well as the tensions and conflicting aspirations among these principles, so that you better understand why the American litigation system works as it does and why it stays in constant motion. Our procedural system is not perfect. But the tradition behind modern American procedure stretches back almost 1,000 years. Procedure has always been the particular ward of the lawyers and judges who work within the adjudicatory system. You are the next generation, about to be entrusted with the task of making this system better. The principles you emphasize and the doctrines you fashion from these principles will determine what American civil procedure will become.

Endnotes

CHAPTER 1

1. William E. Nelson, *Americanization of the Common Law* 72-73 (1975). Nelson was describing the law of Massachusetts in the 1770s and 1780s, rather than of England, but the former was derived from (and almost identical to) the latter.

2. Jay Tidmarsh & Roger H. Trangsrud, *Complex Litigation and the Adversary System* 32-33 (1998).

3. Theodore F. T. Plucknett, *A Concise History of the Common Law* 685 (5th ed. 1956).

4. William E. Nelson, *Americanization of the Common Law* 78 (1975).

5. Charles E. Clark, *Handbook on the Law of Code Pleading* 29 (1928).

6. Roscoe Pound, *The Causes of Popular Dissatisfaction with the Administration of Justice*, 29 Rep. A.B.A. 395, 406 (1906), reprinted in 35 F.R.D. 273, 282 (1964).

7. *Id.* at 397, 35 F.R.D. at 275.

8. Roscoe Pound, *Enforcement of Law*, 20 Green Bag 401, 405 (1908).

9. Charles E. Clark, *The Handmaid of Justice*, 23 Wash. U. L. Q. 297, 297 (1938) (quoting In re Coles, 1 K.B. 1, 4 (1907)).

10. Roscoe Pound, *Some Principles of Procedural Reform*, 4 Ill. L. Rev. 388, 402-403 (1910).

11. Act of June 19, 1934, Pub. L. No. 73-415, 48 Stat. 1064 (current version at 28 U.S.C. §§2071-2077 (2000)).

12. Fed. R. Civ. P. 2.

13. Stephen N. Subrin, *How Equity Conquered the Common Law: The Federal Rules of Civil Procedure in Historical Perspective*, 135 U. Pa. L. Rev. 909, 922, 925 (1987).

CHAPTER 2

1. *Mathews v. Eldridge*, 424 U.S. 319 (1976). We have more to say about this essentially economic understanding of due process in Chapters 5 and 6.

2. Fed. R. Civ. P. 1.

3. *See* Fed. R. Civ. P. 26(b)(1)-(2). Rule 26(b)(2)(C)(iii) contains the principal proportionality requirement. In 2006, the Supreme Court also added a new Rule 26(b)(2)(B), a proportionality rule that deals specifically with one category of

information that can be very expensive to retrieve: electronically stored information. In a turnabout from the usual presumption of broad discovery, Rule 26(b)(2)(B) permits a party to refuse discovery of electronically stored information that is "not reasonably accessible due to undue burden or cost." The judge can still order production of this information for "good cause, considering the limitations of Rule 26(b)(2)(C)," but can also order the requesting party to share the cost of disclosure or discovery.

4. Fed. R. Civ. P. 26(b)(1). Until 2000, parties could liberally obtain disclosure or discovery of information "relevant to the subject matter" of the case. The amendment continued to allow such liberal disclosure or discovery of information relevant to a party's "claim or defense"; the amendment constrained only discovery relevant to the subject matter. The distinction between information "relevant" to a "claim or defense" and information "relevant" to the "subject matter" of the case is not an easy one. For some guidance, see p. 123, n.*.

5. Specifically, a party can ask no more than 25 interrogatories, Fed. R. Civ. P. 33(a); and take no more than ten depositions, none of which may last more than seven hours, Fed. R. Civ. P. 30(a), (d).

6. Fed. R. Civ. P. 26(b)(5)(A).

7. Fed. R. Civ. P. 26(a)(1)-(3).

CHAPTER 3

1. Fed. R. Civ. P. 49(b).
2. Fed. R. Civ. P. 49(a).
3. *See* Fed. R. Civ. P. 2.
4. Fed. R. Civ. P. 38(b), (d).
5. *See* Fed. R. Civ. P. 38(a).
6. 396 U.S. 531 (1970).
7. 492 U.S. 33 (1989).
8. 526 U.S. 687 (1999).
9. 481 U.S. 412 (1987).
10. 517 U.S. 370 (1996).
11. *See* Fed. R. Civ. P. 18(a).
12. 359 U.S. 500 (1959). *See also Dairy Queen, Inc. v. Wood*, 369 U.S. 469 (1962).
13. Fed. R. Civ. P. 59(a)(1). Rule 59(a) requires a party to file a motion for a new trial within ten days of the entry of the judgment. An amendment to Rule 59 pending at the time of this writing will slightly change the language in the text ("for any reason for which a new trial has heretofore been granted in actions at law") and renumber the rule to Fed. R. Civ. P. 59(a)(1)(B).
14. Fed. R. Civ. P. 59(a)(2). Rule 59(a) requires a party to file a motion for a new trial within ten days of the entry of the judgment. An amendment to Rule 59 pending at the time of this writing will slightly change the language in the text ("for any reason for which a rehearing has heretofore been granted in suits in equity") and renumber the rule to Fed. R. Civ. P. 59(a)(1)(B).
15. Fed. R. Civ. P. 50(a)(1). The same standard applies to a renewed motion for judgment as a matter of law. Like a motion for new trial, a renewed motion for

judgment as a matter of law must be filed within ten days of the entry of the judgment.

16. For a case that usefully applies these principles, *see Reeves v. Sanderson Plumbing Prods., Inc.*, 530 U.S. 133 (2000).

17. *Galloway v. United States*, 319 U.S. 372 (1943).

18. Fed. R. Civ. P. 52(c).

19. *Anderson v. Liberty Lobby, Inc.*, 477 U.S. 242 (1986).

20. 477 U.S. 317 (1986).

CHAPTER 4

1. *See* Fed. R. Civ. P. 2.

2. 355 U.S. 41 (1957).

3. 507 U.S. 164 (1993).

4. 534 U.S. 506 (2002). As this book went to press, the Supreme Court was considering another case raising the same issue in a similar context. The basic analysis in the text applies as well to that case, *Bell Atlantic Corp. v. Twombly*; however the Court rules will add to our understanding of Rule 8(a).

5. 355 U.S. at 47.

6. 355 U.S. at 45-46. In determining whether a complaint meets this requirement, courts have developed some interpretive rules. Most significantly, a court must assume that all well-pleaded factual allegations are true, although any legal conclusions can be ignored.

7. Fed. R. Civ. P. 12(a).

8. An amendment to Rule 8 pending at the time of this writing will slightly change this language ("an allegation . . . is admitted if a responsive pleading is required and the allegation is not denied") and renumber Rule 8(d) to Rule 8(b)(6).

9. *See, e.g., King Vision Pay per View, Ltd. v. J.C. Dmitri's Restaurant, Inc.*, 180 F.R.D. 332 (N.D. Ill. 1998); *Sinclair Refining Co. v. Howell*, 222 F.2d 637 (5th Cir. 1955).

10. *See, e.g., Carter v. United States*, 333 F.3d 791 (7th Cir. 2003).

11. 371 U.S. 178 (1962).

12. Fed. R. Civ. P. 30(a), (d).

13. Fed. R. Civ. P. 33(a).

14. Fed. R. Evid. 401.

15. 329 U.S. 495 (1947).

16. *See Upjohn Co. v. United States*, 449 U.S. 383 (1981) (declining to decide whether core work product should receive absolute protection).

17. An equivalent to the Rule 12(b)(6) motion to dismiss is the Rule 12(c) motion for judgment on the pleadings. The Rule 12(c) motion asks the judge to examine both the complaint and the answer in dismissing a claim in the complaint. Because the standard for judging the complaint's sufficiency under a Rule 12(c) motion is identical to that under a Rule 12(b)(6) motion, however, the two motions are effectively identical from an issue-narrowing viewpoint. A Rule 12(c) motion is also the appropriate device to use on the rare occasion when a plaintiff believes that, in light of the defendant's answer, the plaintiff is

entitled to judgment (maybe the answer admits all the allegations of the complaint and raises only a spurious defense), or when a plaintiff seeks to dismiss a counterclaim. In these situations, the high bar of the Rule 12(b)(6) motion remains intact.

18. 477 U.S. 317 (1986).

19. An amendment to Rule 16 pending at the time of this writing will slightly change this language ("take appropriate action on . . . formulating and simplifying the issues, and eliminating frivolous claims or defenses") and renumber Rule 16(c)(1) to Rule 16(c)(2)(A).

20. *See, e.g., Acuna v. Brown & Root Inc.*, 200 F.3d 335 (5th Cir. 2000). *See also* Fed. R. Civ. P. 42(b).

CHAPTER 5

1. *Pennoyer v. Neff*, 95 U.S. 714, 733 (1877).

2. *Int'l Shoe Co. v. Washington*, 326 U.S. 310, 316 (1945) (quoting *Milliken v. Meyer*, 311 U.S. 457, 463 (1940)).

3. *See, e.g., Asahi Metal Industry Co. v. Superior Court*, 480 U.S. 102 (1987); *World-Wide Volkswagen Corp. v. Woodson*, 444 U.S. 286 (1980).

4. *See, e.g., Phillips Petroleum Co. v. Shutts*, 472 U.S. 797 (1985) (striking down application of state's law in a nationwide class action, but reiterating that ordinary limits are few).

5. *Mullane v. Cent. Hanover Bank & Trust Co.*, 339 U.S. 306, 314 (1950).

6. *Id.* at 315.

7. *See id.* at 306 (publication sufficient for some parties, insufficient for others); *Dusenberry v. United States*, 534 U.S. 161 (2002) (certified mail sufficient); *Jones v. Flowers*, 547 U.S. 220 (2006) (certified mail insufficient); *Greene v. Lindsey*, 456 U.S. 444 (1982) (posting on apartment door insufficient).

8. 397 U.S. 254 (1970).

9. 424 U.S. 319 (1976).

10. *Id.* at 335.

11. *Lassiter v. Dep't of Soc. Servs.*, 452 U.S. 18 (1981).

12. *See, e.g., Parklane Hosiery Co. v. Shore*, 439 U.S. 322, 327 n.7 (1979) ("It is a violation of due process for a judgment to be binding on a litigant who was not a party or a privy and therefore has never had an opportunity to be heard"); *Chase National Bank v. Norwalk*, 291 U.S. 431, 441 (1934) ("Unless duly summoned to appear in a legal proceeding, a person not a privy may rest assured that a judgment recovered therein will not affect his legal rights").

13. *Parklane Hosiery Co. v. Shore*, 439 U.S. 322, 330-331 (1979).

14. *See, e.g., Conley v. Gibson*, 355 U.S. 41, 48 (1957); *Schiavone v. Fortune*, 477 U.S. 21, 27 (1986).

15. *See, e.g., Carter v. United States*, 333 F.3d 791 (7th Cir. 2003).

16. Judith Resnik, *Managerial Judges*, 96 Harv. L. Rev. 374, 378 (1982).

17. Andrew McThenia & Thomas Shaffer, *For Reconciliation*, 94 Yale L.J. 1660, 1665 (1985).

18. Grant Gilmore, *The Ages of American Law* 111 (1977).

19. 311 U.S. 32 (1940).

20. 472 U.S. 797 (1985).

21. *See, e.g., Epstein v. MCA, Inc.*, 179 F.3d 641 (9th Cir.), *cert. denied*, 528 U.S. 2004 (1999); *Stephenson v. Dow Chemical Co.*, 273 F.3d 249 (2d Cir. 2001), *aff'd in part by an equally divided Court and vacated in part*, 539 U.S. 111 (2003); *Wal-Mart Stores, Inc. v. Visa U.S.A., Inc.*, 396 F.3d 96 (2d Cir.), *cert. denied*, 544 U.S. 1044 (2005).

CHAPTER 6

1. 424 U.S. 319 (1976).

2. A few federal trial courts with specialized expertise in certain subject matters (the Court of Federal Claims is one example) are not geographically confined, but have a nationwide jurisdiction.

3. 28 U.S.C. §1391(a)(1)-(3). The rules of venue for federal cases not founded on diversity of citizenship are contained in §1391(b)(1)-(3). In nearly all cases, these rules are identical to the rules stated in §1391(a). There are also special venue rules that affect corporations, *see* §1391(c). In addition, Congress has enacted literally hundreds of specialized venue rules for specific types of cases.

4. Fed. R. Civ. P. 60(b).

5. 28 U.S.C. §§651-658 (2004).

6. James S. Kakalik et al., *An Evaluation of Mediation and Early Neutral Evaluation Under the Civil Justice Reform Act* (1996).

7. *McNabb v. United States*, 318 U.S. 332, 347 (1943).

8. *See, e.g.*, Fed. R. Civ. P. 1, 16(c), 20, 26(a)-(d), 42(b), 45, 53(a)(3), 65, 71, 78.

9. *See, e.g.*, 28 U.S.C. §1404(a).

10. *See, e.g., United Mine Workers v. Gibbs*, 383 U.S. 715 (1965) (creating supplemental jurisdiction); *Alexander v. Fulton County, Ga.*, 207 F.3d 1303 (11th Cir. 2000) (interpreting joinder under Rule 20 to achieve judicial economy).

11. *See Manual for Complex Litigation, Fourth* (2004).

CHAPTER 7

1. *Restatement (Second) of Judgments* §24(1).

2. *Id.* at §24(2).

3. *See, e.g., Parklane Hosiery Co. v. Shore*, 439 U.S. 322, 326 n.7 (1979) ("It is a violation of due process for a judgment to be binding on a litigant who was not a party or a privy and therefore has never had an opportunity to be heard"); *Richards v. Jefferson County*, 517 U.S. 793, 797 n.4 (1996) (a state "cannot, without disregarding the requirement of due process, give a conclusive effect to a prior judgment against one who is neither a party nor in privity with a party therein").

4. *Nuesse v. Camp*, 385 F.2d 694 (D.C. Cir. 1967).

5. *Donaldson v. United States*, 400 U.S. 517 (1971).

6. There are cases holding that a defendant impleading a third-party defendant on an indemnity claim can join unrelated claims to the indemnity

claim. *See, e.g., Lehman v. Revolution Portfolio LLC,* 166 F.3d 389 (1st Cir. 1999). Under Rule 14(a), an impleaded third-party defendant is able to assert transactionally related claims against the plaintiff. It is not clear whether, once the third-party defendant has done so, the third-party defendant can also assert unrelated claims against the plaintiff. The spirit of Rule 18(a) would seem to suggest so, but the language of the rule is ambiguous.

7. We thank our colleague Steve Gensler for this wonderful analogy.

8. *Owen Equipment & Erection Corp. v. Kroger,* 437 U.S. 365 (1978). *See also Moore v. N.Y. Cotton Exchange,* 270 U.S. 593 (1926) (describing ancillary jurisdiction in terms of a "close . . . connection" between the original and the ancillary claims).

9. 383 U.S. 715 (1966).

10. 437 U.S. 365 (1978).

11. 89 F.3d 379 (7th Cir. 1996). *Accord, Jones v. Ford Motor Credit Co.,* 358 F.3d 205 (2d Cir. 2004).

CHAPTER 8

1. James Madison, *Notes of Debates in the Federal Convention of 1787,* at 319 (Koch ed. 1966).

2. An Act to Establish the Judicial Courts of the United States §§2-3 (establishing districts and district courts), §4 (establishing circuits and assigning district court judges and Supreme Court Justices to staff them), §§9-10 (jurisdiction of district courts), §11 (jurisdiction of circuit courts), 1 Stat. 73, 73-79 (1789) (not currently in force).

3. An Act to Establish the Judicial Courts of the United States §11, 1 Stat. 73, 79 (1789) (not currently in force).

4. 1 Stat. 122 (1790). The modern version is codified at 28 U.S.C. §1738.

5. An Act to Establish the Judicial Courts of the United States §34, 1 Stat. 73, 92 (1789). The modern version is codified at 28 U.S.C. §1652.

6. An Act to Regulate Processes in the Courts of the United States §2, 1 Stat. 93, 93-94 (1789) (not currently in force).

7. 1 Stat. 275, 276 (1792) (not currently in force).

8. *Wayman v. Southard,* 23 U.S. 1, 32 (1825).

9. 1 Stat. 196 §5 (1872) (not currently in force).

10. *Republican Party of Minnesota v. White,* 536 U.S. 765, 788 (2002) (O'Connor, J., concurring).

11. *Rose v. Giamatti,* 721 F. Supp. 906, 910 n.2 (S.D. Ohio 1989).

12. *Exxon Mobil Corp. v. Allapattah Servs., Inc.,* 545 U.S. 546 (2005).

13. Martin H. Redish, *Judicial Parity, Litigant Choice, and Democratic Theory: A Comment on Federal Jurisdiction and Constitutional Rights,* 36 U.C.L.A. L. Rev. 329, 333 (1988).

14. Burt Neuborne, *The Myth of Parity,* 90 Harv. L. Rev. 1105, 1121 (1977).

15. 211 U.S. 149 (1908).

16. *Osborn v. Bank of the United States,* 22 U.S. 738 (1824); *Bank of the United States v. Planter's Bank,* 22 U.S. 904 (1824).

17. 241 U.S. 257 (1916).

18. 255 U.S. 180 (1921).
19. *T.B. Harms Co. v. Eliscu,* 339 F.2d 823, 827 (2d Cir. 1967).
20. 291 U.S. 205 (1934).
21. 478 U.S. 804 (1986).
22. 545 U.S. 308 (2005).
23. 95 U.S. 714 (1877).
24. 326 U.S. 310 (1945).
25. 444 U.S. 286 (1980).
26. 456 U.S. 694 (1982).
27. Linda Silberman, Shaffer v. Heitner: *The End of an Era,* 53 N.Y.U. L. Rev. 33, 88 (1978).
28. 41 U.S. 1 (1842).
29. 304 U.S. 64 (1938).
30. 2 Jonathan Elliot, *Debates in the Several State Conventions on the Adoption of the Federal Constitution* 491 (1888, 1987 reprint edition) (Fri. Dec. 7, 1787) (also found in 2 *The Documentary History of the Ratification of the Constitution* 519 (Merrill Jensen, ed. 1996)). The Rhode Island legislature was notorious for enacting laws favorable to debtors and unfavorable to creditors, as well as for frequent changes of law. It was often referred to as "Rogue's Island."
31. See Wilfred J. Ritz, *Rewriting the History of the Judiciary Act of 1789: Exposing Myths, Challenging Premises, and Using New Evidence* 126-148 (1990). No court has accepted this interpretation, but it indicates that there is still a great deal of uncertainty about the founding generation's views on judicial federalism.
32. *Hanna v. Plumer,* 380 U.S. 460 (1965).
33. *Klaxon Co. v. Stentor Elec. Mfg. Co.,* 313 U.S. 487 (1941).
34. *Van Dusen v. Barrack,* 376 U.S. 612, 639 (1964).
35. *West v. Conrail,* 481 U.S. 35 (1987).
36. *Walker v. Armco Steel Corp.,* 446 U.S. 740 (1980).
37. 380 U.S. 460 (1965).
38. John Hart Ely, *The Irrepressible Myth of* Erie, 87 Harv. L. Rev. 693 (1974).
39. *See, e.g., Felder v. Casey,* 487 U.S. 131 (1988); *Dice v. Akron, Canton & Youngstown R.R.,* 342 U.S. 359 (1952); *Brown v. Western Railway of Ala.,* 338 U.S. 294 (1949).

Glossary

Abuse of discretion. *See also* discretion, standard of review. The standard of review that allows a lower court judge the most leeway. A court of appeals will reverse a judgment for abuse of discretion only if the lower court exceeded its authority.

Accuracy. Correspondence between events in dispute in the litigation and the factual findings concerning those events, where the findings are made after considering relevant information and excluding irrelevant information.

Additur. *See also* new trial, remittitur. A judicially ordered increase in the amount of damages awarded by a jury, which a defendant can accept as a means of avoiding an order for a new trial.

Adjudication. The resolution of disputes by judges and courts.

Administrative proceedings. Hearings and other proceedings before an administrative agency.

Admiralty. Law relating to the oceans and other navigable waters.

Adversarial (adversarial system, adversary system). *See also* inquisitorial. A description of the Anglo-American legal regime, in which the opposing parties rather than the judge are in charge of decisions such as choosing the claims to assert, the parties to join, and the court to file in; researching the law and investigating the facts; and presenting the evidence and the legal arguments to the decision maker.

Advisory (opinion). Not binding; for guidance only.

Affirmative defense. A defense that essentially admits that the defending party acted as alleged, but provides a reason why the plaintiff nevertheless should not prevail; pleading governed primarily by Fed. R. Civ. P. 8(c).

Alternative dispute resolution. *See also* arbitration, court-annexed ADR, mediation. The resolution of disputes by decision makers other than judges or juries in a forum other than a courtroom.

Amendment. *See also* as a matter of course, leave of court, relation back. Changes in a pleading; governed primarily by Fed. R. Civ. P. 15.

American Rule. The rule that each party pays its own attorneys' fees, regardless of who prevails.

Ancillary jurisdiction. *See also* pendent jurisdiction, pendent party jurisdiction, subject matter jurisdiction, supplemental jurisdiction. Jurisdiction that a court had to hear claims over which no original jurisdiction existed, but that were closely or logically related to claims over which original jurisdiction existed; today a part of supplemental jurisdiction.

Answer. *See also* pleadings. A defending party's response to the complaint; governed primarily by Fed. R. Civ. P. 8(b), 8(c), and 8(d).

Appeal. The process of requesting a higher court to correct an error made by a lower court.

Arbitration. *See also* alternative dispute resolution, arbitration agreements, mediation. A process for resolving disputes in which the disputants permit a private third person, the arbitrator, to make a final decision; can be a binding or nonbinding decision, depending on the agreement of the parties.

Arbitration agreements. *See also* arbitration. Agreements in which the parties specify the terms under which they agree to arbitrate their disputes.

As a matter of course. Describing an action that may be taken without the permission of the judge, such as certain amendments to the pleadings under Rule 15(a).

Attachment. *See also* sequestration. A process by which property is brought under control of a court.

Attorney-client privilege. *See also* privilege. The absolute privilege that attaches to communications between an attorney and his or her client, as long as the communication is for the purpose of seeking legal advice or representation and is not disclosed to third parties.

Bench trials. *See also* jury, trial by. Trials held in front of a judge sitting without a jury.

Bifurcation. Division of a trial or pretrial process into two or more separate parts (such as dividing the trial on liability from the trial on damages, or separating the discovery against one defendant from that against another defendants); governed primarily by Fed. R. Civ. P. 16(c) and 42(b).

Case management, judicial. *See* judicial case management.

Case management conference. *See also* pretrial conference. A conference between the judge and the lawyers for the parties, at which one or more techniques to reduce expense and delay are discussed.

Case management order. A judicial order seeking to manage some aspect of the pretrial process, usually entered after a case management conference.

Chancellor. *See also* chancery, equity. An advisor to the king, who originally controlled access to the royal courts and later decided cases outside the jurisdiction of the courts of law.

Chancery. *See also* chancellor, equity. The court of the chancellor, which decided cases outside the jurisdiction of the courts of law.

Choice of law. *See also* horizontal choice of law, vertical choice of law. The determination of which jurisdiction's substantive law governs, often difficult if the case has connections to multiple jurisdictions.

Civil law (civilian law). *See also* common law, inquisitorial. A legal regime in which judges rely only on statutes or codes rather than on prior cases as a source of law, typically employing an inquisitorial rather than adversarial method for adjudication.

Civilian. *See* civil law (civilian law).

Claim. *See also* counterclaim, cross-claim. The formal allegation of a legal wrong.

Claim joinder. *See also* joinder, party joinder, permissive joinder. Bringing more than one claim in the same lawsuit; governed primarily by Fed. R. Civ. P. 18.

Claim preclusion. *See also* claim splitting; merger and bar, preclusion (preclusive), res judicata. A prohibition on bringing a claim because it was or should have been litigated in a prior lawsuit.

Claim splitting. *See also* claim preclusion, merger and bar, preclusion (preclusive), res judicata. Attempting to bring related claims in two separate lawsuits; prohibited in most circumstances by all American jurisdictions.

Class action. *See also* class members, class representative, mandatory class action, opt-out class action. A lawsuit brought by or against a representative party who represents similarly situated plaintiffs or defendants; governed primarily by Fed. R. Civ. P. 23.

Class members. *See also* class action, class representative. All of the plaintiffs or defendants who are represented in a class action.

Class representative. *See also* class action, class members. The plaintiff or defendant who represents the class members in a class action, and whose name appears on the case.

Clear error. *See also* standard of review. Standard under which an appellate court affords great deference to a trial court's findings of fact.

Code pleading. *See also* fact pleading, Field Code, issue pleading, notice pleading. A form of pleading, governed by legislatively enacted codes, that stressed the presentation of facts rather than the presentation of issues; abandoned in the federal system with the adoption of the Federal Rules of Civil Procedure in 1938, it is still in use in some states.

Collateral estoppel. *See also* defensive non-mutual issue preclusion, issue preclusion, mutuality, offensive non-mutual issue preclusion, preclusion (preclusive), res judicata. A prohibition on relitigating issues that have been previously litigated in connection with a different claim.

Common law. *See also* civil law (civilian law). A legal regime in which judges rely on prior cases in determining the substantive content of the law.

Complaint. *See also* pleadings. The plaintiff's initial pleading, containing the claims against the defendant; governed primarily by Fed. R. Civ. P. 8(a) and 9.

Complete diversity. *See also* diversity jurisdiction, minimal diversity. The jurisdictional requirement (in certain federal court cases) that no plaintiff be a citizen of the same state as any defendant.

Compulsory counterclaim. *See also* counterclaim, permissive counterclaim. A counterclaim that is forfeited if not brought; governed primarily by Fed. R. Civ. P. 13(a).

Conclusions of law. *See also* bench trials, factual findings, findings, mixed questions of law and fact. The legal principles that a trial judge uses to resolve a dispute in a bench trial; governed by Fed. R. Civ. P. 52(a).

Concurrent jurisdiction. *See also* exclusive jurisdiction, subject matter jurisdiction. The existence of jurisdiction in both state and federal courts, allowing the parties to litigate in either set of courts.

Contribution. *See also* implead (impleader), indemnification. The claim that another person is responsible for a portion of the defendant's liability to the plaintiff, because that person also caused the plaintiff's harm.

Core work product. *See also* work-product doctrine. The mental impressions, conclusions, opinions, or legal theories of an attorney; protected under Fed. R. Civ. P. 26(b)(3).

Counterclaim. *See also* compulsory counterclaim, permissive counterclaim. A claim raised by a defending party against an opposing party; governed primarily by Fed. R. Civ. P. 13.

Court-annexed ADR. *See also* alternative dispute resolution. An alternative method of dispute resolution that a court sponsors and makes available to litigants as a means of avoiding adjudication.

Court of Chancery. *See* chancery.

Courtiers. French for advisors to the king; the derivation of the English word "court."

Cross-claim. A claim by a party against a co-party, that is, against a party on the same side of the lawsuit; governed primarily by Fed. R. Civ. P. 13(g).

Cross-examination. Examination of a witness — at trial or in a deposition — by a party other than the party who called the witness.

Damages. The payment of money in compensation for a harm.

Default judgment. A judgment issued against a defending party who does not respond to or contest a lawsuit.

Defendant. The party who responds to the plaintiff's claims, and from whom the plaintiff typically is seeking some remedy, in a lawsuit.

Defensive non-mutual issue preclusion. *See also* collateral estoppel, issue preclusion, mutuality, offensive non-mutual issue preclusion. The prohibition against a plaintiff relitigating an issue that it had previously litigated against a different defendant.

De novo review. *See also* standard of review . Review of a lower court's decision that gives no deference to that decision.

Deposition. *See also* discovery. An oral or written examination of a witness prior to trial; governed primarily by Fed. R. Civ. P. 27, 28, 30, 31, and 32.

Direct examination. The first examination of a witness — at trial or in a deposition — by the party who called the witness.

Directed verdict. *See also* judgment as a matter of law, judgment notwithstanding the verdict, renewed motion for judgment as a matter of law. The former name of the device now generally called judgment as a matter of law.

Disclosure. *See also* discovery, discovery request, initial mandatory disclosure, relevance. The process by which one party must provide certain information relevant to a lawsuit to another party without awaiting a discovery request for that information from the other party; primarily governed by Fed. R. Civ. P. 26(a).

Discovery. *See also* deposition, disclosure, discovery request, interrogatories, motion to compel, privilege, proportionality. The process by which one party can obtain, on request, relevant, nonprivileged, and proportional information concerning the lawsuit from another party or a third person; primarily governed by Fed. R. Civ. P. 26-37 and 45.

Discovery request. *See also* discovery. A party's demand to obtain information relevant to a lawsuit.

Discretion. *See also* abuse of discretion. The authority of a judge to make a particular decision with few or no legal constraints. One example is the decision of what sanctions to impose on a party who has violated Fed. R. Civ. P. 11.

Dismiss (dismissal). The termination of a lawsuit by judicial order.

Diversity jurisdiction. *See also* complete diversity, federal question jurisdiction, minimal diversity, subject matter jurisdiction. Subject matter jurisdiction in the federal courts based on the citizenship of the parties rather than on the source of the legal claims.

Due process (due process of law). *See also* Due Process Clause, notice, opportunity to be heard. Constitutionally sufficient procedural protections.

Due Process Clause. *See also* due process. The clause, in both the Fifth and Fourteenth Amendments to the United States Constitution, that prohibits the taking of life, liberty, or property without due process of law.

Efficiency. When used to speak of legal procedures, the idea that courts should maximize social welfare by minimizing the costs of litigation and the costs caused by erroneous decisions.

Equity. *See also* chancellor, chancery. A name for claims or remedies that were not originally within the authority of the English courts of law, but were instead decided in the Court of Chancery.

Ex parte. Involving only one party to a lawsuit, such as an ex parte order (an order made without hearing from both sides) or an ex parte communication (a private communication from one party to the judge).

Exclusive jurisdiction. *See also* concurrent jurisdiction, subject matter jurisdiction. The congressional limitation of jurisdiction in particular cases to the federal courts, preventing state courts from hearing those cases.

Fact finder. The person or persons who determine which disputed facts are true; in adjudication, either a judge or a jury.

Fact pleading. *See also* code pleading, issue pleading, notice pleading. Pleading that focuses on presentation of the facts.

Factual disputes. The disagreements among the parties about which events actually occurred, or will occur, that bear on the resolution of the lawsuit.

Factual findings. *See also* bench trials, conclusions of law, fact finder, factual disputes, findings, mixed questions of law and fact. The fact finder's conclusions about which events actually occurred, or will occur, that bear on the resolution of the lawsuit; in bench trials, governed primarily by Fed. R. Civ. P. 52(a).

Federal question jurisdiction. *See also* diversity jurisdiction, subject matter jurisdiction, well-pleaded complaint rule. Subject matter jurisdiction in the federal courts based on the federal derivation of the legal claims rather than on the citizenship of the parties.

Federalism. The interrelationship between the state and federal governments, and among the states.

Field Code. *See also* code pleading. The first major pleading code, written by David Dudley Field and enacted in New York in 1848.

Final judgment rule. A doctrine that prohibits a party from filing an appeal from an adverse ruling until the final judgment has been entered in the case.

Final pretrial conference. *See also* final pretrial order, judicial case management. A conference between the judge and the lawyers or parties conducted shortly before trial, during which the plan for the trial is finalized; governed primarily by Fed. R. Civ. P. 16(d) and (e).

Final pretrial order. *See also* final pretrial conference judicial case management. An order from the court, usually entered after the final pretrial conference, that governs the course of the trial.

Findings. *See also* conclusions of law, factual findings, mixed questions of law and fact. The determinations about the facts and mixed questions of law and fact made by a judge or jury to resolve a disputed mater in a case.

Formal sufficiency. *See also* answer, complaint, pleadings, substantive sufficiency. The compliance of a pleading with the requirements of the rules for pleading, such as the requirements of simplicity and brevity in Fed. R. Civ. P. 8.

Forum non conveniens. A doctrine that allows a court to dismiss a case because it would be more conveniently and appropriately litigated in another jurisdiction.

General verdict. *See also* general verdict accompanied by interrogatories, special verdict, verdict. A jury verdict that specifies only the winning party and the amount of damages (if any).

General verdict accompanied by interrogatories. *See also* general verdict, special verdict, verdict. A jury verdict that specifies the winning party and the amount of damages (if any), and also answers other questions that the judge submitted to the jury; governed primarily by Fed. R. Civ. P. 49(b).

Heads of jurisdiction. The listing in Article III of the United States Constitution of the types of cases that federal courts can hear.

Heightened pleading. *See also* notice pleading. Requiring a party to plead with greater detail or specificity.

Horizontal choice of law. *See also* choice of law, vertical choice of law. Choice of law among different states, as opposed to vertical choice of law, which is between state law and federal law.

Horizontal forum shopping. *See also* choice of law, horizontal choice of law, vertical forum shopping. Litigants choosing among courts (whether state or federal) in different states because of a perceived advantage in particular courts.

Implead (impleader). See also contribution, indemnification, party joinder, third-party claim, third-party defendant. The act of a defending party bringing a third party into the case because the defending party alleges that the third party is liable to the defending party if the defending party is liable to the complaining party; governed primarily by Fed. R. Civ. P. 14.

Indemnification. *See also* contribution, implead (impleader). A claim that another party is liable to cover all of a defending party's liability.

Independent jurisdiction. *See also* subject matter jurisdiction, supplemental jurisdiction. Federal court jurisdiction over a claim, independent of whether it is related to another claim over which the court has jurisdiction.

Indispensability. The determination that a party who cannot be joined is so vital to the resolution of the case that the case must be dismissed due to that party's absence; governed primarily by Fed. R. Civ. P. 19(b).

Initial mandatory disclosure. *See also* disclosure. The disclosures that a party must make to other parties early in the case; governed primarily by Fed. R. Civ. P. 26(a)(1).

Injunction. *See also* equity, permanent injunction, preliminary injunction, temporary restraining order. A court order requiring a party to act or refrain from acting.

In personam jurisdiction. *See also* in rem jurisdiction, personal jurisdiction. Jurisdiction over a person, for claims unrelated to claims of ownership or possession in a specific piece of property that is brought within a court's jurisdiction.

Inquisitorial. *See also* adversarial (adversarial system, adversary system). A description of legal regimes in which the judge, rather than the opposing parties, is in charge of developing the factual and legal issues in the case.

In rem jurisdiction. *See also* in personam jurisdiction. Jurisdiction over a specific piece of property, enabling the court to decide disputes relating to ownership or possession of the property even if it would not otherwise have jurisdiction over the parties who claim an interest in the property.

Instruct (instructions). The judge's directions to the jury.

Interlocutory appeal. An appeal that is filed before the case has concluded and a final judgment has been entered in the trial court.

Interrogatories. *See also* discovery. Written questions directed by a party to another party, prior to trial; governed primarily by Fed. R. Civ. P. 33.

Intervention. *See also* intervention of right, party joinder, permissive intervention. The voluntary act of a third party in joining a lawsuit already filed; governed primarily by Fed. R. Civ. P. 24.

Intervention of right. *See also* intervention, permissive intervention. The entitlement of a third party to join a lawsuit already filed; governed primarily by Fed. R. Civ. P. 24(a).

Issue pleading. *See also* code pleading, fact pleading, notice pleading. Pleading focused on presenting the legal issues to be decided.

Issue preclusion. *See also* collateral estoppel, defensive non-mutual issue preclusion, mutuality, offensive non-mutual issue preclusion, preclusion (preclusive), res judicata. The prohibition on relitigating an issue that was previously litigated.

JNOV. *See* judgment notwithstanding the verdict.

Joinder. *See also* claim joinder, party joinder, permissive joinder. The joining of multiple claims or parties in a single lawsuit.

Judgment. The final decision of a court on the merits of a claim or case.

Judgment as a matter of law. *See also* directed verdict, judgment notwithstanding the verdict, renewed motion for judgment as a matter of law, scintilla rule. A judgment in favor of a party issued by a judge in a jury trial; either preempting or displacing the jury's verdict; primarily governed by Fed. R. Civ. P. 50.

Judgment on partial findings. The equivalent of a judgment as a matter of law in a case tried to a judge; a judgment issued in favor of a party before the conclusion of a trial before a judge; primarily governed by Fed. R. Civ. P. 52(c).

Judgment non obstante veredicto. *See* non obstante veredicto.

Judgment notwithstanding the verdict. *See also* directed verdict, judgment as a matter of law, renewed motion for judgment as a matter of law. Formerly, a judgment in favor of a party issued by a judge in a jury trial, displacing the verdict issued by the jury; this device now called judgment as a matter of law in the federal courts.

Judicial case management. *See also* final pretrial order, managerial judging, scheduling conference, scheduling order. The theory that judges should actively attempt, during the pretrial process, to help the parties fulfill their adversarial responsibilities to gather evidence and shape the legal issues; governed primarily by Fed. R. Civ. P. 16.

Jurisdiction. *See also* personal jurisdiction, subject matter jurisdiction. The authority of a court to decide a case.

Jurisdiction over the person. *See* personal jurisdiction.

Jurisdictional amount. *See also* diversity jurisdiction. The statutory amount that must be in controversy for a case to be within federal court diversity jurisdiction.

Jury, trial by. *See also* bench trials, jury demand, jury nullification. A trial to a jury rather than to a judge.

Jury demand. *See also* jury, trial by. A party's formal request for a trial to a jury.

Jury nullification. *See also* jury, trial by. A jury verdict based on the jury's disagreement with the applicable law rather than on factual findings.

Law French. The language used in old English courts after the Norman invasion, from which many of our legal words are derived.

Leave of court. Permission of the judge.

Limited jurisdiction. *See also* subject matter jurisdiction. Authority to decide only specified types of cases; federal courts are courts of limited jurisdiction because they may only decide the types of cases that are specified in both Article III of the United States Constitution and federal statutes.

Long-arm statutes. Statutes conferring personal jurisdiction over persons outside the geographic boundaries of a state.

Managerial judging. *See also* judicial case management. The actions of a judge who engages in judicial case management.

Mandatory class action. *See also* class action, class members, opt-out class action. A class action in which the class members lack the ability leave the class, thus binding them to any judgment entered in the case; governed primarily by Fed. R. Civ. P. 23(b)(1)-(2).

Mandatory disclosure. *See* disclosure.

Master of the complaint. The principle that, within the legal constraints of the rules of joinder, jurisdiction, and venue, the plaintiff decides the claims and parties that should be joined, and the court in which the case should be filed; usually regarded as an optimal attribute of an adversarial system.

Matter of course. *See* as a matter of course.

Mediation. *See also* alternative dispute resolution, arbitration, settlement. A dispute-resolution process in which a neutral third party tries to facilitate a settlement between the disputants.

Merger and bar. *See also* claim preclusion, preclusion (preclusive), res judicata. An older name for claim preclusion: A prohibition on bringing a claim because it was or should have been litigated in a prior lawsuit. If the party won the first lawsuit, the subsequent claim is merged into the first judgment, and if the party lost the first lawsuit, the subsequent claim is barred by the first judgment.

Minimal diversity. *See also* complete diversity, diversity jurisdiction. Less than complete diversity. At least one plaintiff and one defendant are citizens of different states, but at least one plaintiff and one defendant are citizens of the same state.

Minimum contacts. *See also* personal jurisdiction. Sufficient connection between a party and a forum to allow that forum to exercise personal jurisdiction over that party.

Mixed questions of law and fact. *See also* conclusions of law, factual findings; findings. An issue determined by a judge or jury that is factual in nature but also controls the determination of a relevant legal matter; for example, a finding of "negligence," which both determines factually the nature of the defendant's conduct and establishes an element of the plaintiff's legal claim.

Moot (mootness). No longer a live controversy.

Motion. A request directed to a judge and seeking an order or other relief from the judge.

Motion for judgment as a matter of law. *See* judgment as a matter of law.

Motion for new trial. *See* new trial.

Motion to compel. *See also* disclosure, discovery. A motion asking a judge to order another party or third person to produce information that the party or person has not produced during the disclosure or discovery process, despite being under an alleged obligation to do so.

Motion to dismiss. *See* dismiss (dismissal).

Mutuality. *See also* defensive non-mutual issue preclusion, issue preclusion, offensive non-mutual issue preclusion, preclusion. In preclusion doctrines, treating both parties alike, even if one was a party to a previous lawsuit and one was not.

Neutral decision maker. *See also* due process, Due Process Clause. A person not affiliated with any of the parties, who will presumably make an impartial decision; required by the Due Process Clause.

New trial. A trial ordered after a court determines that a legal error impermissibly affected the result in an earlier trial concerning the same dispute; governed in part by Fed. R. Civ. P. 59.

Non obstante veredicto. *See also* judgment notwithstanding the verdict. Latin for notwithstanding the verdict, the source of the abbreviation JNOV for judgment notwithstanding the verdict.

Notice. *See also* due process, Due Process Clause, notice pleading, opportunity to be heard. Providing a party with the information that a court is going to take an action that might affect the party's legal rights.

Notice pleading. *See also* code pleading, fact pleading, issue pleading. Pleading focused on stating the parties' legal and factual allegations in very brief terms that do no more than put an opposing party on notice of the general outline of the party's claims or defenses.

Object (objection). *See also* discovery. The assertion that the disclosure, discovery, or examination of a party seeks information that should not, under governing law, be disclosed.

Offensive non-mutual issue preclusion. *See also* collateral estoppel, defensive non-mutual issue preclusion, issue preclusion, mutuality, preclusion. The prohibition against a defendant relitigating an issue that it had previously litigated against a different plaintiff.

Officer of the court. Attorney.

Opportunity to be heard. *See also* due process, Due Process Clause, notice. A constitutionally protected right, under the Due Process Clause, as a prerequisite to judicial action affecting any person's legal rights.

Opt-out class action. *See also* class action, mandatory class action. A class action in which the class members are given an opportunity to leave the class, after which they are no longer parties in the case and cannot be bound by the judgment entered in the case; governed primarily by Fed. R. Civ. P. 23(b)(3).

Order to show cause. A judicial order requiring a person to present arguments why a proposed judicial action should not be taken.

Original jurisdiction. *See* independent jurisdiction.

Party (parties). *See also* defendant, plaintiff, third-party defendant. The participant(s) in a lawsuit.

Party joinder. *See also* implead (impleader), intervention, joinder, permissive joinder. The joining of multiple parties in a single lawsuit; governed primarily by Fed. R. Civ. P. 13(g), 14, and 19–24.

Pendent jurisdiction. *See also* ancillary jurisdiction, independent jurisdiction, pendent party jurisdiction, subject matter jurisdiction, supplemental jurisdiction. Federal court jurisdiction over a party's claims that are related to claims over which a federal court has independent jurisdiction, but that are not themselves within the subject matter jurisdiction of the federal courts; now included within supplemental jurisdiction.

Pendent party jurisdiction. *See also* ancillary jurisdiction, independent jurisdiction, pendent jurisdiction, subject matter jurisdiction, supplemental jurisdiction. Federal court jurisdiction over the claims of a party that are related to the claims of another party, when a federal court has independent jurisdiction over the claims of one party but does not have independent jurisdiction over the claims of the other party; now included within supplemental jurisdiction.

Permanent injunction. *See also* equity, injunction, preliminary injunction, temporary restraining order. A final judicial order requiring a party to act or refrain from acting.

Permissive counterclaim. *See also* counterclaim, compulsory counterclaim. A counterclaim that may but need not be brought; governed primarily by Fed. R. Civ. P. 13(b).

Permissive intervention. *See also* intervention, intervention of right. Intervention at the discretion of the judge; governed primarily by Fed. R. Civ. P. 24(b).

Permissive joinder. *See also* claim joinder, joinder; party joinder. Party or claim joinder that is permitted but not required.

Personal jurisdiction. *See also* due process, Due Process Clause, minimum contacts, notice, opportunity to be heard. The power of a court to exercise authority over a person.

Petition. A formal request for official action.

Plaintiff. The complaining party in a lawsuit.

Pleadings. *See also* answer, complaint, reply, response (respond). The formal papers filed in a case that set out the allegations of a party; under Fed. R. Civ. P. 7, only complaints, answers, and replies are pleadings.

Precedent. *See also* stare decisis. Prior decisions by the same court or a court that is superior in the judicial hierarchy.

Preclusion (preclusive). *See also* claim preclusion, collateral estoppel, issue preclusion, res judicata. The doctrine that governs the effect of a prior lawsuit on subsequent suits involving some or all of the same parties.

Prejudice. Harm to one's ability to adequately prosecute one's case.

Preliminary injunction. *See also* equity, injunction, permanent injunction, temporary restraining order. A judicial order requiring a party to act or refrain from acting while the case is pending.

Pretrial (process). *See also* disclosure, discovery, judicial case management. The period between the initiation of the lawsuit and the beginning of trial.

Pretrial conference. *See also* final pretrial conference, judicial case management, scheduling conference. Any conference between the judge and the lawyers before the trial, including but not limited to the scheduling conference and the final pretrial conference, concerning the management of the case; governed primarily by Fed. R. Civ. P. 16.

Prima facie case. Production of sufficient evidence to shift the burden of production to the opposing party.

Privilege. *See also* attorney-client privilege, discovery, scope of discovery. Protection of information from disclosure or discovery.

Privity (privies). A relationship between two parties that is sufficient to bind one by the acts of the other.

Procedural fairness. *See also* due process, notice, opportunity to be heard. The ability of a party to participate in an appropriate way in a lawsuit that affects his or her interests.

Process. *See* due process.

Proportionality. *See also* discovery, relevance, scope of discovery. The requirement that the potential benefit of compliance with a discovery request outweighs the burden of producing the requested material.

Quash. To invalidate an official document.

Relation back. *See also* amendment. To deem a later-filed document as having been filed at an earlier time.

Relevance (relevant). *See also* disclosure, discovery, scope of discovery. The ability of a piece of evidence to help prove or disprove a disputed matter of consequence to a lawsuit.

Remittitur. *See also* additur, new trial. A judicially ordered decrease in the amount of damages awarded by a jury, which a plaintiff can accept as a means of avoiding an order for a new trial.

Removal (remove). *See also* subject matter jurisdiction. Moving a case from state court to federal court pursuant to federal statute.

Renewed motion for judgment as a matter of law. *See also* directed verdict, judgment as a matter of law, judgment notwithstanding the verdict. A request that a judge overturn a jury's verdict and issue judgment for the losing party, when an earlier motion has sought judgment prior to the jury's verdict; governed primarily by Fed. R. Civ. P. 50(b).

Reply. *See also* pleadings. The complaining party's response to the defendant's answer, if ordered by a judge.

Repose. The interest in not having the status quo disturbed by a lawsuit, an interest protected by statutes of limitations.

Res judicata. *See also* claim preclusion, collateral estoppel, issue preclusion, preclusion. Another name for preclusion generally (the doctrine that governs the effect of a prior lawsuit on subsequent suits involving some or all of the same parties) or for claim preclusion in particular (prohibition on bringing a claim because it was or should have been litigated in a prior lawsuit).

Response (respond). *See also* discovery request, motion. A party's reply to another party's discovery request or motion.

Ripe. Sufficiently developed that it is appropriate for a court to hear the case.

Safe harbor. Protection from sanctions for violation of Rule 11 if the offending document is withdrawn or corrected within a specified period of time; governed primarily by Fed. R. Civ. P. 11(c).

Sanctions. Punishment for violation of a Rule or court order.

Scheduling conference. *See also* judicial case management, scheduling order. A conference between the judge and the lawyers for the parties conducted shortly after all pleadings have been filed to establish certain pretrial deadlines; governed primarily by Fed. R. Civ. P. 16(b).

Scheduling order. *See also* judicial case management, scheduling conference. A judicial order setting forth deadlines for pretrial activity, ordinarily issued after the scheduling conference; governed primarily by Fed. R. Civ. P. 16(b).

Scintilla rule. *See also* judgment as a matter of law, summary judgment. The doctrine that summary judgment or judgment as a matter of law cannot be granted if there is any evidence, however unpersuasive, in favor of the nonmoving party.

Scope of discovery. *See also* discovery, privilege, proportionality, relevance. The extent of information that a party can obtain by using one of the discovery devices; generally, the information must be relevant, nonprivileged, and proportional to the needs of the case.

Sequestration. *See also* attachment. A process by which real property is brought under control of a court.

Service of process (serve, service). *See also* notice, summons. The formal mechanism used to inform a defending party of the lawsuit; governed primarily by Fed. R. Civ. P. 4.

Settlement (settle). An agreement reached among the parties to a dispute, obviating the need for judicial resolution.

Show cause order. *See* order to show cause.

Special verdict. *See also* general verdict, general verdict accompanied by interrogatories, verdict. A verdict in which the jury determines specific facts but does not indicate which party should win, thus leaving to the judge the task of applying the verdict to the legal principles and determining the winner; governed primarily by Fed. R. Civ. P. 49(a).

Standard of review. *See also* abuse of discretion, clear error, de novo review. The degree of deference that a court of appeals gives to a determination made in the proceeding now on appeal.

Standing. A determination that a party has a sufficient interest in a particular dispute to ask the court to resolve it.

Stare decisis. *See also* precedent. The presumption that a court will follow its own earlier rulings.

Subject matter jurisdiction. *See also* diversity jurisdiction, federal question jurisdiction, removal (remove), supplemental jurisdiction. The authority of a court to adjudicate a particular type of dispute.

Subpoena. A document issued by a court ordering a person to appear or to produce documents.

Substantive due process. *See also* Due Process Clause. The doctrine that the Due Process Clause prohibits the government from depriving individuals of certain rights beyond those enumerated in the Constitution.

Substantive law. The law that governs the parties' rights and obligations, as distinguished from procedural law.

Substantive sufficiency. *See also* formal sufficiency. The compliance of a complaint with governing legal principles, so that the complaint appears to state a valid legal claim.

Summary judgment. *See also* scintilla rule. A judicial order terminating the lawsuit in favor of one party, prior to trial, after consideration of the evidence; governed primarily by Fed. R. Civ. P. 56.

Summons. *See also* service of process (serve, service). The formal document that commands a defendant to appear before the court to respond to the plaintiff's complaint.

Supplemental jurisdiction. *See also* ancillary jurisdiction, pendent jurisdiction, pendent party jurisdiction, subject matter jurisdiction. Authority to adjudicate a claim that would not otherwise be within the court's authority, on the ground that it is sufficiently related to a claim that is within the court's authority.

Temporary restraining order. *See also* equity, injunction, permanent injunction, preliminary injunction. A very short-term, emergency judicial order requiring a party to act or refrain from acting.

Third-party claim. *See also* impleader (implead), party (parties), third-party defendant. A claim asserted by a defending party against a third party alleging that the third party is liable to the defending party if the defending party is liable to the complaining party; governed primarily by Fed. R. Civ. P. 14.

Third-party defendant. *See also* impleader (implead), party (parties), third-party claim. A person brought into the lawsuit by a defending party.

Transactionalism. The principle that claims (and parties) in a lawsuit should be related through the events that gave rise to them.

Transfer of venue. The movement of a case from one judicial district within a court system to another judicial district within the same system.

Trans-substantivism (trans-substantive). The principle that rules of procedure should apply consistently regardless of the subject of the lawsuit.

Trial by jury. *See* jury, trial by.

Trial to the bench. *See* bench trials.

Unripe. Not sufficiently developed to allow a court to adjudicate.

Venue. The doctrine that determines which judicial district(s) within a court system can hear a particular case.

Verdict. *See also* general verdict, general verdict accompanied by interrogatories, special verdict. The determination by the jury.

Vertical choice of law. *See also* choice of law, horizontal choice of law, vertical forum shopping. Choosing whether to apply state or federal law.

Vertical forum shopping. *See also* choice of law, horizontal forum shopping, vertical choice of law. Choosing between state court and federal court based on the expected advantage of litigating in the forum.

Voir dire. Questioning potential jurors to determine that they are impartial.

Well-pleaded complaint rule. *See also* federal question jurisdiction. The requirement that a federal claim be a necessary element of the plaintiff's claim.

Work-product doctrine. *See also* core work product. The protection afforded against the mandatory disclosure of materials prepared in anticipation of litigation; governed primarily by Fed. R. Civ. P. 26(b)(3).

Writ. In common-law pleading, the formal document that stated the type of claim a plaintiff was asserting against a defendant.

Zealous advocate. A term often used to describe the central ethical obligation of a lawyer in an adversarial system to protect the interests of the client.

Index